The Time of My Life

The Time of My Life

A Spiritual Pilgrimage Grounded in Hope

Bennett J. Sims

The Bennett J. Sims Institute for Servant Leadership
Hendersonville, North Carolina

The Bennett J. Sims Institute for Servant Leadership
P.O. Box 1007
Hendersonville, NC 28793-1007
www.servleader.org

Printed in the United States of America

ISBN: 0-9778568-0-1

Frontispiece photograph by William H. Logan.

Barbara J. Kuyper, Ph.D., Editor
Design by Six Penny Graphics
Print Coordination by April Huguenin, Print Works

Financial Gifts toward Publication

Frank and Susan Bishop, Atlanta, Georgia
Erskine and Crandall Bowles, Chapel Hill, North Carolina
Frederic and Regan Burnham, Flat Rock, North Carolina
Frank and Ruth Butler, Topsfield, Massachusetts
Julie C. Clarkson, Charlotte, North Carolina
Lawrence and Kathleen Cowart, Atlanta, Georgia
Dale and Lila Critz, Savannah, Georgia
Martin and Loretta Darby, Greenville, South Carolina
James and Eulalie Fenhagen, Georgetown, South Carolina
Thomas and Margaret Harney, Atlanta, Georgia
Amory and Priscilla Houghton, Corning, New York
Bill and Kennon Jamieson, Asheville, North Carolina
Robert and Florence Lee, Asheville, North Carolina
Donald and Alice McDonald, Davenport, Iowa
John and Patricia Moore, Charlotte, North Carolina
Richard and Elaine Morrison, Gilbert, Arizona
David and Peggy Prescott, Princeton, New Jersey
B. D. and Patricia Rodgers, Charlotte, North Carolina
Linda Anne St. Clair, Gabriola Island, British Columbia
Susan Sherard, Southern Pines, North Carolina
Bennett and Mary Page Sims, Hendersonville, North Carolina
Bill and Patty Turney, Houston, Texas
Deborah Little Wyman, Cambridge, Massachusetts

**All proceeds from the sale of this book will go to
The Bennett J. Sims Institute for Servant Leadership.**

Dedication

**To my parents, Lewis Raymond Sims and
Sarah Cosette Jones Sims**
My parents' unfailing welcome of me to life and love
grounded me in hope, thereby enabling the gift
of coping with all the tumults of personal
and global circumstance.

**To my children, Laura Scott Sims Boucher,
Grayson Bennett Sims, and David Lewis Sims**
My children are all conspicuously gifted, loyal, and
loving to their families and to their parents in the
sorrow of their divorce after 42 years of marriage.

**To my wife of our second adventures in marriage,
Mary Page Welborn Sims**
Mary Page's luminous love and vigor of spirit opened
in me even deeper springs of hope and moved me to
higher levels of joy than I had thought possible.

You will forget your misery; you will remember it as waters that have passed away. And your life will be brighter than the noonday; its darkness will be like the morning. And you will have confidence, because there is hope; you will be protected and take your rest in safety. You will lie down, and no one will make you afraid. — Job 11:16–19

Contents

Preface

Challenging American Cultural Captivity

Stories are the heartbeat of all lively communication. This is my story. I share it partly because writing has become a personal fulfillment through the years. But even more, in public terms, I share my story in the hope of coaxing a care for all life in a world imperiled by terrorist ambitions and American political captivity to the blandishments of money, imperial ambition, and violence. It is my conviction that this self-aggrandizing posture is held in place by subtle and pervasive fears that are supported by fundamentalist expectations of world-ending calamities and manipulated by privilege-preoccupied forces that seek to perpetuate incumbent political power.

In America, we need reliance on the forces of hope, a sturdy hope that grasps the unity and interdependence of all life in preference to strategies that rely on proud blaming and warfare. Our present excesses of partisan preference for wealth over commonwealth could eventuate in the loss of all our stories. The advent of nuclear weaponry and its competitive stockpiling means that the future will never again arrive automatically. The years ahead for the children of the world must now be created by human wisdom, passion, and resolve. Otherwise, the universal longing for peace has no chance of fulfillment.

This progressive accent runs like a unifying axis through most of my story. It starts with a childhood and young manhood of unexamined conservatism and develops into a chronicle of advancing freedom from what seems to me an ominous captivity to religious and political retrogression from the noble American experiment in personal freedom and painfully advancing social justice. The opening years of the twenty-first century find the United States being led in a creeping and shameless repudiation of the bold conviction that all of humanity is equal in divine value and endowed with public entitlement to "life, liberty, and the pursuit of happiness" — all in a divinely fashioned holograph of creation that cries out to live in freedom from arrogant exploitation of the uniting earth from which all life derives. Sound religion teaches this, and sound politics protect it. "The earth is the Lord's and all that is in it, the world, and those who live in it" (Psalms 24:1).

Everyone's reservoir of memories must be far fuller than casual remembering ever suspects. A deliberate calling on my recollections, as in writing this odyssey, reveals their astonishing bulk. The more I tapped into my old storehouse at age 85, the more it yielded, and the more I had to winnow the harvest lest it load the barn beyond its capacity to invite inspection. A special yield is Chapter 1, "Trading Limericks with an Old Master." The opening chapter puts my story on a wide stage and begins with a comic prophecy about my pilgrimage of living into controversy and liberation with the help of a famous friend.

The freedom-freighted term *liberal*, from which the ringing word *liberation* derives, describes my view of life. I would like to retain the word as distinguishing my stance on most issues, but ultraconservative invective and secular desacralizing have trashed the term to such an extent that *liberal* now suggests irreligion, lack of patriotism, and scorn of morality. So, grateful for the flexible richness of the English language and for the forward thrust of the term *progressive*, I stand with the public trailblazers of the American start-up who fashioned a masterful United States Constitution and its amendments — a bold progressiveness without which there would be no "land of the free and home of the brave."

When I reached the end of these long looks astern and ahead, it occurred to me how much more there remained of what could be told. My life has been rich and memorable literally beyond words. My ardent hope is that my tale will enrich the lives of others, as the records of other lives have rewarded me. So I serve up what follows as a droll and serious thank-you offering for the privilege of a flawed, forgiven, and fabulous journey into old age.

Special thanks are due to my friendly computer and to my faithful family and friends. Of course, the latter outnumber the word processor by multiple hundreds. They are the ones who people, with affection and vibrancy, this reservoir of memories and forecasts. Still, my computer is cherished because it has saved hours of the tedium that accompanied my writing as a parish priest, seminary teacher, diocesan bishop, and leadership educator. So this roster of gratitude includes a long parade of gratefully remembered personal secretaries who typed and retyped my scribbling for years. When I left Emory University where the Institute for Servant Leadership was founded and no longer had a private secretary, I finally learned to touch-type, albeit very slowly. In spite of my ponderous personal use of the electronic wizard, the instrument has blessed me.

As for my nonelectronic friends, they include colleagues in ministry and education, especially my successor as president of the Institute for Servant Leadership, the Reverend Deacon Bill Jamieson. Bill is widely and brilliantly gifted, tirelessly energetic, and grandly generous to his old predecessor. He and his gracious wife Kennon, the institute's administrator for many years, have moved the enterprise into enlarged fields of action and influence. With Bill and Kennon deciding to devote their energies to a new servant enterprise, the Reverend Frederic B. Burnham, Ph.D. joined the institute in 2005 as senior fellow and conference director. Fred, who retired in 2003, comes to us from Trinity Church in New York City, where his energy and scholarship built and led the Trinity Institute for 20 years and established a world-renowned Christian continuing education enterprise. Martin R. Darby will join the management and teaching leadership of the institute in 2006 as president and executive director. His leadership role will be expanded to that of teacher as he joins with others in presenting small-group workshops on the theory and practical application of servant leadership. He has recently conducted two church vestry retreats in North Carolina and Georgia that were enthusiastically received. For the past 20 years, Martin has been managing director of Coates Inks, a subsidiary of Sun Chemical Corporation located in Greenville, South Carolina.

Special acknowledgment needs to be given colleagues who have spent their time and skills on the development of this book. Sally Cook Parsons has handled administrative details and Richard Parsons preliminary work on production of the book. Barbara Kuyper, Ph.D., scholar and writer, has done all the brilliant and tedious work of editorial scrutiny on every page. Barbara has also assisted me in checking all the citations and passing on the suitability of the title and subtitle. Jeanne Galbo of Chapel Hill, North Carolina was our meticulous and intelligent proofreader. April Huguenin of Print Works in Greer, South Carolina managed the final design, production, and printing of the book.

Others deserving of thanks include those presently in membership on the institute's Board of Trustees as well as those who have served generously and since rotated into the distance. My brother Edward has encouraged this work from its beginning and offered occasional critiques. Like me, he is a retired Episcopal clergyperson, although his brains and charm could have made him big bucks as a trial attorney.

Several others have my warm thanks for help in bringing this book to birth. They include the Reverend Isabel Carter Hayward, Ph.D., professor of theology in the Episcopal Divinity School of Cambridge, Massachusetts; and Bishop William H. Folwell, colleague for many years in the House of Bishops of the Episcopal Church and golf partner since we both retired to Hendersonville, North Carolina. My special friend Fran McKendree, virtuoso guitarist and Christian composer, and his wife Diana have contributed their assessments of the book. John and Patricia Moore of Charlotte, North Carolina have been lavishly generous with gifts of time and money to the institute and have contributed their enthusiasm to the writing of this chronicle. Other generous friends include Frank and Susan Bishop of Atlanta, Georgia; the Reverend Julie Clarkson of Charlotte, North Carolina; and the many friends of the institute whose names appear on the financial gifts page at the front of the book.

As with so many who write books, it is my wife who has given the most encouragement. Mary Page and I, married now for nearly 18 years, share two capital gifts, one of them quite astonishing. The first is that we have the same birthday, August 9, although I arrived 22 years earlier. The other gift rises from a greater mystery than coincidence. It goes to the realm of the miraculous and has the same force for us as for the village tailor Motel Kamzoil in *Fiddler on the Roof.* That exultant young man, just engaged to his beloved, ran in circles through the birch grove near his home singing, "It's a miracle!" Our supernal gift is that both of us have reached maturity in second marriages and have never known such a steady abundance of love and joy and the exquisite freedom to be growing into the patterns of personhood that we believe God intends for us.

One final prefatory word. To be alive to write this chronicle at age 85 has been a special gift of God. I no longer walk steadily, nor can I play the fetching golf course just across the road from our front door. So in spite of good fortune to have lived so long, I sometimes feel like the aged Israeli who exclaimed, "I'm so old that when I was young the Dead Sea was only sick!"

Chapter 1

Trading Limericks
with an Old Master

America's foremost limericist somehow knew that I had begun to out-grow a conservative upbringing. The poet and I became friends in my first parish church during the 1950s. He must have sensed that I had become impatient with some rigid traditions and wanted to claim the freedom to push the boundaries of my perceptions of truth outward to new and larger dimensions. His limerick pushes those boundaries out to the point of absurdity, but the exaggeration fits a liberated spirit.

> There was an old parson named Sims
> Who astonished the church with his whims.
> When he read the Epistle,
> He gave a loud whistle
> And stood on his head for the hymns.
> — Ogden Nash, *The Saturday Evening Post*, 1965

As with most octogenarians, I am given to massaging my memo-ries. In these dwindle-down days of diminishment, I think more often of my first parish church than any of the several other ecclesial posts I was privileged to hold in a ministry that now spans 56 active years.

My ardent attachment to a first parish is true even when I sleep. Every vocational night dream that involves me as a clergyperson locates me in some wildly distorted shape of the Episcopal Church of the Redeemer in Baltimore, Maryland, my enduring home parish. I own a niche in the burial wall of its columbarium.

Founded in 1855, the Episcopal Church of the Redeemer is situated on nine acres in the prominent northwest corner of the rolling country estate of its principal benefactor. Most of its years were spent in relative quiescence as a small and contented cluster of Maryland gentry — until Baltimore began marching into its northern suburbs following World War I. By the end of World War II, the city had camped around its lovely nine acres in an expansive network of fine homes and gardens and upscale schools.

In 1948, when I was a senior student at Virginia Theological Seminary in Alexandria, I was asked to join the rector and his staff as the weekend assistant to help with the growing Sunday school and to assume responsibility for a Sunday evening ministry to young people. Upon graduation from seminary a year later, the rector, Richard Henry Baker, asked me to move to Baltimore with my little family to become what was then called a curate, an old Anglican designation adapted by the Episcopal Church to mean an ordained deacon or priest who was assistant to the rector. The title is no longer in fashion in the United States.

A year later, my great friend and mentor Dick Baker was elected a bishop, and I was asked by the vestry to be his successor. Even before much inner wrestling and consulting with my bishop and former professors at Virginia, I knew I would consent. The call spoke seductively to my need to succeed. As I look back, that consent was anything but liberation from cultural captivity. It was, in fact, yielding to the premium that culture attaches to upward mobility and achievement. On the other hand, to post a 31-year-old with less than a year's experience in priest's orders as head of the most prominent parish in the Diocese of Maryland defied all church convention. A bumpy history of several such moves out of the ordinary, one of them a deliberate choice of downward mobility, is the substance of this chronicle of liberation.

In the 1950s, the Redeemer congregation was an almost uniformly privileged population. It still is. During my years as rector, the largest single vocational group in the parish was made up of medical doctors, several of them professors in the various medical disciplines at the Johns Hopkins School of Medicine. The second largest vocational group was comprised of attorneys. Next were business leaders along with investment and commercial bankers, among them the presidents and vice presidents of three of Baltimore's biggest banks. The president of Johns Hopkins University and the mayor of Baltimore (earlier the governor of Maryland) were both regular worshippers. Architects of reputation were there, one of them an occasional lecturer in the architectural schools at Yale and Harvard, and in the Sunday congregation now and then would be the famous Ogden Nash. The wives and children of these prominent and gifted men were all handsome people, and any of the women who fell short of physical beauty were rich in strength and beauty of character.

It is easily imagined that such a congregation would carry heavy conservative baggage, and so did I as their rector — for awhile. I even voted for Richard Nixon over John Kennedy in 1960. But on the heels of JFK's stirring inaugural address, I knew that my vote had betrayed the liberal currents that had begun to churn in my soul in the late 1950s. By then the parish had grandly outgrown the limited-seating country church erected in 1858, and now it had to accommodate four consecutive Sunday morning services. In 1958, exactly 100 years after the first church was built, a contemporary and heavily controversial new church rose on our nine-acre tract. The story of that bright and painful shift is told in detail later in this chronicle. Suffice it to say here that presiding over the building of a large church which deviated sharply from prevailing convention was the first significant and defining move of my long and bumpy ride from right to left.

The chapters that follow comprise the tale of a charmed life of pilgrimage from conservative bias to a muted liberal passion — muted because I was deeply immersed as the principal leader in a conservative constituency. The second great defining move to a larger embrace of truth came in 1963 when I participated in the nonviolent March on Washington and heard Martin Luther King, Jr. deliver his history-altering address, "I Have a Dream." On the following Sunday, I reported the experience from the pulpit. Ogden Nash, in the congregation that morning, must have divined that I was headed for trouble with tradition. It is clear from his humor-driven genius that he understood better than I the beckoning horizon toward which my life was tending.

In 1965, when Ogden's limerick appeared in *The Saturday Evening Post*, I had become the rector of a smaller and very different church in the radically dissimilar setting of Corning, New York. That move to a more provincial parish, which followed a graduate fellowship at Harvard, precipitated a season of sharp spiritual pain. The move confronted me with my capitulation to the lures that fit Marcus Borg's three As of cultural captivity: achievement, affluence, and appearance. It drove me to seek the spiritual direction of a marvelous monk of the Benedictine monastery near Elmira, New York. It was a relationship of deep girding, and the Corning episode became the third great shaping experience in my odyssey of liberation. I came to know in greater depth the bold, inclusive companionship of Jesus Christ.

From a steadily developing liberated spirit, I fashioned an answering limerick to the one about old Parson Sims and sent it to the editor of the same magazine.

To the whims of old Sims drink a toast;
They're amusing and harmless to most.
But if you're perplexed
About what's coming next,
Just read Ogden Nash in the *Post*.

Ogden must have read my doggerel because he sent me another of his limericks soon afterward, two of them in fact. His reference to Mack Sennett in the first one harks back to a silent movie producer of the old black-and-white comedy series featuring the Keystone Kops.

Your reverend namesake dear Bennett
Upheld each Episcopal tenet.
But some traces remained
After he was ordained
Of his earlier years with Mack Sennett.

In the spirit of longing for liberation from certain ecclesiastical and cultural imprisonments, this was Ogden's second offering, accompanied by a personal note.

A mother still groping for hope
Addressed a request to the Pope:
Could she try birth control
Without losing her soul?
The pontifical answer was "Nope!"

Almost all the Christian denominations are changing, some ponderously and at great risk of schism like my own Episcopal Church, as we have moved to ever-larger boundaries of inclusion. In the years since my first ordination in 1949, we have opened our common life to racial differences, liturgical reform, women in holy orders, and gay and lesbian legitimacy. But other church bodies, especially the Roman Catholic Church for all its greatness, continue to be shaped by medievalist and male-dominant rigidities. The Southern Baptist Convention, filled with earnest believers, seems to me even more fearfully mired in a fierce fundamentalism that insists on historical inerrancy with regard to the Bible — a position that seems riven with hopeless contradictions. Later chapters will elaborate my understanding of the ominous worldwide rise of fundamentalism in our time.

Meanwhile, I am deeply glad and grateful to have lived long enough to see my church risk severe internal distress in deciding to honor the legitimacy of homosexual identity and fidelity in same-sex relationships. This is my take on the meaning of the decision in 2003 by both houses of our General Convention to confirm the choice of an openly gay man to be bishop of New Hampshire. That singular diocese, along with majorities in the General Convention, rang a loud and liberating gong for hosts of Episcopalians. Large numbers of saddened exiles from the Episcopal Church may now take heart that their church can be home again after years of temporizing resistance to the costly inclusivity of Christ. We have at last embraced justice and love for great numbers of its faithful gay and lesbian communicants. Again, I am buoyed and grateful to have lived long enough to participate in this bracing age of convulsion and renewal — this vast turning point through which the human pilgrimage now moves.

They say that long lives are the gift of good genes. Happiness and hope must have something to do with it, too. But the real grounds for the truth and buoyancy that prompt this saga of recollection and forecast are deeper than genes and joy. I am grounded in the unmerited bestowal of love and forgiveness by vividly remembered grandparents and parents, one brother, two wives, three children, four grandchildren, and an extended family of aunts, in-laws, and cousins. Joined by a long parade of pals and parishioners, all have been my cherished companions along the way. They fill the years of a pilgrimage from birth in New England through three Midwest boyhood cities and eventually into all the states of America as well as wide stretches of the Caribbean and Central America, east and west across the great oceans several times, and around the world once by ship, air, and rail.

To have been given a lifetime that participates in our present tumultuous turning point in human experience is a matchless privilege. Ours is a moment of seismic shift in history, a time so vastly significant as to compare with the development of agriculture and the emergence of conquest empires soon thereafter. For me, the meaning of that earlier turning point, around 10,000 years ago, is that it gradually redefined the human understanding of power. Power became male dominance, control, and subjugation. Power has remained so until our own time when it begins again, as it did for most of human prehistory, to mean, not male dominance and competition, but cooperation and a corrective feminine quality of sensitivity to the interwoven web of oneness in the depths of all life. Enlightened theology and ethics, along with archeology, astronomy, and contemporary physics, have become partners in laying out a new and beckoning road for the human odyssey. Only a refusal to awaken to the truth of human and cosmic interdependence can abort a march into a world liberated from centuries of stubborn fascination with war and violence. Science and religion are now arm in arm with this great truth: while conflict is inevitable, violence is optional. It is a bracing time to be alive.

At the same moment, this is an ominous time. Our vast addiction to violence, especially in the United States, makes it so. This blistering addiction, harnessed to the science-developed means of unimaginable destruction, has landed the human odyssey on the brink of self-extinction. As was claimed in the Preface, any long tomorrow will never again come automatically for the planet as it has for 3.5 billion years. August 1945 seems the precise break-over point, changing the timetable from a divinely automatic future to a future become humanly problematic. Of course, that moment on the calendar of life had multiple antecedents in the slow development of the weapons of warfare, but the end of an automatic future erupted in an instant when two atomic weapons fell from the sky over Japan by calculated design and decision. From now on, the future must be created. The morally and politically arduous task of creating the future is now ours to consciously undertake. On this epic turning point of time, the very existence of a human future demands that we risk the longest stride we have ever attempted in the perennial business of growing up.

If there is to be an equivalent high adventure of life for my children and grandchildren, humanity must come to grips with the absolute requirement for global mind change — from a very long adolescence of resorting to violence to a new maturity that repudiates violence as a problem solver. *Human being* has given way to *human becoming* as a statement of deepest reality. If human life in the planet can be seen as in process and not fixed in static unchangeability, then the future is open. These memoirs argue that the human parade is not trudging in a rut to its ineluctable demise. We are still exploring and adventuring. Tomorrow beckons both from behind and ahead. It will be guided by great memories to be sure, but the future is not preshaped by a static past. History is loaded with the advancing dynamic of constant change. In a word, there is hope.

Chapter 2

"I Wet My Pants"

A few of my earliest years were spent in the little city of Chanute, Kansas. From that setting, I ingested some recollections that my amused parents told and retold. My favorite involves father, mother, and high-chair-size first son at meals in a variety of restaurants, some in the old Fred Harvey restaurants in Midwest railroad stations. Impervious to the nearby crowded tables, little Bennett, in his rompers, wiggles to his feet and, standing in his baby chair, begins an impassioned speech of babbled incoherence. Waving his teddy bear for emphasis, he concludes the address with a clearly enunciated "Conch!" and pounds the bear on the tray table with a resounding thud. The exclamatory *conch* has never been deciphered. It remains a mystery as deep as the sarsen rocks of Stonehenge. If reincarnation were a cherished family belief (which it isn't) we might want to claim that *conch* is a preconscious remnant of the *amen* that functioned in a prearticulate child as a forecast of his profession as a pulpiteer.

While Chanute is mostly a compound of oft-told tales from amused parents, there does remain in memory one vivid, fear-charged recollection that comes directly from my brain. My earliest clear recollection is of panic at a picnic as a two-year-old on the flood plain of a swollen

Kansas creek. I wonder if most of our earliest memories are rooted in fear. The churning brown boil of creek water rose so suddenly that it caught picnickers' cars submerged to their hubcaps. With a grinding of gears, my father's black Dodge coupe got us safely to the country road above us, but a nearby truck was stalled and stuck in the swirling current. I can still see the pattern of the open wire siding above the bed of that truck and the tortured faces of the people in the cab.

I hope that I am not the only one whose earliest recall is locked in panic rather than in the love and safety of the nursing breast and bottle. Whether or not I am joined by others in remembering fear first, my earliest memory raises a lively question. What does this say about my belief that there are only two great forces driving the human odyssey, namely love and fear? Why don't I remember first the warmth of love and the comforting embrace of tenderness and delight that enfolded me as a newborn?

In addition to the reasonable theory that fear is first because of the trauma of leaving the womb at birth, I confess to a deeper and more socially grounded prehistorical theory to explain the priority of fear over love. This personal assumption is lightly held because I do not know how correct it may be, but the earliest of our species must have had to rely on some instinct of fear to survive the perils of marauding beasts and harsh environments. Perhaps that instinct lives at the root of human consciousness. This theory is supported by the fact that distrusting others and despising them seems easier in real life than assuming the best in others and being quickly forgiving. Otherwise, violence and warfare would not be more lavishly recorded on the pages of history than human reconciliation and peace, and forgiving would come more naturally than fuming. Also, rage would not be the subject of so much therapeutic counsel and admonition, as in St. Paul, who knew the healthy habit of letting anger out while refusing to nourish it: "let not the sun go down upon your wrath" (Ephesians 4:26, KJV).

I acknowledge that I obey Christ's admonition to love our enemies, especially political enemies, with almost automatic reluctance. As a progressive Democrat in these opening years of the twenty-first century, I have to pray hard when I petition God to "forgive us our trespasses as we forgive those who trespass against us." That incisive qualification is a bother. It seems to condition God's forgiveness on the basis of our readiness to forgive. But as a theologian, I do not believe that God withholds mercy until we forgive. It is not God's withholding but our withholding of forgiveness to others that diminishes our capacity to be forgiving, especially of ourselves. Our ability to experience deep down the forgiveness of God undoes our guilt and bestows the serenity and courage of reborn people who reach out to others with the offer of reconciliation and healing.

> So if anyone is in Christ, there is a new creation: everything old has passed away; see, everything has become new! All this is from God, who reconciled us to himself through Christ, and has given us the ministry of reconciliation; that is, in Christ God was reconciling the world to himself, not counting their trespasses against them, and entrusting the message of reconciliation to us.
> — 2 Corinthians 5:17–19

The strange priority of fear over love is not really different in the case of my computer. A first lump of angst had to be dissolved to experience the electronic marvel as a helper to cherish. But love came quickly and easily. This proves that a warm relationship with a machine is deeply different than with people. I suppose that is because a machine lacks the living ego to insult and offend you with a contrary value system or a nasty grudge. Still, there is something alive and animate about any prized inanimate thing. That may be why we never call a seagoing vessel a *thing* but always a *she*. I loved the 60,000-horsepower destroyer on which I sailed at the close of World War II. She was a living and beautiful beast. Quantum theory explains this by the conviction that the tiniest component of the cosmos interacts with all other components with some measure of feeling.

According to the physicist Brian Swimme, gravity, which works to hold a star system such as our own solar system together, remains a good but inadequate explanation. Better, he says, to hold that mystic forces such as intimacy, attraction, and even affection lie below the level of gravity and electromagnetism. Could this be the reason that human imagination and impulse force the gargantuan cost and risk of space exploration? Could humans be the self-conscious expressions of that same mystic draw that compels all the star systems to cohere over unimaginable distances? I believe that the congruence of science and spirituality is precisely here. We humans are enmeshed in an interwoven web of life that includes the whole range of reality from subatomic invisibilities to the wheeling spangle of stars in the undiscovered darkness.

In this chronicle of confessions, it is time to speak of the arrival of my only sibling, Edward Raymond Sims. He was born on August 14, 1923, five days after my third birthday. Our mother returned from Chanute to her girlhood home in Davenport, Iowa for Edward's birth. On a downtown sidewalk in Davenport, I made my first confession at age three, and the confession suggests the refreshing freedom of children. By contrast, our adult years tend to turn us away from candor, moving us to handle embarrassing personal truth by concealment or exaggeration. Mother's younger sister by three years, Alice Hills, had me in hand as my babysitter during the birth of my little brother. She tells of meeting a very tall lawyer friend nicknamed Sky Lohmiller on a downtown Davenport street the day of Edward's birth. I was at sidewalk level as a toddler beside Alice. Following what was probably a cheerful greeting to her tall friend, she looked down and invited a greeting from me. "Tell

Mr. Lohmiller what happened this morning." Lifting my face to address the tall man, I spoke the truth nearest to consciousness: "I wet my pants!" I had not yet learned the constraints of embarrassment.

It seems a significant loss in the quality of relationships that propriety and shame must forbid so much of the plain honesty of childhood. This phenomenon may lie at the base of Jesus' admonition that the Kingdom of Heaven belongs to us as we recover the self-honest freshness of the little child in each of us. This cannot mean making public announcements of toilet training failures, but there is a clue about the disarming power of openness in my confession of August 14, 1923 — especially of openness to one's real self. Rigid defenses, which are almost always born of some quotient of dread or ambition and which are so inimical to personal, interpersonal, and global peace, tend to dissolve when risks are taken to be honest in relationships. That must be why third-party intervention is employed in getting beyond the hiding and blaming that prohibit reconciliation.

The Wizard of Oz may be the great American myth. It is a trenchant favorite of mine because it endures as a drama of the power of truth to activate freedom and widen the experience of peace and joy in a whole circle of relationships. The Wizard, earlier a manipulator of people, became an instant giver of good gifts when he forsook the sham of hiding behind the curtain that concealed the technology of his pretense to supernatural powers. The Wizard's intimidating voice and the frightened circle of immobilized supplicators before his throne were joined by an unintimidated third party who opened the frozen circle with barks and, with a fierce tug, opened the concealing curtain for Dorothy and her friends. The dog Toto became the rescuing third party. Emboldened by the sight of the Wizard at his technical control panel and microphone, Dorothy confronted the fake Wizard and, stamping her foot, leveled him with an angry frown. "Oh, you are a bad man!" she said. "No," replied the unmasked manipulator, "I am not a bad man, just a bad Wizard."

And lo, the supplicants received their grand desires. The Cowardly Lion got his roar, the Tin Man got a heart, the Scarecrow was handed a certificate testifying that he had a brain, and Dorothy awoke at home in Kansas with her little dog.

Charmed by this classic most all of my remembered life, I was in late adulthood before the depth of its mythic truth came home to me. Suddenly it dawned on me that the subtlety of the Wizard's magic was not to create what did not exist. What the Wizard wrought was not something absent but what already lay present, although hidden and unsummoned. Dorothy had been in Kansas all along but was simply knocked unconscious by the Kansas tornado that had lifted and tumbled her house. What this must mean is that disarming honesty does not implant what is absent, like gifts of courage and a heart and a brain and a homecoming. Whatever the cost in surrendered fear or bombast, the risk to be real simply evokes the gifts and virtues awaiting the honest relationships that call them forth.

As Pascal wrote, those whom we love the most are not those who give us something we never had before, but those who show us the richness of what we already possess.

Chapter 3

Family Values

One of the capital traits that mark the conservative catalog of virtues is commitment to family values. I was brought up on this virtue. Never a matter of didactic instruction, family values enveloped me from earliest remembrance as gossamer wings of the spirit. Those nurturing wings trained me to the values of loyalty, self-discipline, truthfulness, and humor. Listening to the current recitations of conservative political merits, I react with sharp resentment to the insinuation that liberals cannot be credited with an equivalent family caring and commitment. Although the years have moved me to a hearty progressive political posture, they have only deepened my appreciation for the tough-and-tender spirit of family allegiance. Of course, that spirit has suffered the usual strains and pains that overtake us all, conservatives and progressives alike, but the bonds of family values that shaped me early have only been sturdied through the highs and lows of the years that followed.

Davenport, Iowa on the Mississippi River is the crucible of my upbringing in a fervently embraced conservatism. The conservative grip came with the territory of home and family and included the solid Christian securities of a Calvinist upbringing in the First Presbyterian Church. I remember vividly the family joy at the triumph of Republican

Herbert Hoover over Alfred Smith, the "dirty Democrat." And I can still repeat the neighborhood boys' political chant of the 1928 election campaign: "Hoover, Hoover, he's our man; Smith was born in a garbage can!"

In 1932, Franklin D. Roosevelt won the White House in a landslide and brought with him a feverish liberal policy sweep. My grandfather, an already somewhat humorless man, filled the family conversations with an equally feverish reaction of Republican moral outrage. I loved Harvey Bennett Jones with a young boy's attachment to a hero and imbibed his conservatism with enthusiasm. Later, while in college during Roosevelt's third-term election run in 1940, I organized a young Republican club among friends in the hope of adding energy to a momentum to elect Wendell L. Willkie, the aggressive Republican candidate. When Willkie lost, I organized an extension of the life of the club by ordering pins and buttons in red, white, and blue letters that said "Keep Awake" and by meeting weekly to resist the blandishments of FDR and encourage my conservative fellow Iowans. Predictably, Keep Awake went sound asleep after the initial impulse died — about two months into 1941.

I have known for years that Franklin Roosevelt was a persuasive and heroic figure. In the year of the great man's second run for the presidency, I was in high school in Kansas City, where our father's work had moved us in 1934, and enrolled in ROTC. My olive-drab-uniformed battalion, all of us shouldering old Springfield rifles, was involved as honor guard for FDR's October 1936 campaign visit to Kansas City. A great horde of 20,000 crowded the new municipal auditorium, where a runway had been installed to help the handicapped president move from his car to an elevated platform fixed with a battery of microphones. The crowd grew restless as we waited and waited. I remember thinking that the president, being a Democrat, was no doubt deliberately testing our patience for effect. When at last FDR appeared, a pandemonium of applause and cheers broke out, not only because he had finally arrived but also because he walked, gallantly smiling, on deformed legs the whole length of the walkway, holding on to no support but the hand rails of the temporary structure. Swept into the cheering of the multitude and instantly moved by the heroic entrance of the crippled president, I found myself roaring approval for a Democrat. I remember feeling both awed and slightly ashamed to have been overcome by public pressure. I resolved not to relate my reaction to any of the family, but the memory of that event 67 years ago is as fresh and vivid as if it happened only yesterday. Something profound happened in my impressionable teen-age soul, and I frankly cherish the memory and the sensation of that moment in which I betrayed my conservative upbringing. It may have been this initial and unbidden impulse that led to a much later realignment of my political convictions and ardor.

Davenport is the cradle of an abiding habit, maybe an addiction, that must have started with a little boy's affliction with colds and coughs. Our mother was a devotee of Vicks VapoRub®, a camphor-laced salve used on chests and below nostrils. More than 80 years later, I can hardly be without Vicks in a drawer on my side of the bed. A Vicks bottle accompanied me around the world in 1962, and a small bottle of the salve belonging to me was confiscated from an overhead beam close to where I had slung my hammock on the battleship *Arkansas* as a naval trainee in 1940. I gladly suffered the scorn and salty profanity of a petty officer to get the bottle back. Much earlier, when about 10 years old, I sent a letter of thanks to the president of the Vick Chemical Company of Greensboro, North Carolina. Vicks has since become a shelf product of the huge company Procter & Gamble, but in 1930 the Vicks outfit was small enough to take a 10-year-old boy seriously. Not only did the company president write me a personal letter in return, but he also sent me a several-year supply in a small carton. Maybe some executive at Procter & Gamble would do the same for a grateful small boy now. P&G could well afford it. In 1930, a small bottle of Vicks VapoRub cost 15 cents.

Today it takes as much as $3.40 plus tax to leave a supermarket with a bottle no bigger.

Davenport is the locus of many golden memories, not only of the intellect but of the senses as well. I can still whiff the pungent odor of the Mississippi River as it lapped the brick pavement of the slope-sided levee where stern-wheel steamers tied up and from which my aunt Alice slid into the turgid water as the first woman to swim the great river between Iowa and Illinois at that location. But all in memory is not golden. Reality requires that recollection take account of both the good and the gloomy. There were times of sadness, the saddest being the death of my beloved grandfather in 1935 of heart disease at age 66. He was a bastion of certainty around whom the whole family revolved — proud, handsome, all-knowing, and always a hearty despiser of Democrats whom he blamed for the income tax that he held to be both discriminatory and confiscatory.

Another major Davenport sadness was the near-fatal accident of my father in 1930. One spring morning, Aunt Alice called me from class at Grant School. She took me to Mercy Hospital on West Locust Street where Lewis lay close to death. At the cement plant where he worked as one of the engineers, he had snagged his trouser leg on an upright peg and fallen from a railroad trestle. Landing on his head, he was rendered unconscious and, with a fractured skull, was not given much hope of recovery. Following several days of our not knowing whether he would live, he did recover full consciousness and was finally discharged with instructions to live virtually motionless for what must have seemed to him an eternity. Lewis did no remunerative work for two years.

Meanwhile, the Great Depression deepened. Were it not for Grandfather's generosity despite his diminished fortune, we could not have remained in our big frame house. We did without a car, a telephone, a daily paper, and even ice for the icebox. Twice daily, either Edward or I would trudge up the narrow alley connecting the rear of the three houses between Grandfather's and ours to use the big General Electric refrigerator in the Jones family pantry. Our mother kept us in slender portions of cash by knitting clothing and accessories for her friends who were less Depression-afflicted than we were.

The rest of the Davenport years remain upbeat in memory. Even the grind of the Depression did not disturb the undercurrents of joy that both Edward and I remember as foundational. We climbed the cherry trees in our back yard, kept white mice in cages at the edge of the property, and put on goofy, made-up, one-act dramas behind our house, stringing a rope between the cherry trees for holding blankets as theater curtains. Folding chairs from somewhere served our audiences at 10 cents per ticket, paid with condescending amusement by neighborhood parents. One of our most successful productions, in which the good guys shot the bad guys, was called "The Gangsters of Chicago." Edward, always given to mischief himself, took the bad-guy roles by choice. Another one-act hilarity was a cowboy and Indian exchange of cap-gun and blunted-arrow violence, Edward again choosing the sinister role as a war-path Indian. All the dimes and nickels we collected went to the Milk Fund for the poor children of Davenport. The Milk Fund was sponsored by the local newspaper, and our dramas were always noted in the paper.

My Davenport pals formed what we called the Gang, allowing little brother Edward occasional entrance into the chicken-coop clubhouse behind Ed Putnam's house. Mr. Putnam had boarded up the chicken-wire front, which made it a snug, slope-roof meeting place with benches on the front and back walls. A small door opened and closed on one side wall, and a half-glassed window occupied the wall opposite. The window frame held a pane only in the lower half since an old cast-iron, coal-burning stove standing near the window was vented by a black chimney pipe running out the upper half of the window frame and then turning and going up beyond the rooftop. In winter, one of us would fire up the stove for thawing out after long afternoons of ice-skating at the nearby park. There would be high and happy comfort on the crowded benches until some scamp started a second winter game of Stink by spitting on the hot stove-top. The rest of us would gleefully join in, spitting until the odor forced departures for relief.

Mischief has got to be a perverse current of joy that runs strong in all boys and probably in girls depending on how widely one applies St. Augustine's dubious doctrine of original sin. Later in this true tale of a very conservatively trained youngster, I want to confront the highly questionable validity of this notion invented by a genius with a troubled conscience. For now, it is clear that conscience, from whatever source, operates to disturb our peace. What follows is an episode seared into memory as a tale of sin and redemption. Although I could not have named them thus at age 12, the deep theological twins of sin and redemption were built-in family values. Even though I knew not the names, I knew them from earliest experience as badness and forgiveness, as doing wrong and being taken back — fundamental descriptions of human proclivity and divinely driven behavior.

Edward and I shared the northwest corner bedroom of 211 East Rusholme Street. Nearest my bed was an old bureau with the top drawer stuffed with socks, handkerchiefs, and a variety of old tickets, rocks, and souvenirs of boyhood cherishing. One day in 1932 or so, I rode my bike from our house to downtown Davenport, about four miles distant, in search of a small paint brush. Edward and I were caught up in using the scroll saw at our basement workbench for fashioning four-inch figures in painted plywood of comic-strip characters of the day — Moon Mullins, Dick Tracy, Popeye, and Andy Gump. I needed but had worn out the last slim brush for painting the details of faces. The nearest Woolworth dime store stood at the corner of Second and Brady Streets. Dime stores in those days displayed their wares in countertop trays, using dividers to separate the small from the larger items. I knew right where to go, but I had a problem. There was no dime in my pocket. So, lurking around the counter and looking as casual as a cat, I waited until no one was watching and quickly snatched a little 10-cent brush. My bike was parked against the store front just outside the main door, and I went for it, walking with studied innocence. Hopping on the bike and racing up the Brady Street hill, I gained the basement workshop at 211 past the Palmer College of Chiropractic for which Davenport was, and perhaps still is, famous. Safely home, I hid the brush beneath a pile of handkerchiefs in that bureau, where it lay hidden in the sock drawer for a full year. I simply could not bring myself to use it. It burned a ragged hole in my Presbyterian conscience, and, before it could burn a hole in the drawer, I hopped on that same bike one Saturday and coasted down Brady Street hill to Woolworth's and their paint brush counter, gingerly replacing the offending 10-cent brush.

Would it not be wonderful if we could cleanse all our stains of conscience by such personal acts of restitution? But no! Most misdemeanors are fixed forever in our personal records. Maybe this is why the world religions scholar Huston Smith contends that Christianity's special gift to the wayward human odyssey is the grace of unconditional forgiveness — and the mystery of the cross.

Chapter 4

Family Follies

Of all my memories of our father Lewis Raymond Sims, his sparkling humor stands out above all other attributes. Although he suffered a crippling lack of self-confidence anchored in a childhood in which he was virtually abandoned, his keen intellect flashed forth antithetically in both withering anger and high good humor. He could reduce us boys to mute fright and our mother to tears, but he could also send us into howls of laughter with quips and quotes and naughty humor. Mother used to sing a bedtime ditty to us as very young boys:

> Little birdies in the tree, in the tree, in the tree,
> Little birdies in the tree, sing a song to me.

From Father the ditty came out a bit differently:

> Little birdies in the tree, in the tree, in the tree,
> Little birdies in the tree, please don't pee on me.

A song learned much later was prohibited from the table by our proper mother:

> Sam, Sam, the lavatory man,
> Assistant superintendent of the Second Street can,
> He brings in the soap and hangs up the towels,

And listens to the music of the moving bowels.

Another quip that attaches to what we called bathroom talk went this way. Father is talking: "You know that the 'g' in the word *Gnostic* is silent, exactly like the 'p' in *swimming*."

This facility for humor must have been what broke through my mother's proper Victorian maidenhood and swept her and my father into romance. It was truly an accident that put them into a serious relationship. There was an officers' dance at the Rock Island Arsenal in 1917, an event which my mother greatly resisted attending but at which she did meet the attractive and charming First Lieutenant Lewis Sims. The next day, my father wanted to claim a horse for riding the island trails, but there were none to be had. All were out of the stables that afternoon, assigned to other officers who had requisitioned them earlier. What to do with a free afternoon? Never without ingenuity, Lewis remembered the dance of the evening before. By telephone across the wide Mississippi, he reached the proper Miss Jones and persuaded her to meet him for a late afternoon date and dinner. Thus Edward and I were born — all for want of a horse!

Our parents lived into old age and kept the vows of their marriage through many reverses of fortune. The faith that they practiced as Sunday school teachers through the Great Depression and cheerful church attendance in all their years built a foundation of fidelity and mutual admiration. The high sense of humor that prevailed in our home was also a source of endurance, not unfailingly, but as an undercurrent that might erupt at any time. Laughter punctuated almost every dinnertime.

One evening, Lewis had us all in stitches and bewilderment with his story about how he and his New England college friend Park Shaw invented a men's club so exclusive that the only members were the two of them even though the club was open to general membership. Their secret of exclusivity lay in the name they gave the club. It was so difficult to pronounce that only those who could repeat it exactly after a first hearing were eligible for membership. Edward and I never qualified. It took us multiple tries, stumbling between misplaced syllables and eruptions of hee-haws:

CONSTANTINOPOLITANISHADOODLESOCKINBOKFIFENKOFF!

As a special tribute to our father, I want to put into narrative the most famous of his stories, one that I have used for years when stuck for a joke but have plenty of time and room for pantomime. In 1962 and again in 1967, I served for many months as a missionary to Japan, working as priest in charge of an English-speaking congregation of the Anglican Diocese of Tokyo. Included in the annual clergy conference in 1962 as a guest, I was invited to tell a story to the several dozen Japanese clergy who comprised the diocese, almost none of whom spoke English. My father's story came to mind since it required more gestures than language. I cleared my throat and began, trusting my father's spirit to carry me through the risk.

There was a little man of singular unimportance who always wanted a tailor-made suit. He regularly took Sunday morning breakfast with a cluster of cronies at a local diner to which he walked each week, having no car. Carefully saving his money, he finally put together enough for a tailor-made suit. Proudly he showed up on Sunday morning, and, before seating himself, he turned fully around in front of his friends, asking, "How do you like my new suit, fellas?" They all exclaimed their approval except for one rather picky pal. "It looks great except for one thing: the left sleeve is shorter than the right." Sure enough. The little man had to admit the flaw. Monday morning found the customer at the tailor's shop complaining about the short sleeve. The tailor, a man of diplomacy, said, "You are right about the sleeve, but you must remember that your suit is not an ordinary garment. It is a living thing and will take some time to adjust to the particularities of your body. However, you can hasten the process if you take the left cuff in your thumb and fingers and, as you wear the suit, pull gently down to bring the left sleeve in line with the right."

Satisfied, the man returned to his gang at the diner next Sunday. Pulling at his left cuff, he addressed his friends, "How do you like my suit now?" Again, everyone exclaimed admiringly save for the picky pal. "It's much improved," he admitted, "but a new problem develops in the left lapel when you pull down on the cuff. Your pull on the cuff forces the lapel out from your body in a most awkward way." Sure enough, the whole left lapel bowed out most unbecomingly. On Monday morning, the customer was again at the tailor's. The craftsman, never at a loss, admitted the problem but reminded the man about living garments. "They all require time to conform to the contours of the human body. However, if you turn your head sharply left and tuck the offending lapel under your chin, it will speed the process of adjustment. But you must continue to pull gently down on the left cuff."

Satisfied, the little man returned to the diner and his friends the next Sunday. Walking up to their table while tugging at his left cuff and tucking the lapel beneath his left chin, he had to growl sidewise, "How about my new suit now, fellas?" Wonderful improvement, they all agreed except for the persistent critic. "Look, friend, when you twist your head so sharply left and tuck the lapel under your chin, the maneuver pulls your suit coat up in the rear and exposes your crotch, making it sag badly." Sure enough, the stride, as it is properly called, hung down shockingly from behind. So back to the tailor went our little man early

Monday morning. "My friend," said the tailor, "the same principle of time required for jackets applies equally to the trousers to conform to bodily contours. However, the process can again be accelerated. This time, while tugging and tucking on your coat, just reach around behind you with your right hand and hitch up your stride, giving it a good hoist."

A lot less comfortable with his walk to the diner next Sunday but obedient to the principle, the awkwardly contorted little man in his tailor-made suit passed between two orthopedic surgeons who, in their astonishment, turned around to stare. "What in the world do you suppose is wrong with that pathetic cripple?" asked one to the other. "I couldn't for the life of me say," was the reply. "But," he went on, "that's the best damn-looking suit I have ever seen!"

It worked. Most of the clergy understood not a word, but they responded with hoots of laughter, some even falling backward on the tatami mats that covered the floor.

Of my mother it must be said that she demonstrated greater strength of character than any of us over the years of our life as a family. She grew in stature and stood against all adversity as an axis around which our little foursome gathered energy and hope. She is the conspicuous hero of our pilgrimage. Mother grew up in protected privilege as the oldest of three daughters of a wealthy and very conservative patrician. Through much personal and family deprivation during the years of her marriage, she emerged a decided liberal in political and social orientation. In her 50s and 60s, long after her comfortable and conservative upbringing, she endured my father's financial reverses in uncomplaining loyalty to him, moving from one small apartment to another in Kansas City. Without her steadfastness as a wife and mother and without her readiness to work, first in Kansas City real estate and later as a salesperson in a fashionable women's clothing store, the family would have suffered real privation.

Much of our mother's need to steady us and contribute to the family fortunes rose from the sharp disconnect between our father's intelligence and the low level of his worldly success. In all his working life, his annual income never exceeded four figures. About our father's keen mind and personal charm there was never a doubt, but brother Edward and I have suffered a long-standing puzzlement over why our father was never a conspicuous achiever. Edward tells about a painful episode in our father's odyssey that he learned years later from our mother. In the dark of one night, when our father was at home between his long trips as a linen salesman, she awoke to hear him sobbing at the bedroom window. Responding to her embrace of comfort, he confessed that his anguish rose from feeling himself a total failure in life and said that he wished himself dead.

This deep sadness in our father is confirmed by a remark I remember hearing him make many times in his later years. Often he would tell me that he believed implicitly in life after death as God's promise of a second chance to make something of one's life. The only sensible explanation of this deep despondency lies in his experience of abandonment as a sensitive and aspiring child. From someone in the family comes this story. When Lewis was 10 years old and living with the Field family in Montague, Massachusetts, his mother promised to pick him up for school one morning. Lewis waited on the front steps all day for the fulfillment of her promise, but no one ever came. Such emotional cruelty must embed itself deep in one's psyche and permanently cloud one's sense of personal worth, especially since the experience may not have been an isolated disappointment.

Mother's second sister, Aunt Dot, held a distinct place in the family as a woman of unique spirituality and love of birds. Late in life she married a Navy cook, Phren Sonier, whom she always referred to simply as Sonier. I remember her best as the spirited singer of a comic ballad about a man who kept a mischievous goat:

> A man named Worth, a friend of mine,
> Had three red shirts on his clothesline.
> He bought a goat just for a kid
> That soon ate up his Sunday lid.
> Worth built a pen, all straight and stout,
> To keep that goat from getting out.
> But that goat got out one night at nine
> And ate those shirts off Worth's clothesline.
> Now Worth, he got mad and vowed and swore
> That he would have the old goat's core.
> He took him by his woolly back
> And tied him to the railroad track.
> And when the train did hove in sight,
> It gave the goat an awful fright.
> He struggled and kicked with might and main,
> Coughed up the shirts and flagged the train.

Humor is a spiritual gift. Strange that we almost have to read into the biblical literature to find flashes of fun and joy. That may be partly why the Christmas story in Luke is so cherished. Above the solemnity and discomfort of the trek by donkey to Bethlehem and the earthy animal odor of the stable, we catch the overarching joy of the angels' anthem. And perennially that crude and humorless birth scene gets translated in pageantry and music with a great lilt. Often it plays out in children's dramas with spontaneous accents on humor. One Christmas Eve at my parish church in Baltimore, the congregation broke up when Joseph, in unrehearsed dialogue and a fake beard, solemnly asked the innkeeper for a room and was answered, "Do you have a reservation?"

Chapter 5

Adolescence, Personal and Cultural

Kansas City had become my father Lewis's home in 1933 when, able to work once again after his fall and skull fracture, he was given a job as room clerk at the upscale, full-service Bellerive Hotel in midtown. Grandfather, who had invested in the hotel, was again the benefactor. Although the Bellerive was in receivership at that time as the result of Depression-induced bankruptcy, it was open and struggling back to life on low wages for its employees. Lewis's salary was $1500 a year in monthly increments of $125. He dutifully sent most of this to Davenport, where his wife and two sons remained without much in the way of amenities. Our father visited Davenport and his family only twice during the year he lived alone in Kansas City. They were exquisitely happy reunions, especially the one at Christmas. Our parents' financially forced separation seems, in retrospect, not to have diluted their devotion to each other and may have even enhanced their love. I remember the wrenching sadness of both parents the day after Christmas when Lewis had to go to the train.

Then came the day in August 1934, following my 14th birthday and Edward's 11th, when we all moved to Kansas City. Grandfather took us to the Rock Island depot where we began an overnight drag in the cheap coach seats. When I complained about the seats, Mother, who was

31

already exasperated by the trauma of moving, upbraided me with an oft-repeated rebuke: "Bennett, you ought to have been born a millionaire's child!" Mother was entirely right. My taste for Pullman accommodations and first-class everything (when I can get it) has always lurked beneath a mildly cultivated habit of trying to live simply and never really succeeding.

After that overnight trip in facing coach seats, Lewis met us at Union Station in the big city. Having no car, we piled into a honking taxi. We were awestruck at the size of everything as the taxi steered us to a destination on Armour Boulevard and Kenwood Avenue about two miles down-distance from the Hotel Bellerive. Lewis had arranged a third-floor, walk-up apartment for us that had one bedroom, a bath, and a little kitchen. Edward and I were given the small bedroom, while Mother and Dad slept in the pull-down Murphy bed in the living-dining room. How we got our furniture from Davenport into that tiny place I can't imagine. Some of it surely went into storage because our mother's Chickering grand piano turned up later when fortune smiled in 1937 and we moved to a three-unit residential complex at the Bellerive after Lewis was promoted to resident manager.

Having admitted to complaints about the overnight coach seats on the Rock Island and a lifelong taste for things of beauty and privilege, I believe it important to record here that at no time do I recall a sense of despondency by any of the four of us at being squeezed into that little apartment. Lewis's two-year work loss after his accident in 1930 and the Depression years that followed must have toughened us spiritually. As I look back, I feel that we were advantaged, not deprived, by the tremendous losses endured by so many in the 1930s. Almost everyone suffered, particularly in the Midwest. Unemployment reached as high as 30% in Davenport, and every bank failed. The newspapers reported so many suicides in our city that we lost count. Yet neither Edward nor I recollect the stringent Davenport and Kansas City years as times of fraying family ties or darkened spirits. Just the reverse. We remember growing up cheerfully through those early teen years. How come?

My foundational happy memory is that love, discipline, and unfailing church attendance shaped our life together. These were our family values. Not for a single good or ill-remembered moment did Edward or I doubt that we were cherished and admired. We were corrected and rebuked, of course, especially for sloppy table manners and dirty hands, but we always knew our parents' pride and joy in us as their sons. I am certain that parental love is the reason for risking uncertainty as a beckoning call to life. Uncertainty is the name for every tomorrow and every major decision, and the freedom to risk must rise from a sense of security anchored and nourished in an unconditional parental embrace. My brother and I were loved. Maybe that is why most people are not in jail! Most of us seem to be motivated by a sense of decency and compassion and the hope of being well thought of.

Penitence is another clue to the nearly universal longing to stand well with one's self, with others, and with God. Even impenitence is a clue. Otherwise, we would not cling so fiercely to the protective habit of blaming others in our desperation to be well thought of. This instinct runs as deep and enduring as the trenchant myth of Adam and Eve, in which Adam blames Eve and even God by implication: "The woman whom thou gavest to be with me, she gave me of the tree" (Genesis 3:12, KJV). Eve follows suit by accusing the snake: "The serpent beguiled me" (Genesis 3:13, KJV). Only those who are blessed with adequate self-esteem and the experience of forgiveness by loved ones can admit to being wrong. Although evil and ugliness infect the human story at every turn, I believe that their grip on the human spirit would not distort human behavior so darkly if all of us could access memories of our childhood and youth with a solid sense of being loved. I know that my odyssey of living into liberation began in the womb. This is not to say that I have never resorted to blaming others, but rather that I know instantly what a cowardly and imprisoning maneuver the blaming of others is. And when I resort to blaming circumstances or other people, I am aware that my guilt remains. The consequence of shifting blame remains even now what it was in the truth of the biblical myth: the man and the woman lost the garden and lived in exile.

Our Kansas City years were mostly bright with joy, as were the Davenport years. In our new home three floors above and overlooking busy Armour Boulevard, I prized the sound of the hot tamale peddler as he pushed his cooking cart ahead of him in a slow trudge back and forth along the miles of that city street. If I try hard, I can still hear the tinkle of the little bell that announced his passing presence every evening, summer and winter. At the dinner table one freezing winter night, I said that I felt sorry for the peddler in the cold dark of the street below. My father responded that I should admire the man, not feel sorry for him. In those hard times, the hot tamale man was making the best of the worst, working at what he could do for himself and for those dependent on him. Furthermore, he was warm out there from the steam in his cart that kept the tamales hot!

From our tiny apartment, I relished the walk to and from Westport Junior High School, presided over by the most patrician principal of my remembrance, the silver-haired Miss Jessie Baker. I deeply admired my teacher of algebra, Miss Sanford, who never graded a test paper herself. She had us kids hand our tests across the aisle so that we could grade one another's papers and learn self-respect from the practice of strict honesty. It was from Miss Sanford that I learned and still remember Shakespeare's advice spoken by Polonius to Laertes. I write here from a memory cemented in place by that noblest of all my teachers at Westport:

> This above all, to thine own self be true,
> And it must follow as the night the day
> Thou canst not then be false to any man.
> — *Hamlet* I, iii

I remember nothing of algebra, only the luminous character of the woman who trusted and taught us. I was astounded to pass the course with a B because I have always been deficient with math and numbers, but Miss Sanford's quality of teaching made the difference. Math took on some kind of high fascination under the influence of a teacher whose reason to be in the classroom was plain and simple love of the subject and care for her students.

When our father was promoted to assistant manager at the hotel, we acquired our first family car in a dozen years. It was a used but shiny Terraplane, a smaller version of the Hudson. It had a real clock and radio, both with circular dials. The windshield was a wonder: it opened out from hinges on the frame above to let the wind blow in for cooling. That small, two-door coach became a chariot for dates with my first real girlfriend, Cordelia Alice Murphy. Cordie was the younger sister to two remarkably able older brothers, Franklin and George. Both brothers followed their late father into the medical field. Franklin achieved notable fame in both the academic and corporate business worlds. He was dean of the University of Kansas School of Medicine and later president or chancellor of two universities (Kansas and the University of California, Los Angeles). Subsequently, he became chairman and chief executive officer of the Times-Mirror Corporation, publisher of the *Los Angeles Times* and other newspapers. In addition, Franklin became a confidant and medical counselor to Henry Ford II and served many years as a director of the Ford Motor Company. George, younger than Franklin by two or three years, followed their father into the practice of medicine and served with distinction as a professor of medicine and cardiology at the Cornell University Medical College in New York City.

My relationship with the Murphy family influenced me both positively and negatively. On the one hand, I felt honored to be a favorite of Cordie and her mother. On the other hand, I felt diminished by her powerful brothers, especially by Franklin whose brilliance in conversation tended to leave me intimidated and speechless. Except for my painful sense of personal and social inferiority as a high school and college boy, I might have sought a mature and lasting relationship with Cordie and been her suitor into marriage. But we would not have made a good match. She was a lovely, intelligent, and patrician young woman, but I often felt a sense of low self-esteem in her presence. Although never conveyed by Cordie, I remember feeling abashed that the little Terraplane was badly outranked by her mother's big LaSalle (a smaller Cadillac in the 1930s and 40s). Her older brothers were both medical doctors, one of them superbrilliant in conversation and professional achievement. Being a Kansas college graduate and a dropout from premedical studies for a transfer to philosophy, I believed that I could not compete, and so I quit the race with the Murphy family. It may be quite telling that I do not recall thinking of Cordie in all the subsequent years of marriage to another, into graduate schools, parish ministries, and a seminary professorship — until I was elected a bishop and moved into a stately house in Atlanta with seven fireplaces, an elevator, and a big white Buick in the garage. This seems striking evidence of a cultivated sense of inferiority in me until I achieved some worldly status to put alongside her brothers and the Murphy family LaSalle.

Adolescent insecurity was a crippling block to my sense of personal worth. This could be every adolescent's bugaboo and the reason why the stretch into maturity can feel like an endless project. My struggle to develop a sense of self-worth probably rose from some causes that will always remain obscure, but three such sources are clear. First, I was physically small. Second, I felt like a dumbbell. I could not play the numbers game in school, and doing arithmetic was like digging a ditch with a stick. Third, there was always the large financial and social distance between me and most of my friends such as Cordie and her cluster of privileged girls and boys at the Mission Hills Country Club. But of the three, the second was the worst and most enduring plague.

Although I had a very happy start in the certainty of parental love, adolescence planted a sense of self-denigration that plagued me all through high school, college, antisubmarine training in the navy, graduate theology schools, and years of preaching and essay writing as a parish priest. All this despite the fact that I graduated second in my class at Virginia Theological Seminary in 1949, was appointed to the teaching faculty of the Virginia Seminary in 1966, and held a visiting professorship in theology at Emory University's Candler School of Theology from 1980 to 1988. As bishop of the Episcopal Diocese of Atlanta and chair of the Pastoral Letter Committee from 1977 to 1982, I wrote all the pastoral letters to the church from the House of Bishops. And in the years since 1972, I have published four books as a theologian. Those who viewed my accomplishments from the outside might never have imagined that I felt so inadequate.

My perennial sense of inferiority has diminished since Kansas City days, but the layers of self-rejection lie deep and readily aroused by the insidious standards of personal worth in the American culture. They keep all of us, in varying degrees, as prisoners of the insidious competitive norms of a fierce financial and appearance-oriented culture. I believe that most Americans suffer a silent psychic bondage exacerbated by the need for self-importance, nonambiguity, and a secure place in heaven. All of these requirements are stridently and successfully addressed by a religious fundamentalism. The war in Iraq is waged by an administration led by a Texas oilman and ranch owner in the name of a domesticated god who blesses America on demand.

What this means socially and theologically is that the present gargantuan military warship of America may be sunk to its gunnels in cosmic idolatry, its decks awash in slippery materialistic greed and sinking for want of compassion for the earth and for one another in the human family. America and its government, at this critical point in our pilgrimage, seem to have backed down into the blind bravado of cultural adolescence. We may be bottom-bound in the ocean of history for want of the rescuing power of public justice and private honor upon which the nation was founded. We are led by a thinly veiled neofascist conspiracy that seeks to run the nation for the benefit of business, the military, and the investor class.

In the year 2006, our nation may have sunk to the lowest level of gluttonous self-serving in all its brave and blemished history, but my ardent hope is that current world-wide contempt for the imperial lust of present American political leadership will hasten the day of that leadership's repudiation. An aroused national and global citizenry has begun, even as I write, to mass in public protest of American bullying across the world. The United States is not detached from a moral universe. We reap as we sow! This truth is far more than a pious motto, far more than a moral mandate in all the world's religions. The truth that we reap as we sow extends now to postmodern science where the same axiom is honored. Quantum physics ratifies the primordial intuition that all things cohere in an interwoven web of living connectivity. All is one, and what we do to other selves and other nations must, in the very nature of things, rebound on ourselves! This is the only proper power politics for the world's lone superpower. The United States of America, with more than 10,000 nuclear warheads in storage, submarines, and launching silos, must one day repudiate its arrogant unilateral and retaliatory violence, or we will bring upon ourselves and the entire world an incinerating apocalypse.

As to the global environment, whatever we do to other organisms in the web of life we do to ourselves, from the pinnacle of the hierarchy of consciousness in the human species to its lowest discernable pulsing structures in the rocks and rills of the living earth. The late quantum physicist David Bohm put the iron paradox of cosmic individuality and universal community in memorable terms: "Everywhere there is separateness without separation." This quantum principle is easily illustrated. Allow your thumbs to overlap and then lock your remaining eight fingers together to make a bowl-like shape in front of you. Eight distinctly separate fingers, when laced together, make an inseparable whole that, when tightly joined, becomes a small container that can hold water for a while. This profound paradox is basic to cosmic order in quantum theory: "separateness without separation."

Progressives in politics might consider a forthright election slogan in 2008. It could read, simply, "Grow up, America."

Chapter 6

Auto Disaster, Sex,
and Evolution Science

In my old age, I look back on a progressive pilgrimage and feel that hope is the soil of my life. I became aware of the irrepressibility of hope in my own embrace of life when, long after my ordination to the ministry of the Episcopal Church, I came upon the writings of the French Jesuit scientist and mystic Pierre Teilhard de Chardin (1881–1955). He is properly called by the second name in that series, Teilhard (pronounced *Tayhar*). Later in this chapter, I will take a brief look at the great man's grasp on the dynamic of evolution and my own dream of the future that is nourished by one of the laws of evolving life that he proposed. Meanwhile, keeping to the sequence of these memoirs, some of my finest memories involve high school and college friendships, along with episodes of note punctuated by a brief stint in the U.S. Navy in late 1940.

My principal friend in high school was Charles Richardson. Chuck, a handsome rake of 17, had a family place with a sailboat at the dock at Lake Lotawanna near Kansas City. The lake was a large body of muddy Missouri creek water formed by an earthen dam downstream. For midwesterners accustomed to Missouri mud, it was a perfect place to fish, swim, and ply the waters in a variety of powerboats and sailboats. Chuck and I were in almost all the same high school classes. Neither of us did very well in our classes because of our specializing in horse play, school plays, dates, and dances. Two of my most vivid recollections of high school days involved the only severe auto accident of my life and my enchantment with the first sensations of adolescent romance and sexual arousal.

The auto accident happened on a 35-mile drive home from Lake Lotawanna with Chuck at the wheel of his father's new 1937 Packard. Barreling down the four-lane section of U.S. Highway 71 south of Kansas City, we passed a slower-moving vehicle that suddenly swerved left into our passing lane. In those days, cars were equipped with exposed, chrome-plated front and rear bumpers that ran parallel to the radiator grill in front and to the trunk at the rear. The outboard ends of each bumper were curved slightly to conform to the shape of the front and rear fenders, forming in each case a kind of exposed hook like the crook of the fingers in a half-closed fist. When the car we were passing moved suddenly left, the right front bumper end of the Packard hooked and locked into the left rear bumper end of the offending car ahead. Both vehicles were clipping along at high speeds when the ominous hooking happened. Chuck panicked, executing precisely the wrong and most perilous maneuver. He hit the brakes, the effect of which was to lock the bumper ends even more securely, pulling the speeding cars into each other. I remember thinking, "For God's sake, Chuck, ease off on your brakes, speed up a little, and steer slightly left." That way, we would be quickly and safely disengaged, particularly since the offending car was slowing, giving us the advantage of easing past him. But my panic rendered me utterly mute, and Chuck's instincts played him false.

With the tires of the Packard squealing, its rear end was jerked off the road to the left by the pulling fulcrum of locked bumper ends. This fatal lock of the bumpers was broken by a force that jerked the Packard off the pavement, making it slide, driver's side forward, while yanking both sets of bumpers from their brackets. The careening Packard was thus released to regain the road, but Chuck's front wheels were turned hard left so that it threw the Packard from skidding left-side forward to a sudden power twist. The car screeched off the pavement and onto the opposite shoulder with the right side moving forward. Still careening sideways at fairly high speed, the Packard, with its rear wheels over the edge of the shoulder and its undercarriage scraping stones and dirt, flipped onto its top twice before coming to rest on its right side. Both the hood and rear trunk lid had twisted open and off in the tumbling twirl, but the roof supports held firm. Even though the tops of cars in those days were fabric-covered (steel turret tops had yet to be developed), our heads had not penetrated the fabric for having hit the crossover steel bars that ran between the interior roof lining and the exterior fabric top.

Both of us climbed out of the carnage through the open window on the driver's side, Chuck going first. He suffered hardly a scratch. When I followed him, hoisting myself through the window, I felt a sharp pain in my right hand. It was bleeding badly. What happened was that I had my right hand on the open windowsill of the passenger side as a way of steadying myself in the tumbling Packard (no safety belts in those days), while Chuck must have been holding the steering wheel to steady himself. When the car flipped on the shoulder, it pinned my right hand under the car for an instant as it rolled. Even in that instant, my hand was pinned long enough to tear the flesh of the two central fingers to the bone and puncture a gash in the back of the hand. By the time Chuck and I gained the side of the highway beside the wreck, a host of cars had stopped, and one man offered to take me to the nearest hospital.

I remember being afraid of losing my hand while it bled on the front floor mat of the kind man's car. But I have no recollection of the hospital except the opaque blur of my distressed parents at my bedside when I awoke from anesthesia. The surgical repair on my hand was done by our family doctor, Sidney Shapiro, MD, a quiet and obviously gifted practitioner. Dr. Shapiro had to sew together all the tendons in the two torn fingers and stitch up the hole in the back of my hand. I had to keep my hand soaking almost every waking moment in a warm solution of Epsom salt for two weeks to forestall infection. My hand healed so quickly that I was gripping a golf club at the Meadow Lake course at 95th Street and State Line in less than three weeks. Evidence of the injury remains by way of long inner-margin scars on the two center fingers and a permanently swollen knuckle region on the back of my right hand. But my gripping facility was unimpaired, and I swung a golf club, never expertly but very gratefully, until my 83rd year when prostate cancer finally weakened an aging body.

There are two reasons for detailing this story of the auto accident. First, in all the rich deposit of recollections of my teenage years, this episode is the most vividly memorable. Second, the miracle of surviving a double-turnover crash in a fabric-top automobile at 60 miles per hour set me to thinking that God had something special in mind for me in the years ahead. There is a text in the gospel of Luke that became a kind of guiding life principle thereafter. It comes to mind unbidden whenever I face a decision at some turn in the road. "For unto whomsoever much is given, of him shall be much required" (Luke 12:48, KJV).

The Depression years with my father's slow drag into financial security and then its sudden loss soon afterward were factors that surely contributed to feelings of adolescent inferiority. But my guess is that, at bottom, all of us are domesticated to vulnerability in a stridently competitive American social order. From childhood, most of us must feel pitted against one another at school for grades and from adolescence onward for pulchritude. My high school romance with Cordie Murphy was a genuine high, a first experience of the blossoming realities of otherness in emotional attraction and sexuality. I came to high school age without the slightest tutelage in sex either from home or school and only the smutty stories that abound in a boys' locker room. I fell into the heated fascination of gingerly groping in Cordie's femininity, but a Presbyterian-shaped conscience raised a brick wall between petting and anything more. So I stumbled into the marriage bed some years later with another love as a virginal ignoramus.

There was a time since then when I said to myself that my virginity at marriage was no blessing. Better to have sewn some sexually instructive wild oats and come to marriage with some experience and wisdom about this most celebrated and impassioned species-perpetuating impulse. Now, in the wake of a social era of wild promiscuity and sexual degradation, my value system has returned to the restraints of my adolescent years. America today is not a happy culture. Our society is traumatized by greed, gore, sex, and war. Little wonder that fundamentalist churches prosper. The longing for moral certainty and a high-minded cultural compass gives conservative religious leadership a wide hearing. The decadence of postmodern culture raises the human fear level to such a degree that biblical interpretations trumpeting worldly doom and heavenly rescue are eagerly heeded and lavishly supported.

The trauma of a culture adrift in hedonistic self-serving accounts for much of the fear and anger that mark the fundamentalist spirit. I have made a personal friend of a gifted biblical literalist and have been consistently bowled over by the fever of his rejection of historical criticism. That a man so intellectually superior could dismiss so hatefully the evolutionary understanding of the history of life on earth continues to surprise me until I examine my own presuppositions and discover in myself the power of emotion over the intellect. Still, it remains to me the profoundest mystery why my inner makeup should lift me to love the progressive view in almost all fields, especially in the realms of theology, politics, and science. I believe I am as aware and as rueful as anyone of the grossly hedonistic turn in American culture, but it has not driven me into moralistic rigidity and biblical literalism. Now I can see better than ever what I believe are the reasons for fundamentalist absolutism, but I am grateful for the grace that has mysteriously moved me to an expansive view of life and the world.

As a resolute theological and political liberal, I remain hopeful. If we can outgrow our fascination with the cowboy strut and imperialist militarism of the Bush administration while preserving as best we can the living environment, I believe that the human odyssey will move from a long-protracted adolescence into an era of advancing maturity. Such a future will be marked by an overtaking value system of nonviolence, a movement to nonviolence already powerful enough to have established an impressive record of nonviolent conflict resolution. Undeniable cases in point are (1) the American civil rights movement of the 1960s, (2) the nonviolent achievement of freedom for the several republics of the former Soviet Union in the late 1980s, and (3) the nonviolent revolution of 1994 in South Africa that shifted political power from a white minority to the black majority. The mounting commitment to nonviolence across the world could be the energy to propel humanity from 8000 years of using power for domination, oppression, and war to a new level of global maturity in using power for partnership, collaboration, and peace.

More than 40 years have gone by since my first adventure into the scientific research and vaulting mysticism of Pierre Teilhard de Chardin (*The Future of Man*, translated from the French by Norman Denny, Harper & Row, New York, 1964). Over those 40 years, I gradually developed a strong conviction that the human odyssey is poised now on a capital hinge of history, a conviction shared by hosts of writers and historians. Along with his accomplishments in science, Teilhard was grounded in the gospel records of Jesus and the defining theology of St. Paul. His digs and research as an archeologist and paleontologist turned his mind to the future. For him, the past truly became prologue. If we can open our minds to the long arrow of cosmic evolution and the brief time line of human presence, we can be prompted to a hopeful sense of history yet to be made.

Teilhard's immersion in the deep past led him to deduce a guiding law of steadily increasing brain specialization that he named the law of complexity-consciousness. According to Teilhard, as the evolutionary thrust of life slowly led to an increasingly complex arrangement of neural and supporting skeletal components in the bodies of all organisms from primordial ooze to human ingenuity, consciousness in the brain stem was advancing in parallel with the complexification process. In humanity, as the species emerged from lower primate forms, consciousness at the instinctual level erupted into reflective self-consciousness. Teilhard wrote over and again, "We are the species that knows and knows we know." Given the dynamic flow of evolution, a highly self-conscious *Homo sapiens* as cunning humanity is only the latest flowering of the evolving life process, not the last. More in the way of human maturation and ingenuity is yet to come. But maturity will emerge successfully only if humanity can perceive and act on our oneness with all of life in time to reverse the planetary plunder that our ingenuity has wrought.

Of this critical moment in the global drama, Teilhard wrote, "The whole future of the earth, as of religion, seems to me to depend on the awakening of our faith in the future." This is Teilhard's way of saying what I mean by living on a hinge of history. In spite of the ominous portents of my own nation's convulsive commitment to war in the year 2006, I believe that the human pilgrimage is turning toward a new world of fulfillment in compassion, justice, and peace. This phenomenon of human behavior has not been widely known since the primordial, feminist-dominated, matrilineal society of premilitarist cultures. Since the emergence of the imperialist, male-dominant social and political orders of 7000 to 5000 BCE, the human experience has known a planetary overrun by an ever-increasingly aggressive, inventive, and violent *Homo sapiens*. But it seems clear to me that we are privileged to be present on the moving arrow of evolution when a new humanity is in the making.

There is now in gestation a higher level of consciousness that knows love to be the propulsive power of all life. This emerging new consciousness has been long in the making, sliding into visibility with the appearance of the Buddha and the Hebrew prophets and climaxed by the coming into history of Jesus of Nazareth. Many energies are now coalescing in a world become too small for violence, energies from the new sciences and the old religions. The human species is evolving from competitive cunning to collaborative compassion, from *Homo sapiens* to what I want to name *Hetero pacificus* using a gender-inclusive prefix and the Latin term for *peaceable*.

From his faith, informed by scrupulous research and field experience in the earth sciences, Teilhard wrote, "Some day, after mastering the winds, the waves, the tides, and gravity, we shall harness for God the energies of love. And then, for the second time in history, man will discover fire." There is much more to write about our turning point in time, and concluding chapters in these memoirs will concentrate on evidence that supports a sturdy hopefulness.

Chapter 7

Minor Triumphs
and a Colossal Failure

Following an undistinguished graduation from Westport High School in 1938, my life was lifted by a first real trip away from home. Three friends from Davenport invited me to accompany them on a two-week toot into the Rocky Mountains of the American West. On Monday, August 15, the three of them started west from Davenport in a 1937 Terraplane, the business car of Donald McDonald's dad. I started north the same morning by train and met them at the Rock Island depot in Des Moines. After a cheap lunch (we were determined to spend sparingly from start to finish), we took off for Omaha, heading for the Badlands and Black Hills of South Dakota. Next were the Big Horn Mountains of Wyoming and the tumbling waters of Shell Canyon. Still ahead of us westward were Yellowstone National Park and Old Faithful. Then we continued south along the east escarpment of the Grand Tetons and into Colorado for a week at Estes Park.

The four of us made a happy quaternity of eager young bucks on the margins of manhood. We were Don McDonald and myself, close friends from childhood and still in regular touch in our mid-80s; Gordon Rock, now deceased but long a medical doctor in Davenport; and Nick Kruse, the tallest and most robust of us all. Nick graduated in architecture from an eastern university and had a distinguished career until his death a few years ago. That trip was a teenage hoot, and I still have the text of the journal I kept every day of the two-week adventure. Looking back 67 years later, the most remarkable feature of that odyssey was the cost of it. We each paid for our own meals and overnight lodging and split the cost of travel four ways. The most we paid for gas was an outrageous 34 cents a gallon at the top of a very steep mountain highway; elsewhere the average was about 18 cents. I took the $50 in damages paid to my father by the insurance company from the accident on Highway 71 the previous summer and came home two weeks later with $3.87. That represents an average of $3.30 a day. Incredible!

Junior college came that fall. My experience there is memorable for two quite antithetical assessments of my personal abilities by two different teachers. One was a chemistry professor whose name, mercifully, I cannot recall. He was a real turd, but I have to take some responsibility. I exercised poor judgment because I knew from high school that I had no talent for the subject and ought to have steered clear of test tubes and Liebig condensers. At least I had the good judgment to seek out the professor for special help in advance of a semester exam. He was an impatient man who went over some material with me by way of review but skipped one section entirely, saying that there was no need to spend time on that material because I lacked the brains to comprehend it. I remember being deeply demeaned. No teacher had ever dismissed me out loud as a dunce, although several in previous years had no doubt privately assessed me similarly. But to be given the back of the hand in such a dismissive way, even though true, was a searing insult. It was a devastating moment of being stabbed in the heart because it confirmed my self-appraisal based on the prolonged experience of being found wanting in personal worth by the competitive grading system from 6 years old to college at 18. As a teacher myself for several years, I never ran a competitive seminar or classroom unless forced to do so by the school administration. I gave only pass-fail assessments. Each one was accompanied, wherever possible, by personal consultation in which there was almost always a way to encourage each student by both challenge and appreciation.

The other personal assessment of my native ability in junior college came from a professor of sociology. His evaluation was a totally unexpected salute to my capacity for absorbing and analyzing course material. Naturally, I remember the professor's name! He was Mr. Lewis, a genial scholar who took the class on field trips, one of them to the Fulton State Hospital for the insane in Fulton, Missouri. We went by a smooth Greyhound charter and stayed in the dorms of Westminster College in Fulton. (Incidentally, Westminster College was the location of Winston Churchill's "Iron Curtain Speech" of March 5, 1946 in which he castigated the Soviet Union for its paranoid isolationism following World War II.) Quite out of the blue one day, Mr. Lewis decided to evaluate about half a dozen of us in the presence of the entire class, probably 35 men and women. I was utterly surprised to be singled out when he came to me and said something like this. "Take young Sims. He is gifted with such keen intelligence that he can report accurately on the reading assignments without giving them more than cursory attention during class time. His problem is that he is intellectually lazy and will never amount to much as a student." The good man meant his evaluation as a wake-up call, and the sorrow of it is that, with a few exceptions, it did not wake me up until enrollment in Princeton Theological Seminary nearly 10 years later.

One of those exceptions was a single junior college course in comparative anatomy. I must have signed on for it because of my mother's hope that I might become a medical doctor and also because of Cordie Murphy and her family of doctors. To my surprise, I relished the course, and it remains in memory as the most exciting exposure to classroom and lab knowledge of all my years as a student. The professor was Overton T. Ballard, Ph.D., about 35 years old with prematurely gray hair and a knee-length white lab coat. He carried a great dignity about him along with the faint odor of formaldehyde. His lab also smelled of that preservative for anatomical specimens. O. T. Ballard quietly inspired careful attention to detail, and he built in me a curiosity about the seemingly miraculous connectivity between anatomies of the life forms that ascended the scale of evolution. I can still remember the names of some bones and muscles in vertebrates and can instantly do crossword puzzles that call for the name of a four-letter arm bone (ulna) and the collarbone that we upright humans have but four-legged creatures lack (clavicle). And I sometimes act the adolescent with my fitness coach in naming one of the principal muscles. The great posterior calf muscle, the gastrocnemius, sounds the most exotic.

Dr. Ballard's principal assignment was to reconstruct the skeleton of a vertebrate from a living specimen that the students, in pairs or singly, had to take alive and kill mercifully. The specimen could be a frog, bird, cat, dog, or any stray and deformed pound animal whose death would be okay. A classmate, Clayton Walker, and I chose a large dog from the pound who had suffered an accident that broke his facial bones and left him looking disfigured. We had to chloroform him, an odious task using a burlap bag. We then boiled his body in an outdoor washtub, removed the flesh, and dried the bones in an oven. We reconstructed the skeleton in fidelity to the damaged structure of the dog, finally mounting it with supporting heavy wire on a beveled and lacquered platform for display in class. Clayton and I scored an A, but I could never again carry out such an assignment. My love for animals would forestall any project that involved killing them.

Still, Overton T. Ballard's polished teaching and quiet demeanor as a scientist pushed me into premedical studies when, after a year of absence from school, I enrolled on a scholarship at Baker University in

Baldwin City, Kansas, 50 miles west of Kansas City. Most of the intervening year between junior college and Baker was spent at Hallmark Cards as an order filler and later at Woolf Brothers as a clothing salesman and general flunkie to the stiffly proud floorwalker Mr. Wyman.

Between the Hallmark and Woolf Brothers jobs, I spent a humbling month on board the old battleship USS *Arkansas* as an apprentice seaman bucking for a commission as an officer in the U.S. Naval Reserve. Easily the most eventful of my three work segments was the 30-day training cruise aboard the *Arkansas*, an ungainly pre-World War I vessel with basket-weave crow's-nest towers that had been reduced to training duty or target towing for gunnery exercises. There must have been 100 recruits for officer's training on the cruise, all of us past our teenage years and with at least two years of college. If we passed muster in the rigors of sea duty aboard the *Arkansas*, we would go to Notre Dame or Northwestern or some such facility for three months of a quick-step training course. Everybody knew the impossibility of reshaping landlubbers for naval leadership in three months, so all new ensigns so trained were wryly designated 90-day blunders.

On the *Arkansas*, we slept in white canvas hammocks slung from hooks in the overheads of several starboard and port-side gun rooms. Each gun room housed a big 5-inch, 38-millimeter rifle mounted on an electrically operated swivel bolted to the heavy deck. Twice during the cruise from New York to Cuba and back, the heavy slide-out sections of the ship's freeboard (above the waterline) were removed, and the guns were exercised using powder and ammunition aimed at a billboard-size target of canvas towed by another vessel about a nautical mile away. This was a fascinating maneuver to watch from the main deck above. Occasionally a gun crew would strike the target, and cheers would resound.

Another fascination associated with the gun rooms occurred whenever the ship hit heavy weather and was pitching and rolling in boiling seas. To operate the 5-inch 38s, the old slide-out panels were removed so that the gunnery crews could swivel and elevate their guns through some 150 horizontal degrees. The panels were designed to fit snugly in their tracks when the guns were not in use, but the fit had loosened over the years in the old *Arkansas*. As a result, the seas would penetrate the loose-fitting panels in heavy weather, and the gun rooms would fill with wildly sloshing saltwater, all of which would eventually drain out to sea through scuppers and drains. In heavy weather, it was grand to be dry and comfy at night in a swaying hammock that was secured to hooks in the overhead.

Another feature peculiar to the old ship was its severely limited capacity for making fresh water from its Kleinschmidt evaporators. This limitation translated into a strict routine for taking showers. Shower times were limited to early mornings and overseen by sentries ordered to use their sidearms on any apprentice seaman found violating the shower drill in which water use was limited to a quick splash before soaping down and a second quick splash for rinsing off. Imagine how delicious it was to get home to a lavish hot bath!

I found the most interesting part of the cruise to be an afternoon of shore leave in the Cuban town of Guantanamo City, a short train ride from the naval base at the deep-water harbor of Guantanamo, a ship and stores facility still in heavy use by our navy. The shocking squalor of that village was my first exposure to degrading poverty. Raw sewage ran in the gutters, and flies swarmed the hanging sides of beef and pork at street-side cafes. Prostitutes with crudely exposed breasts loitered at the open doors of some of the hovels that passed for homes. My encounter with human degradation was so brutal and unexpected that I remember feeling healed by my return to the clean and tidy gun room.

The 30 days of training concluded with a private interview in the forward section of the ship. Each trainee stood before two somewhat scowling officers of senior rank who sat behind a steel table covered with a green cloth. One looked me up and down disdainfully, noting out loud that my weight was below the allowed limit. I had to be 135 pounds and had weighed in at only 126 in the ship's sick bay a few days before. The officer pointed out that I looked skinny and measly-muscled but said that I could go home and eat bananas to qualify for the 90 days of midshipman's school. He then went on to say that midshipman's school was open to those people willing to accept assignment to sea duty as commissioned ensigns in the U.S. Naval Reserve. Stupidly but earnestly, I said I'd be happy to eat bananas and that I would be willing to accept sea duty if I could be assured of an assignment limited to six months so that I could return to college and complete my degree work. The other examining officer exploded at my impertinence, insisting that "no one could predict what that maniac Adolf Hitler would do if the Battle of Britain ended with the invasion and defeat of England!"

The next day, a list of the 100 or so apprentice seaman trainees appeared on the ship's main bulletin board. The names were arranged alphabetically in four sections. Most of the names were in section one. They had qualified for midshipman's school and would be sent orders accordingly. In section two were a dozen or so names of those who failed to qualify physically. I looked in vain for my name in that section, hoping not to have to go home to a diet of bananas. In section three were another dozen names of men who had failed to qualify on psychological grounds. Still my name was not there. In the final section were three lone names of those who had failed to qualify on both physical and psychological grounds. Sure enough, the final name on the last list was "Sims, B. J."

Chapter 8

Fraternity House Mischief

Three years before Kansas was admitted to statehood, Methodist enthusiasts for advanced education staked out a tract at the center of the tiny town of Baldwin City, 50 miles west of Kansas City. The year was 1858, and the pioneering Christians named their new school Baker University to honor Bishop Osmon Cleander Baker, the cleric then presiding over a western Methodist missionary jurisdiction. To have called the new institution a university was a bit of chutzpah, a high, hopeful stretch. Not only did the charter include an undergraduate curriculum, but also included plans for postgraduate education in a school of theology where frontier, circuit-riding Methodist ministers could be trained and dispatched. Thus the proud appellation of university.

When I matriculated in 1941 as a junior, I had no aspiration for the ministry and would have been in the wrong place had I so aspired. By 1941, Baker had no school of theology. In my student days, the school was a university in name only. Between its founding and my arrival, the growth of Baker had been an undulating curve of small peaks and comfortable valleys. A few buildings did mushroom in an off-campus location after the abandonment of the original single building called Old Castle. On-campus construction began with Old Science Hall in 1863 from subscriptions that included $100 from President Abraham Lincoln. It was grandly planned as a four-floor building of stone to be situated at or near the center of the campus. It held a chapel, laboratory and lecture rooms, and a small office for the president. Old Science was later renamed Parmenter Hall for Dr. Charles S. Parmenter, a professor of earth sciences who taught in the building for 39 years. Later came Centenary Hall, a two-story brick building with tall windows that housed an enlarged new chapel on the second floor. After Centenary came Taylor Hall, a classroom building and gymnasium, and then Case Hall, a three-story library building with administrative offices. Later still, a splendid stone structure rose for the sciences named Mulvane Science Hall. As for the student population, 999 were enrolled at Baker in 1906 but fewer than 300 of us in the fall of 1941. We were taught by a faculty of not more than 20 men and women. Small potatoes it was, but a vibrant little crucible for the cultivation of both sound learning and good friendships. In my case, one of those friendships blossomed into high romance and eventuated in marriage two years later.

Today Baker can rightly claim its university status. It is now comprised of three schools of certified academic standing, and there are modern buildings as well as completely renovated old ones on the campus. This splendid cluster of new and vintage facilities in Baldwin City, where the College of Arts and Sciences is located, is the hub of Baker University. The Baker University School of Nursing is located in nearby Topeka, the state capital, while the School of Professional and Graduate Studies uses a multicampus arrangement in Wichita and Kansas City. Total student population now numbers over 2700 with more than 100 full- and part-time faculty. One of my most outstanding young scholars, George Bell Wiley, Ph.D., has been a professor of philosophy and religion at Baker for 25 years. I ordained George to the priesthood while bishop of the Episcopal Diocese of Atlanta, and his old bishop is proud of our university. But Osmon Cleander Baker, the founder whose name the school bears, would probably frown at Baker today. Gone is the old vow to abstain from all alcoholic beverages while enrolled as a student that I had to take. And gone is the prohibition of smoking on campus, although something of that rule may still be intact. While folks smoke on campus these days, it happens nowhere in any of the campus buildings, perhaps not so much a sign of piety as of good manners and good health.

My on-site Baker experience began in 1941 with a preclassroom social whirl called rush week. Students new to Baker were introduced to the fraternity and sorority houses by way of parties and picnics. There were four fraternities and four sororities: Delta Tau Delta, Kappa Sigma, Sigma Phi Epsilon, and Zeta Chi for men and Delta Delta Delta, Alpha Chi Omega, Phi Mu, and Zeta Tau Alpha for women. For me, it was a bewildering week of being rushed by three of the four fraternities. There was plenty to like about each one, and I received invitations to pledge and move into all three that rushed me. The Sig Eps ignored me completely as unqualified, I suppose, since Sig Ep was a muscle and brawn gang. The Sig Eps were almost all varsity athletes, and they must have had me pegged correctly as a skinny squirt. How to choose between the three invitations? I chose Kappa Sigma but knew within a couple of weeks that Kappa Sig was never going to be home. I can't say whether this was a considered judgment, but it probably wasn't. Sometimes you have to go with mounting inner sensations, and I felt a real inner dislocation. I asked for a release from my pledge and sought out the person in the Zeta Chi house to whom I felt most drawn during rush week. Zeta Chi took me in as a kind of second-hand pledge and installed me in a third-floor room. I began to feel at home, even though I was assigned menial chores and subjected to the moderate hazing that goes with being a pledge.

Zeta Chi, the only Baker fraternity not affiliated nationally, calls its chapter Alpha Omega, a sassy foreclosure on its multiplication elsewhere. The house was then, and still is, a much-renovated, three-story frame building that looks as if it were originally a big family dwelling. It conveniently stands a block or two down the main street from campus. In my day, it had second- and third-floor rooms where clothes, books, and desks were kept for pairs or trios of men. For sleeping, we all had steel-framed bunks with shallow mattresses on a large, open-air screened porch that was entered from the rear of the second floor. One of the more odious of the menial tasks assigned to pledges was called rooster duty. Each night every brother noted on a bulletin board the hour of his preference for a wake-up call, and the rooster on duty was required to go to each man separately and give him an on-time shake. There were always two or three among the brothers for whom several shakes were required, and one of the men was inclined to be vicious when awakened. Most every morning, this ill-tempered brother would swing a heavy fist at the rooster while still half asleep. Most of us pledges quickly learned a safe maneuver when approaching his bunk. It involved the use of an elevated broom handle accompanied by the hope that the brother would strike his wrist while swinging and learn some good manners.

Attending a small, denominational college in a thimble-sized village when most of my friends at junior college went directly to state universities in Kansas and Missouri was a bit humbling. Several former classmates also made it to places like Northwestern and Michigan, and one friend won a scholarship to Harvard. But I grew to love the Baker setting in a village with only a few paved streets, most of them brick. In the center of town where the two main streets intersected stood a simple, tapered stone marker mounted by a stout, vertical metal rod capped by a black steel orb. One could stand at the base of the stone structure, called the shepherd's monument, and see in all four directions into rural Kansas. I believe that Baker and Baldwin City wove its charm precisely because of such simplicity. At sunset in the spring and fall, I would occasionally climb out the dormer window of my third-floor room and, gaining a safe spot on the old roof, gaze in solitary delight at the lavish splash of reds and oranges on the darkening western horizon. Now widely traveled, I have seen nowhere in the world more heart-soaring sunsets than in eastern Kansas as a very young man. "Tis the low sun that makes the color." (That was Tennyson's language for King Arthur when he forgave Lancelot's treachery in his adultery with Arthur's queen. This does not make a virtue of betrayal or justify treachery, but it does represent the kind of last word on sin that was uttered for human liberation from the Crucified.)

Physics and chemistry, which were required subjects for premed students, bewildered me. Of the sciences, only biology and geology were natural interests, and I continue into old age with a lively love of archaeology and paleontology, disciplines in which Teilhard de Chardin is a first-magnitude star for me. No wonder I couldn't put his books down when I first encountered his soaring spirit in the mid-1960s! There were college courses that did excite me, though, mainly philosophy and literature. This interest fulfilled the prophetic claim of the Western Auto store manager who, two summers before, believed that I would do okay as a philosopher but not as a wrestler of tires and batteries. The philosophy courses were taught by a favorite professor, Hiram Chester Weld, a youthful Ph.D. not much older than his students. Hi Weld and I arrived at Baker simultaneously, he from the completion of his doctoral work at Boston University and I from a year divided among Hallmark Cards, Woolf Brothers, and a failed try at a naval career.

Instant fascination with philosophy and related subjects prompted my faculty advisor to recommend shifting my major from premed to what really interested me. I had gifts for contemplating life's meaning and for writing papers, and these attributes were nourished and sharpened at Baker, leading ultimately to a life-long vocation in the Christian ministry. However, my commitment to the ministry did not happen until much later. That decision required a galvanic spiritual experience at the naval base in Hawaii following the close of World War II. That episode, which shook my foundations, deserves an emphasis of its own in this chronicle, and I will describe it later in this record of a contemporary pilgrim's progress.

Two more experiences at Baker need to be noted. The first is an episode of indulgence in forbidden wickedness. Six of us Zeta Chi brothers dared to violate the Baker University nondrinking vow. The rule, which was strictly applied, forbade the sale and consumption of alcoholic drink within five miles of the campus. Kansas had been teetotal-dry for years until shortly before my college days when 3.2 beer was allowed by license in little bars. From the beginning of prohibition until the early 1940s, Kansans did their swilling in secret, which prompted the renowned editor of the *Emporia Gazette* William Allen White to write satirically that "every two years Kansans would stagger to the polls and vote dry." But nobody drank in Baldwin City, or, if anyone did, it was never spoken of until six Zeta Chi seniors sneaked out of town in Bill Hoopingarner's Chrysler once a week to a 3.2 beer joint exactly five miles away at a major highway crossroads. We wolfed down peanuts and beer and shared lubricated jollity around a red-checkered tablecloth. Our truancy into late-night boozing might never have been discovered and reported to the dean's office had we been canny and kept to the beer joint at the crossroads. But success in forbidden tomfoolery emboldened the six of us to start using Hoopingarner's big Chrysler trunk as a refrigerator. It was winter, and the beer acted as hidden antifreeze for vow violators. We started to sneak our libations into the Zeta Chi house, where a cozy circle of revelers gathered around the light of a big candle in a dark corner of the dirt-floor basement.

It didn't take long before word came from the dean's office summoning the six of us to a disciplinary meeting with the Reverend Doctor Benjamin A. Gessner in the dining room of the fraternity house. Ben Gessner was the protector of college behavioral traditions and a formidable cleric. Our own fraternity president had snitched on us with no prior warning. I remember being torn between fury and penitence. The man might have put in-house brotherly loyalty before the priggish satisfaction of telling on his friends. On the other hand, what would my parents think? As the dean informed us, letters were being sent to all our homes stating that each of us was henceforward on probation and would risk summary expulsion from school if we ever drank anything stronger than grape juice between then and graduation in May.

Some years later, when I knew more of the scriptures, it occurred to me that Jesus had spoken about the inescapable justice of the moral universe:

> There is nothing covered up that will not be uncovered, nothing hidden that will not be made known. You may take it, then, that everything you have said in the dark will be heard in broad daylight, and what you have whispered behind closed doors will be shouted from the house-tops. — Luke 12:2–3, NEB

But a last word from the cross is not ruthless exposure and condemnation. It is mercy, even before there is penitence. The gift of the grace of forgiveness is never something one has to summon from afar. Forgiveness waits at the door, and it is like a bracing wind when the courage of truth opens the flawed human heart to the healing power of love. In fulfillment of the divine promise, the fraternity president's blue-nose betrayal turned into the bestowal of freedom. My father was instantly amused, not outraged, when the Dean's letter came. He had been a surreptitious beer drinker in college, too. As for Ben Gessner, he and I had a warm reunion when the university invited me back as a lecturer years later. Not only that, but Baker singled me out in 1985 for the honorary degree of Doctor of Humane Letters.

Baker remains a rich source of great and enduring memories, and there is one more to report. The greatest of my memories is a warm cluster of recollections around a lovely girl with a beautiful name. I met her one day on the Zeta Chi bulletin board where her name appeared beside Scoot O'Bryhim's as his date for the autumn hayride a few weeks hence. She was an alumnus of Baker who was teaching school in the dirt-street town of Olivet, Kansas and planned to return for the fall fraternity event. Her name was Beatrice Wimberly, and I had never read a more instantly lovely name. However, names are seldom predictive, and the images they conjure do not often prove true. But in Bea's case, I was bowled over to find, on meeting her, that the person and the name were totally congruent. She was beautiful. Thus began an epic of my life involving a smitten courtship, marriage 2 years later, and 42 more years of a mostly cheerful and productive partnership until I was led to face the mounting disaster of a mismatched pair of one-time lovers. Despite the strange undercurrent of insecurity that plagued our relationship from the beginning, we weathered storms and reared three wonderful children who are strong, loving, and loyal to us both. But the long, rolling waves of insecurity slowly swept away our early resolves to make a life-long marriage, and we agreed in sorrow to divorce in 1985.

The paragraph above compresses loads into little, saying far less than could be recorded if everything were told, but enough has been written to give thanks for years of shared joy. I will chronicle some details later but want to add here my ardent thanksgiving for our three wondrous children. They are, first, the lovely and brainy Laura, then tall and tender Grayson, followed by our gifted writer and exemplary parent, the caboose on our train, David Sims. There will be more about each of them in chapters that follow.

Chapter 9

Return to the Navy

As recounted earlier, I flunked my first attempt to become a naval officer, not unfairly since I was judged unfit on both physical and psychological grounds. But everything changed after Pearl Harbor on December 7, 1941. The armed services suddenly became voraciously hungry for recruits. The saying was that if you could see lightning and hear thunder, man, you were in. The navy must have lost all track of the last name on that fatal list of 1940 rejectees because they took me back. Early in 1942, the navy instituted an officer training program that granted deferments of up to two years for college juniors and seniors who, upon successful graduation, became eligible for midshipman's school at several university sites. Of course I applied, hoping that records from the USS *Arkansas* had been deep-sixed. I wanted to finish college, and I wanted that gold stripe of an ensign in the U.S. Naval Reserve.

My longing for a second chance at the navy came alive at the only gas station in Baldwin City, Kansas. My father had generously loaned me his Oldsmobile for the pre-Christmas dance at the Zeta Chi house on Saturday, December 6. Bea was my date for the dance, and I had taken the Olds to the dirt-street town of Olivet to fetch her. As we drove back to Baldwin City from Olivet, her remarkable intuition kicked in. Out of the blue, she said, "I feel that something momentous is soon to happen in the world." The very next noon, as I was filling the tank of my father's Oldsmobile at the station in Baldwin City, we heard about Pearl Harbor, and I thought to myself, "How did she know?" It was there, on that corner, that I heard the radio announcement of the Japanese attack on Pearl Harbor. The phenomenon of remembering one's precise location when something momentous is announced is well known to all who can recall exactly where they were when they heard that President John Kennedy had been shot.

Upon graduation from Baker University 18 months later (with another undistinguished record), five of us in the class of 1943 who were members of Zeta Chi entrained for South Bend, Indiana for midshipman's school at the University of Notre Dame. I did surprisingly well, relishing the military and academic experience and landing a commission in September as an ensign. Bea and I were affianced at the time. Toward the end of midshipman's training, all of us (about 400 men) heard a lecture from an active submarine commander. The much-decorated officer made it clear that the war was going to be very long. We would have to get our troops from England into the heart of Europe, slugging our way into Germany, and also island-hop in the Pacific until we could survive the carnage of a landing on the islands of Japan. He hoped that some of us would make it home again years down the road.

I went to the telephone immediately afterward to call Bea, who was now back at Baker to finish her degree work. I proposed that we get our relationship cemented by marriage as soon as possible lest I never be seen again. She agreed, and we were married in the Baldwin City Methodist Church with Hiram Weld officiating during a two-week leave between the close of training at Notre Dame and the next assignment. We spent our honeymoon at a fine old hotel in Excelsior Springs, Missouri.

Bea and I then entrained for Miami, Florida, where I had been assigned further training in small-ship naval warfare. I was one of several hundred new ensigns. Most of us were from colleges and universities in the Midwest and had never seen a deep blue sea. I was the exception and had to hide my sense of superiority for having endured Atlantic and Caribbean waters on the old *Arkansas*. At one point in the small-ship training routine, all of us were subjected to an IQ test. I dimly recall taking it, but not seriously. IQ tests had punctuated school days from junior high onward. At the close of the two-month course in Miami, every ensign was given orders to a ship or to some further special training. My orders sent me to Key West for advanced training in antisubmarine warfare, and it included a day on board a real submarine.

Two Key West recollections stand out. One memory clusters around an experience of high drama the day several of us spent as passengers and trainees on an antique World War I submarine. Like the *Arkansas*, the submarine had been relegated to training exercises. We were miles out at sea, in a dive that called for leveling off at 90 feet, the standard operating depth for the old so-called R-boats. Built long before the new fleet submarines then operating in the forward areas of both oceans, R-boats were not designed to withstand ocean pressures below 150 feet. We trainees had been told the story of one old R-boat stationed at Key West that had violated the 150-foot limit and had gone to the bottom with no survivors. On the day of our R-boat cruise, I was standing in the conning section where the periscope is housed when the captain ordered a dive. I felt the deck tilt decidedly down, and I watched the depth gauges slowly register our descent. When the gauges registered just above 90 feet, I expected, along with everybody else, that the boat would begin to level off. Not so. We kept going down, the gauges registering 100, then 110, and then 120. Alarms were clanging, and anxiety mounted in the room while the captain kept ordering a halt to the descent in a strained voice. Everyone knew that it was curtains if we sank below 150. My grip on the nearest stanchion tightened to the point of white knuckles. Suddenly the deck began shifting toward the level. We were at 135 when the boat began to halt its descent. Slowly, at 145, the deck started to up-tilt. The alarms ceased, and the strained and sweaty silence was broken by resounding cheers.

The second memory has to do with an announcement by the senior training officer when our class of 20 first assembled. He gravely pointed out that we constituted the cream of the crop of several hundred officers who had taken the IQ test in Miami. Soon thereafter, I discovered that I was the lone philosophy major of the 20 men. Everyone else held a math or advanced science degree. I thought, "Here we go again, back to Western Auto where I never made it wrestling tires and batteries." How well I did during those four weeks at Key West I was never told, but I remember my bewilderment over the equations and computations about distances and relative speeds at sea between a submerged submarine and an attacking surface vessel.

But the Key West experience was a memorable joy. The only clue about my performance as a student was that all but one of us went from Key West to new destroyers in forward areas of the Pacific. I was that one, assigned to a creaky old World War I destroyer refitted with modern antisubmarine gear. Fair enough. As a philosophy major, I was about as well-fitted for high-tech antisubmarine duty as a carpenter in a space capsule.

The old destroyer was in the Boston Navy Yard at that time. On the way to Boston, I was assigned to a firefighter school in the Brooklyn Navy Yard with a room in the Sand Street YMCA. Despite the simulated hot blasts of live shipboard oil fires, I relished the experience at firefighter school because it made me feel like a real veteran of the ocean-going navy. Bea had gone to Washington, where she had found work in an army cryptographic facility. She was living across the Potomac in Arlington, Virginia, and we kept in daily touch by telephone.

After a week of grime and heat, I went by train from Brooklyn to Boston to find the USS *Badger, DD-126*. It must have been late on a Saturday evening when I phoned the personnel office at the Boston Navy Yard. I was told that the office was manned with only a stand-by crew for the weekend and that I should go to the Parker House across from Boston Common for two nights and then report in first thing on Monday morning.

After a good night's sleep at the Parker House and a Sunday brunch, I ambled to the hotel desk for suggestions about what to do that day. The clerk recommended a special recital by the classical African-American soloist Roland Hayes. Mr. Hayes was scheduled that early afternoon in concert at the Boston Museum of Fine Arts. Service people were always welcome at no charge for such events. It was an arresting afternoon of spiritual enrichment. The man's singing moved me, not only for his commanding presence and the beauty of his voice, but also because I was alone in a strange city and was aroused by some measure of loneliness to feel a special nourishment of soul. The March day had turned to early dusk when I got to the hotel for an evening meal.

After dinner, I started down Tremont Street looking for a movie when I heard the bells of the Park Street Church at a nearby corner of Boston Common. I had not been to church that day, and I remember thinking that I could save money by going to worship. A Presbyterian growing up in the 1920s and 30s would be quite at home in a Sunday evening church service, so I kept my money and walked up to the second-floor worship auditorium of the Park Street Church. The service turned out to be the climax of a missionary week of testimonies arranged for the purpose of raising money for overseas missions. Baskets were passed between ardent testimonials by seven or eight missionaries home from a foreign field, all seeking to arouse monetary generosity. I had some dimes and quarters for each passing. Throughout the congregation were fair numbers of us service men and women, and I remember feeling heart-warmed and fully at home. At the close of a final moving testimony, the resident minister, whose name was Harold Ockinga, asked those to stand who were willing to go into the mission field if there were enough money to send and support them for a year. Moved by the Spirit and memories of Roland Hayes that afternoon and overtaken by the warmth of the service, I could not resist the impulse to stand — in full naval uniform — along with many other uniformed men and women, all the while emptying my wallet and pockets into the passing basket. Instead of saving money at a movie, I returned to the hotel within an ace of being broke but high in heart.

That well-remembered Sunday in the gloom of a late New England winter connects with my early upbringing in the First Presbyterian Church of Davenport. The Spirit had hold of me from childhood years under Dr. Leroy Coffman and his director of religious education, Miss Alfreda Zarges. Both my parents taught Sunday school under Alfreda, and I remember having to memorize the 23rd Psalm under my mother's tutelage. To this day, I can recite that psalm from the old King James Version flawlessly. As I describe later in these memoirs, the 23rd Psalm became a deeply saving spiritual resource in September 1945 when I suffered a severe depression near the end of a three-year naval career.

Before closing this part of the saga, I need to indulge a retromemory. At the First Presbyterian Church in Davenport, Dr. Coffman had another gifted staff member, the Reverend Oscar Gustafson, who was the director of youth ministries. He formed a boys' club called the Friendly Indians. About 40 of us preteenagers were divided into four tribes: the Mohawks, the Iroquois, the Sioux, and the Apaches. My tribe was the Apache, although I had hoped to be assigned to the Mohawks. It sounded to me, at 12 years old, more impressive to be a Mohawk! Each tribe had an upper teenager as its chief. Harold A. McIntosh, whose initials spelled his nickname, was our Apache head man. Each of us new Friendly Indians was given burlap sacking at the opening meeting on a

Saturday morning and helped to fashion and decorate an Indian poncho. The poncho, along with headbands and feathers, was to be worn at weekly tribal meetings. I have no recollection of what we did at those Indian powwows except, no doubt, to remain at all times friendly! But I do recall an overnight encampment at Duck Creek complete with a great campfire and individual cooking, especially breakfast with greased cast-iron skillets. Most memorable of all is the before-breakfast song we learned from Ham McIntosh, our chief. He led the singing:

> Ham and Eggs, Ham and Eggs,
> Some like theirs fried nice and brown,
> Some like theirs turned upside down,
> Ham and Eggs, Ham and Eggs,
> Flip 'em, flop 'em,
> Just don't drop 'em,
> My Ham and Eggs.

Why record this Duck Creek doggerel? There are two reasons. First, the breakfast ditty became a hit around the early morning meal table in more than one Episcopal rectory in later years. Second, the song symbolizes the best in my religious experience and education as a youngster. In my growing years, the church was a glowing place, and time happily colors my memories of church. I would have to dig deeply into recollection to find an impression in childhood or youth of religion as a grind, even when the sermons may have been tedious without drawing supplies for Edward and me. (Our parents separated us in Sunday morning pews as a child management maneuver.) I grew up experiencing religion as a distinct girding, almost never as tedium.

I suspect that this flavor of church life still marks the Southern Baptist youth experience, symbolized for me by the lively church buses that pepper the weekend highways and byways of the Bible-serious South. I have only a single answer to the question of why our progressive, nonfundamentalist religious traditions seem far less able to communicate the same religious glow and girding that moved my heart as a youth and young man. My adult progressive tradition seems to have moved me so far in the conceptual direction that the experiential dimension has been too much sacrificed. How this imbalance can be redressed without embracing a mindless, dehistoricized version of the Bible remains for me a large question. Surely we don't have to park our brains at the church door to feel again the warmth of the Spirit's fire.

This challenge suggests two things. First, at the opening of the twenty-first century we live on the cusp of a seismic shift in the world view of human experience. Finding a seriously cheerful stance that takes the exploding global reality hopefully is less easy now than when I was a youngster. We now live on a huge swinging hinge in human history, and the old moorings are so loose that the temptation to resist the swinging is very great. Fundamentalism looks to me like a refuge for the fearful religious heart that demands the certainty and security of an infallible Bible. Fundamentalism seems disabled by the change and flow of history that marks the very writing of the Bible — which is a genuine historic production from the true hearts of our fallibly faithful forbearers. God did not write the Bible. We did. Great and fallible people wrote scripture, and a progressive faith in God has the freedom to understand the Bible as the progressively constructed record of developing faith that took more than 1000 years to evolve. Our sacred record moves forward in history from portions of Old Testament oral sources in the ninth century BCE to late portions of the New Testament dating to the second century CE. The Bible itself represents the vigorous reality of an historical progression.

Second, the mainline churches must continue to authorize fresh expressions of their worship, music, and theology that can move the human spirit with warmth and zesty enthusiasm. The good news is that this progressivism and courage have been decidedly forthcoming in many sectors of organized religious life despite accusations of apostasy from the sequestered backwoods of nervous church authority. The official brave actions of the Episcopal Church since my first ordination 56 years ago prove that my church has grown young as I have grown old. We have refused the fossilizing impulses that go with great age by courageous inclusive decision making since the mid-1960s. We have (1) embraced black civil rights at every level, (2) included women in holy orders, (3) contemporized our liturgies and music, and (4) legitimized gay and lesbian identity as bestowed, not chosen, sexual identities. Now we need to go forward in embracing the new world view that modern science offers in the post-Newtonian insights and discoveries of quantum physics. These expressions of rebirth will furnish the church with both the conceptual and experiential forces to move us into our rightful role as peacemakers in the pattern and power of Jesus of Nazareth. All that the churches need is the courage to embrace the perennial challenge of Christ to be reborn.

Chapter 10

Ungainly Bucket of Rivets and Rust: USS *Badger, DD-126*

I found the USS *Badger* on Monday morning after a taxi ride to the Boston Navy Yard. The receiving officer directed me to a dry dock in the Yard and had a sailor-driven jeep take me and my gear to the ship. In dry dock, the *Badger* was undergoing repairs to the hull, engine rooms, and topside rigging. Her sides were hung with painting crews on suspended platforms, and her decks were awash with greasy steam lines, dirty power cables, and untidy heaps of naval stores that included crates of lettuce and other fresh vegetables for a ship's complement of 12 officers and 200 crew. After months of convoy sea duty in the winter turbulence of the North Atlantic, the *Badger* was a bucket of rust. I was appalled and offended. The very nerve of the U.S. Navy to send me, an antisubmarine specialist, to this foul vessel! Even before walking the narrow, swaying gangway across the deep chasm of the dry dock, I wanted immediate reassignment. But over the ensuing months that stretched into two years, I came to love the old bucket and to trust the competence of every, or almost every, officer and crewman who sailed the ship.

The *Badger* was built in 1919 at the Camden, New Jersey shipyards as a fast torpedo-boat destroyer with depth-charge and K-gun
launchers and two heavy, 3-inch rotating rifles, one mounted on the
forecastle forward of the bridge and the other on an elevated gun deck
just forward of the stern. Originally, the ship carried four boilers and
four smokestacks, one for each boiler, giving that old destroyer class the
nickname "Four-Stacker." Many of the old four-stackers, including the
Badger, had been modified to become three-stackers. One boiler and its
stack were removed and replaced with a large fuel tank so as to increase
the cruising range. Even with more fuel for longer stretches of sailing, a
three-stacker had to be refueled at sea at least twice to make an Atlantic
crossing. Sometimes the heaviness of the seas and the amount of zig-
zagging in the pattern of steaming that was needed to protect a convoy
required three refueling maneuvers, each one difficult and often perilous. Later in the war, this limitation relegated the *Badger* and others
like her to coastal convoy work. Newer ships with larger fuel reserves
replaced them on the trans-Atlantic run.

After the *Badger* was overhauled in Boston, we sailed as antisubmarine protection for troop and supply ships from Newfoundland north as
well as to Trinidad and the Canal Zone south. Memories abound of those
great months on the *Badger* that turned into two years of being stretched
and rewarded. On a naval vessel, the captain is king, a monarch by navy
regulations. His presence and interior qualities define the character of
his ship, be it cheerful and steady or flinty and unreliable. His personal
strength and abilities establish the spirit of the vessel he commands. Our
captain, a Naval Reserve lieutenant commander, was a thoroughly decent
and intelligent man of privileged New England upbringing. Educated at
Groton and Harvard and experienced in seamanship from his youth for
having sailed the Long Island Sound, he was a superb ship handler. He
could bring the *Badger* to the dock in any wind or weather and against
a contrary tide. But at some deep level, he lacked the secret quality of

command. My sense is that he feared close relationships. There is something that can be deeply unmooring for those who live above most other people in a caste system such as the subtle American separation between Ivy Leaguers and the middle- and lower-income levels of an ostensibly egalitarian society. I believe that our captain was essentially an insecure commander for all his sterling qualities. This insecurity showed up in his unpredictability. He could be cheerfully avuncular one day and a martinet the next. The result was a slightly uptight officer wardroom and a strangely unhappy ship.

The crew tended to be troublesome on board and particularly on shore leave. Among the crew returning to the ship late at night from shore leave, some of the men would always be under arrest by the shore patrol for drunken and violent behavior. Two or three would be totally blotto and would have to be hauled on board with cargo nets attached to the crane-like boat davits.

The officer complement was far better behaved, and I recall only one of them as an ornery sort. Aside from Rodney Boynton, with whom a relationship came with effort, the other officers were easily likeable, Billy Kee from Rock Hill, South Carolina the easiest of all. Billy was a big, muscular teddy bear. He and I drank ourselves into a stupor at the officers' club one night in Bermuda, behavior that contradicted our shared habit of daily Bible reading and prayer time. It seems important to note at this point that each of us carries a persona, a projection of ourselves designed for at least two dynamics: (1) to protect us from disfavor and (2) to project qualities that we believe will enhance our standing with ourselves and others. I suppose we indulge in contradictory behavior as a way of relaxing the strain of persona projection, or of letting it all hang out. This may explain a lot of adolescent rebellion against the boundaries imposed by parents and other institutions such as church, school, and the navy! Another close friend in the wardroom was Douglas Folsom of Alabama, the communications officer. Doug was a devout southern gentleman with a tender spirit that often seemed out of context on a warship. There will be more about Doug and our chance meeting at Pearl Harbor in a later chapter.

The executive officer on a naval vessel is second in command. On the *Badger*, Lieutenant Daniel Donahue of Waterbury, Connecticut was executive officer. Danny, a math major in college, was easygoing and brilliant as a celestial navigator. He functioned as the steadying counterpoise to the volatile unpredictability of our patrician skipper. Even now I know the names and heavenly locations of many of the great stars and constellations for having stood night watches with Danny under the clear Caribbean skies as his junior officer of the deck. The ones I remember are Cassiopeia, Ursa Major (the Big Dipper), and Orion, my enduring favorite. Orion is the Great Hunter who, accompanied by his trailing dog star of binary brightness Sirius, chases the Seven Sisters of the Pleiades across the deep cosmos. Betelgeuse, on the right shoulder of Orion, is a supergiant at 220 times the brightness of our sun.

As I write in the year 2005, I wonder if any of these splendid men who served in World War II are alive. At 23, I was the youngest officer. The captain was the oldest at 32, which would bring him to 93 in 2005. All the rest would be in their middle to late 80s. Maybe we will meet in a promised afterlife, that hoped-for state that my father Lewis so keenly embraced as a second chance to make it in another go at life. My ardent hope for Lewis in such a second chance is that he would turn a happy back on business and go for a Ph.D. in math or history. As a teacher, he'd have been a smash.

Of the *Badger* crew, I clearly remember only two. The first is Guillermo Cresente LaPuglia, a heavily muscled fireman who tended the boilers below decks. He was known on board as Willie Puglia since almost none of his shipmates could remember, let alone pronounce, his pure Italian name. I remember him as a cheerful giant of a man, swarthy, smiling, and greasy as he came topside through the air locks that sealed the boiler rooms against blowbacks. The boiler rooms carried an internal air pressure a few pounds per square inch above the outside air pressure to keep the roaring boiler fires pointed inward under the honeycomb of boiler tubes. The boilers transformed the desalinated water running through these tubes into 125 pounds of steam pressure. The steam moved through heavily insulated pipes to the turbines and rotated the two monster drive shafts that spun the big brass propellers at the stern. The *Badger*, 300 feet long and 21 feet wide at the beam, was originally rated at 1200 tons and drove through the sea like a steel pencil. She could make 32 knots at flank speed, or about 37 miles per hour. Willie Puglia and I exchanged Christmas cards at his initiative for several years following the war until we lost track of each other in the late 1950s.

The second memorable enlisted man on the *Badger* was Carl W. Borho of Louisville, Kentucky. Carl held the singular job of ship's laundryman and worked two big washing machines in a crowded little compartment called a shack on the afterdeck, or fantail. He and I formed the habit of putting our backs against the bulkhead of his laundry shack on a Caribbean night at sea to talk and talk. One of our conversations turned to what each of us wanted to do at the end of the war. Carl's plan was crystal-clear. He intended to return to Louisville, marry his fiancée Doris, and buy a neighborhood bar. He would make it his life's work to encourage the friendships that can develop in the atmosphere of a public house, as he called it, a term that the British have elided into *pub*. For him, relationships were the heart of a happy life. Carl had it precisely right, and he prospered.

My aspirations were far less clear. I do not remember what I shared on the fantail, probably something about doing graduate studies in business and personnel psychology under Dale Yoder, a professor at the University of Minnesota with whom I had been in correspondence before graduating from Baker. This ambition, vague as it was, must have grown

out of a pipe dream of becoming a vice president of personnel at the
Ford Motor Company, which, in turn, was the outgrowth of a lifelong
romance with cars. I wish I could recover the considerable losses suffered in owning and disposing of a 1929 four-door, canvas-top Model A
Ford called a Phaeton. Among antique car owners, there is a spiritually
healing routine of balm for the not-so-savvy owners of these costly big-
boy toys. It goes this way. When you purchase an antique car, you put
the sales invoice into a large paper bag and add to the bag all the invoices
for parts, body work, licenses, tires, batteries, tools, antique car clubs,
and police and parking tickets that you accumulate over the period of
ownership. Then when you sell the car, you take the bag to your driveway and set it afire as a sacrifice of incense to the voracious gods of the
internal combustion automobile.

At the war's end, Carl did get his bar, actually several of them, in
Louisville. He retired to Florida as a man of wealth and was succeeded
by his sons in bar ownership and management. He and I sustained an
annual exchange of news every Christmas for many years. Our correspondence lasted into the early 1990s when a letter came from Doris
that Carl had died. Once while driving through Louisville in the 1950s, I
phoned Carl at one of his taverns. He invited me to visit, but my trip was
a hurried affair with children in the back of a station wagon. So we didn't
meet, but our phone conversation conjured memories under Caribbean
skies at sea and no doubt fed the energy of exchanges every Christmas
for years thereafter.

The aftergun deck is the location of another memorable relationship, this one exclusively within myself. The captain gave me an assignment that opened an intellectual and relational relish I did not know
existed until it was revealed in my deep interior self by carrying out the
captain's orders. My assignment was to assemble all the enlisted personnel not on watch duty to the gun deck for the purpose of teaching
them the details of the ship's construction as well as how to protect its

watertight integrity and fight shipboard fires while engaged with an enemy at sea. I had been promoted to first lieutenant by then and was, by navy command structure, in charge of the ship's hull — all its fittings and exterior appearance. In reality, the first lieutenant is what I came to call the commissioned janitor. The first lieutenant's job is impossible because everything topside is exposed to the captain's eagle eye. For that reason, I wished I were an engineering officer whose spaces were below deck and far from the captain's daily scrutiny. But as the ship's head janitor, what I discovered that first morning with the crew on the aftergun deck made up for the odious burdens of my job. I discovered in instructing the crew that I loved to teach. Teaching was meat and drink to my mind and soul. Nothing I ever did later as parish priest, professor, or bishop nourished me so profoundly as the interpersonal dynamics of knowledge and insight-sharing with eager fellow learners. To teach is to learn. The Iroquois tribes of our own northeast United States know this truth very well, so well that they are reported to have 35 words for *learn* and not a single term that means *teach*.

The USS *Badger*, named for a distinguished admiral of the nineteenth-century United States Navy, was in and out of Atlantic ports until the ship was designated a laboratory for the development of special noisemaking gear. This gear was to be trailed 100 yards astern a ship as a decoy to the sound-homing torpedoes shot from their tubes by the German U-boat fleet prowling the Atlantic. The homing torpedo was a deadly undersea weapon. Its miniature sonar in the nose cone was aimed at the turbulence of the rotational swish and thud of a ship's propellers. For this technical research duty, the old *Badger* was stationed at Port Everglades just south of Fort Lauderdale on the east coast of Florida. It was a delight to live there for four months in the winter and spring of 1944–1945. Fort Lauderdale was then a smallish retirement and resort village with some unpaved streets and almost everything within walking or cycling distance. Today Lauderdale bears no resemblance to that vintage village of World War II.

On board the *Badger* each day for its experimental cruise in the Gulf Stream was a specialist in industrial physics whose job it was to invent and perfect an aft-streaming noisemaker as a decoy for homing U-boat torpedoes. Before the development of these canny weapons, deck officers and lookouts on antisubmarine vessels were trained to sight oncoming torpedoes by the visible wake of the compressed air exhaust that propelled the weapon at speeds far greater than most surface ships, about 35 knots. Attacking torpedoes from U-boat positions were often aimed ahead of the targeted ship so as to increase the speed of the closing distance between the sub and the victim ship, often a convoy escort vessel like the *Badger*.

Before our research duty out of Port Everglades, the *Badger* prowled the Atlantic as a convoy escort vessel, and many nights at sea I prepared myself for the hero's role as I stood watch on either the starboard or port wing of the bridge. As officer of the deck on the midwatch (midnight to 4 a.m.), I would imagine sighting a torpedo wake aimed at a point just below the bridge aft of the port bow. Quickly and smoothly, I would order the helmsman "left full rudder" and the engine room telegraph operator "port engine back full, starboard engine ahead full." This maneuver would twist the ship swiftly in a direction parallel to the course of the oncoming torpedo, forcing the deadly weapon to run harmlessly along the port side and out to the unoccupied sea where it would exhaust its fuel supply and sink. I had this series of confident commands memorized cold, only to be reduced to mute terror one night in the Gulf Stream when a telltale wake appeared off the port wing of the bridge. The wake was headed for the skin of the ship at a point just below the waterline and precisely beneath my conning station on the port wing. I could open my mouth, but nothing sounded. Terror struck me completely dumb. After what seemed a suspended eternity and nothing had exploded, I peered gingerly over the side of the bridge to the waterline below. Behold, there at the port bow was a cavorting dolphin! Several weeks probably went by before I could muster the embarrassed nerve to tell this tale at the wardroom mess table.

The best moment of all the months aboard the *Badger* came in the dark of a day in May 1945. Doug Folsom had taken a coded dispatch to the captain who, in turn, went to the ship's bullhorn with the announcement that the darkened ship was to be lighted from stem to stern, all the guns were to be run out and elevated to fire safely into the night with blank ammunition, and all who smoked could light up and puff furiously. The Germans had surrendered unconditionally, and Hitler was presumed dead.

Soon thereafter, the ship was ordered to the Philadelphia Navy Yard and into dry dock for decommissioning. She would be retired from service and reduced to scrap. As first lieutenant, I was ordered, along with three other officers and the captain, to remain on board with a skeleton crew, while all others were discharged for reassignment to the Pacific fleet. The process of decommissioning took a month. It was a time of both sadness and gladness. I was sad to see a beloved old ship stripped of her rigging and fighting gear but at the same time felt muted gladness in knowing that the fullness of victory in World War II was only a matter of time. The *Badger* died in Philadelphia just across the Delaware River from her birthplace in the Camden shipyards. Mercifully, none of us decommissioning officers were there to see acetylene torches cut her into chunks for recycling.

All of us were awarded 30 days decommissioning leave, and I was at home in Kansas City when Japan suffered the incineration of two of its cities and the ultimate death of several hundred thousand of its old men, women, and children. Grim details of the Japanese defeat were not immediately apparent or felt. What was felt in America at the end of World War II defies description. The emotional release sent Americans at home and throughout the world into paroxysms of exuberance and celebration.

But sobriety soon returned for me. My leave ended only a few days after the second bomb drop on August 14, 1945, and my orders had me flying to a holding station at Pearl Harbor, Hawaii, where I experienced my life's lowest and highest points of soul time in less than 24 hours. All the years since, 60 of them, have been shaped and girded by those twin experiences of black depression and soaring liberation on the beach at Waikiki.

Chapter 11

A Born-Again Christian

The Douglas DC3, the small, two-engine, 25-passenger, tail-wheel workhorse of World War II, was equally popular as a commercial airliner of the day. I experienced my first airplane ride in a DC3 when I flew by TWA from Kansas City to San Francisco in 1945. We took off at dusk for an overnight flight and made fueling stops in Wichita, Kansas and Amarillo, Texas since the DC3 was not fuel-fitted for much nonstop duty. First flights must be anxiety-inducing for lots of tenderfeet in the air. I was one such. Nobody ever bothered to tell me things about airplanes at takeoff and cruising. I had a moment of panic when, in gaining altitude over the Missouri River, the plane appeared to be losing speed as the passing earth below slowed perceptibly. I was certain we were going to crash and sink in the Big Muddy. Serenity returned, however, when a bit of delayed thinking assured me that ground speed and air speed are relative to each other. The higher you are above the earth, of course, the slower the plane seems to be moving. I settled back and dozed through the night.

When dawn came over what was probably Arizona, I glanced out the window and noticed the starboard wing dancing in moderate turbulence. Panic again. I have already confessed to being deficient in physics and math, and it may have been hours before I realized that airplane wings would snap off like stick candy if they did not dance in turbulence. Much later, it struck me that rigidity is probably important in some structures such as rocks, although rocks suffer from rigidity in having to yield to the shattering power of expanding ice and the slow disintegrating force of running water. So it must be that adaptability and flexibility are keys to survival, health, and longevity in all forms of nature and human nature as well as in human structures such as tall buildings and airplane wings.

After a day and a night in San Francisco, I reported to Military Air Transport in Alameda across the bay. A long flight that night in early September 1945 would get me and a planeload of other in-transit military personnel to Hickham Air Field in Honolulu. The plane was a DC4, a big brother to the old DC3 with four engines and a nose wheel to keep the aircraft level on the tarmac. After an early-morning landing at Hickham Field, a bus took the navy people to their base at Pearl Harbor, scene of the Day of Infamy on December 7, 1941. I was deposited at ComDesPac (Commander, Destroyer Force, Pacific), which is the other-ocean equivalent of ComDesLant, destroyer headquarters in Casco Bay, Maine.

Later that morning, I found my name on a ComDesPac bulletin board that notified in-transit officers of their new assignments. By then I was a lieutenant junior grade, which is a rank above the entry level for naval officers. Although not a big leap, my new rank did mean another half-gold stripe and escape from the demeaning rank of ensign, the lowest rung in the navy officer ladder. My rank also meant that I would be eligible for release from active duty since the war was over by several weeks and I had more than two full years as a commissioned officer with most of that time at sea on an old destroyer. Any new posting for me would be orders to proceed to a discharge station in the United States and assignment to inactive status in the U.S. Naval Reserve. This easy assumption was further strengthened by the fact that my orders sending me to Pearl Harbor were dated several weeks ahead of the date in August when the Japanese surrendered. At the time, this meant to me that any new orders would surely reflect the radical downturn in the need for active-duty personnel, and I believed that I was going to be headed home from Honolulu.

All these assumptions deeply accentuated the shock and distress I felt when I found myself assigned to the USS *Caperton, DD-650* in the forward areas of the far Pacific. This was an ocean away in the opposite direction from the home that I longed for and felt I deserved. Inquiry disclosed that the *Caperton* was then stationed at the Yokosuka Naval Base a few miles south of the Japanese capital in Tokyo Bay. Before departing Pearl Harbor, I was handed a thick bundle of orders that entitled me to transport on a series of ships from Hawaii to Japan with several transfer stops in between.

The steady advance of despair that overtook my spirit in the course of that day is difficult to describe in writing. Along with hordes of other officers in transit, I was to be billeted in a big, ill-lit barrack building called a BOQ, a mnemonic for bachelor officers' quarters. Didn't the navy know that I was not a bachelor, but a man two years married almost to the day on September 25, 1943? The gloom deepened when I saw where I was to be housed while awaiting transport on ships headed for Tokyo Bay. Home for awhile was up a flight of darkened stairs to the second deck of the barnlike BOQ where I would find my assigned upper bunk on a numbered iron bedstead equipped with a waferlike, lumpy mattress. I remember the desperation I felt when I heaved my Val-Pak onto the bunk, along with the bed sheets and blanket that were handed me at the BOQ desk. How could I bear this palace of gloom and the detestable prospect of another seagoing bucket far from home? At some point in that protracted day of despair, I gave in to the pain of advancing depression and determined that I would declare myself a defeated veteran of the heaving Atlantic. The very next morning I would go to the naval hospital and turn myself in to the psychiatric clinic for warehousing.

It was late afternoon by then. In search of some distracting activity, I returned to the reception desk where I had seen some notices of activities at the officers' club on the base as well as in downtown Honolulu, a streetcar ride from the main gate of the base. As I made inquiries at the desk, someone called my name in evident excitement from behind me. Turning to the voice, I recognized a shipmate from the *Badger*. It was my good friend Douglas Folsom, our communications officer. Seeing Doug was a boost, tiny but timely. He was also looking for some distracting activity that evening. He suggested a movie at the downtown Hawaii Theater across the boulevard from the famed Royal Hawaiian Hotel on Waikiki Beach. The hotel was leased at that time to the U.S. Navy as a submarine officers' rest and recreation facility. Like a forlorn, lost dog, I followed Doug to public transportation and some eatery near the theater and then on to the theater box office. There we could buy tickets, but we would have to wait for the next showing of the film, scheduled an hour later at 8:00 p.m.

To pass the time, Doug proposed an interim visit to the Royal Hawaiian Hotel directly across the boulevard from the theater. As naval officers, we could walk into the famous navy-leased facility without any question. Entering the lobby, I spied a large poster behind the glass case of what must have been the daily-events bulletin when the facility operated as an upscale tourist mecca. It was characteristically situated between the elevator doors. I guessed that the bulletin board was now used by the resident chaplain because the poster held a five-line verse in large Gothic print:

I said to the man who stood at the gate of the year,
"Give me a light that I may tread safely into the
    unknown."
He replied, "Go out into the darkness and put your hand
    into the hand of God.
That shall be to you better than light and safer than a
    known way."
So, I went forth and, finding the hand of God, trod
    gladly into the night.
— M. Louise Haskins, from the poem "God Knows"

Instantly I knew this was for me. The verse did not banish my deepening depression but struck home as a gift from a kindly Providence.

Doug took us out to a promontory where deck chairs overlooked the surprisingly shallow Waikiki Beach, not an impressive stretch of sand when you have cavorted on the deep, white beaches of Fort Lauderdale. But the Pacific beyond the breakers was a matchless blue as far as one could see to the unbroken circle of the horizon. Still, in desperate despondency, I could not respond to beauty. My sickening gloom only deepened. I recall seeing a lone ship far out and hating the idea that I would have to be a miserable sailor again. Doug must have sensed my depression because he was quiet. My spiritual misery had lowered me into a black hole, but some impulse of health drove me to a slow repetition of the Sunday school memory exercise that my mother had made me learn. "The Lord is my shepherd; I shall not want" (Psalm 23, KJV). I could get no further into the 23rd Psalm, not because I'd forgotten it, but because I had never before noticed the unequivocal affirmation of the declaratory words "I shall not want." I repeated those four words over and over. This declaration of absolute spiritual certainty has been translated from the Hebrew over and again in the many variant ways of saying it in English. But at the time, I knew only this 1611 King James Version, and it was enough — and totally arresting. The psalm must have gone deeply into my unconscious and registered there secretly.

I had begun to feel a bit lifted from the black hole, but not greatly, when Doug nudged me for the walk across the streetcar tracks to the theater. We found two seats on the aisle, my place outboard Doug. The film was an early Technicolor feature starring Betty Hutton as a trapeze performer in a circus story. She wore pink tights, but I remember nothing else about the film. During the welcome distraction of the movie, something grandly mystical had moved in my deep unconscious. Since reading the Louise Haskins verse between the elevators and my despondent stare at the sea, some profound mystic energy had moved in my soul, entirely imperceptibly and totally unmanaged by my conscious mind. When the movie ended and the lights went up in the theater, I rose from my seat — and kept on rising. Heaven had come to earth and set me soaring. I can still recover the sensation of walking on air up the sloping aisle to the theater lobby.

When Doug and I were straphangers on the trolley headed back to Pearl Harbor a short while later, I can almost hear what came to me as a voice. It was my own voice, and I was saying, "If anyone feels aimless and lost, just take my hand. I know the way." Later, as one reborn to joy and waiting for sleep on the top bunk at the BOQ, I sat bolt upright in a dazzling darkness, whispering "I love you, Lord," and then slept unwaking through the night. What I experienced was exactly a fulfillment of the prescription that Jesus provided the night visitor Nicodemus when he asked how he might gain eternal life (John 3:7–8). Jesus answered, "You must be born from above. The wind blows where it chooses, and you hear the sound of it, but you do not know where it comes from or where it goes. So it is with everyone who is born of the Spirit."

There are important sequelae to this experience of spiritual transport, this highest mystical peak on the skyline of remembrance. First is the fact that not even a whisper of depression overtook me in coming down to the earth and the sea for many weeks in the Pacific on many ships and jeep rides. The sickness of brutal despair was gone, never to return in any equivalent intensity in all the 60 years of traceable ups and downs since. I have had times of what my psychiatrist in Baltimore, Wendell Muncie, MD, called anxiety attacks, but nowhere along the road to old age has there been even a faint recurrence of the depression that drove me to plan a selfcommitment to a psychiatric hospital. And now, as an old man, I feel at the top of psychic health. Another sequel to that mystical moment of rebirth in Honolulu was my complete release from the occasional seasickness that sometimes made life miserable on the *Badger*. After my rapture, I relished the sea and the U.S. Navy, along with all the ships on which I rode and stood watches in pursuit of the *Caperton*. It was a chase that required two months of shiphopping and strange ports of call. I loved it all and write of it with relish.

From Pearl Harbor, I was a passenger on an aircraft carrier to the mid-Pacific atoll of Eniwetok, an amphitheatrical formation of coral and sand a few feet above sea level with a great, placid inner stretch of the sea known as a lagoon. Eniwetok had become a refueling and transfer station, and ships of all sorts and sizes were in the lagoon. They rode at anchor for a day or more as they took on fuel and discharged supplies and such in-transit people as I was. Some ships took on more cargo for occupation duty in forward areas, while others sailed back to the American west coast with discharged military personnel or even for major navy yard overhaul. A few years following the war, that serene, coral-embraced blue lagoon at Eniwetok was fouled by U.S. Armed Forces in a massive test of hydrogen nuclear weapons many times more destructive than the dinky ones used to incinerate Hiroshima and Nagasaki. I will say more about Nagasaki in the next chapter when I recount a surreptitious personal visit to that brutally demolished city of 400,000 only weeks after the drop on August 14, 1945.

Returning to the lovely lagoon, hundreds of U.S. Navy ships were steaming from Eniwetok after the war to forward areas of U.S. occupation duty or back to navy yards on both U.S. coasts for demolition or for temporary decommissioning and anchorage in nests of mothballed vessels. Years later, while Bishop of Atlanta and wearing my clerical collar, I was in the window seat of a Delta jet as it flew low over the Philadelphia Navy Yard for a landing at the airport across the Delaware River. There, in the very navy yard where the *Badger* had died, were mothballed clusters of World War II destroyers neatly tied in nests of six to eight vessels. Suddenly I saw the big painted number 650 on the bow of the outboard destroyer in a nest. Straining the seat belt and craning around to see behind me as the plane sped past, I hollered in a shameless whoop, "That's my ship!" It was indeed my ship. Many weeks after my arrival in Eniwetok and my status as passenger on three more navy vessels in sequence, I found the USS *Caperton, DD-650* in Tokyo Bay.

When I disembarked the aircraft carrier in Eniwetok in late September 1945, some odd-looking vessels were riding at anchor, entirely stationary and lacking motive power for steaming. They functioned as two-deck dormitory barges, accommodating the almost endless parade of personnel going to and coming from the forward areas of American military occupation in such places as Okinawa, Iwo Jima, the Philippines, and the home islands of Japan. I must have spent a week on one of those barges awaiting transportation by the next appropriate ship heading west toward Tokyo Bay and the *Caperton*. Those stationary barges were furnished with galleys manned by navy cooks, heating and cooling equipment, bunks, heads (navy talk for toilets), and showers. They also included a library and game tables in a central recreation area.

One day I noticed a strikingly handsome full lieutenant wearing a U.S. Naval Academy ring in the recreation area of the barge to which I was assigned. Every day he read the Bible. Curious, I introduced myself one evening, and thus began one of those interludes that is forever well-remembered. In this case, our conversational exchange did not end until almost dawn. I remember the starry sky wheeling over us while we spent most of the night talking. Although he wore the ring of a U.S. Naval Academy graduate, I sensed at some point that he did not talk as if the navy were his permanent career choice. His name was James Muncaster Reeves, Lieutenant USN from West Virginia. I risked a bold question. Was Jim going to remain in the navy? He answered quickly. No, he had decided to enter seminary and prepare for the ministry of the Episcopal Church as soon as he could arrange a discharge. I warmed to this disclosure and shared with him that I, too, hoped for the ministry on discharge from the navy, mine to be in the Presbyterian Church since that was my upbringing under Dr. Coffman, Oscar Gustafson, and the Friendly Indians. The next morning, Jim boarded a motor whaleboat with his gear for assignment to a heavy cruiser in the Puget Sound Naval Shipyard near Seattle. My turn for catching a ride en route to the *Caperton* came a couple of days later when I joined the officer wardroom of a snail-paced landing craft vessel on its way to Buckner Bay in Okinawa. Two Septembers later, almost to the day, Jim Reeves and I dramatically reconnected.

Meanwhile, I believe it to be divinely designed that we shared a secret piece of information in the course of our first connection. That was the first time either of us had spoken aloud of our hopes for the ministry. Our exchange of nonnavy career aspirations took place on the slim balcony of a bleak dormitory barge at Eniwetok under the slowly rotating magic of a mid-Pacific spangle of stars.

Chapter 12

Atomic Incineration: Nagasaki, Japan, October 25, 1945

The U.S. Navy accommodated me with a sluggish ride from Eniwetok to Okinawa. A World War II landing ship tank (LST) could make 10 or 11 knots at cruising speed and was designed to carry, among other things, a battalion of soldiers or marines in its dormitory spaces as well as tanks and battle equipment in its great cargo area below the main deck. The vessel loomed large at sea, with a vulnerable freeboard the size of a two-story building at the bow. In an assault on enemy-held territory, an LST would make its way under reduced power, slide onto a beach, come to rest, and swing open its bow doors to discharge tanks, other vehicles, and armed men. Because of its bulk and sluggishness, an LST was known by the unappreciated nickname "Large Stationary Target." A passenger on board one of these ugly ducklings ought never to joke about the nickname. It would be an insult that risked cold disfavor.

I kept discreetly quiet about my experience on a swift destroyer, and my ride on the LST was a pleasure. The company was splendid, especially the marine officers on their way to occupation duty in Okinawa. They would encamp in tents on the island, where they were to secure the now-defeated Japanese garrisons and take prisoners for return to Japan. The marine officers spoke enviously of naval personnel assigned to ships. They knew that we had staterooms on the newer vessels and were treated to clean sheets on comfortable bunks, while they often had to fight their way onto an unfamiliar shore in the face of enemy fire and make do with whatever they could pitch by way of a tent or makeshift shelter. But the marine officers on the LST asked me not to mention their secret envy of naval personnel. That would bring down the scorn of their peers and make a lie of the cultivated reputation of the U.S. Marine Corps as the toughest and proudest branch of the military.

From Okinawa, the LST plodded north to the Japanese naval base at Sasebo on the southernmost main island of Kyushu. The harbor at Sasebo is almost entirely landlocked. It is reachable only through a narrow defile in the high surrounding hills through which the swift tides of the Korea Straight daily pour in and out. The LST had to wait for entrance until the tide turned from ebb to flood to make headway with its limited diesel power. When the ship rounded the last turn in the channel entrance, I could scarcely believe the devastation that our B29 bombing had wrought. It was a bleak and broken scene of half-sunken and beached Japanese naval vessels. One was an aircraft carrier, run high up on the beach in a cove and burned to death. For the LST to reach an assigned anchorage, the captain had to thread his way through and around clusters of steel superstructures punching above the surface of the harbor, solemn grave sites of big and little warships.

Disembarking for a look around the town of Sasebo, another officer and I walked through the commercial district, although there is little distinction between residential and business sections in most Japanese cities. We were astounded at the quiet of a bomb-disfigured and busy city, mostly women and children and older men shuffling to work and shopping in their stilted wooden clogs. Only necessaries seemed available at the sidewalk shops and green grocers. A tiny taxi here and there chugged the narrow streets propelled by a wood- or coal-burning steam engine, smoking furiously on its way. I recall marveling at the serene ingenuity of a war-devastated people and their resolute demeanor. Although the two of us wore uniforms of the conqueror, we were ignored as if we were not there. We felt no outward animosity, just determined nonrecognition. I found this astounding. It was my first experience of the unwelcoming remoteness of the Japanese character when circumstances and the presence of strangers evoke it.

The real unmasking of the stoic spirit of the Japanese came a day later when three of us junior naval officers, using forged orders, took the train to Nagasaki, a two-hour ride up and down the coastal hills of Kyushu. I was the forger. Occupation regulations forbade any but senior U.S. military officers to visit the scene of the second atomic bombing by our U.S. Air Force. We were keen to go, but we knew no officer of adequate rank to appeal to. So, with unaccustomed brashness, I signed my name, B. J. Sims, Commander USN. (I hope for another loss of records by the navy.) The orders got us round-trip tickets to Nagasaki by steam locomotive pulling a long string of old cars.

The Japanese are inveterate travelers. Quiet pilgrims and tourists crowd all forms of public transport, even in the wake of a crushing national disaster. As I can reconstruct the calendar, the day was October 25, 1945, only a dozen weeks after a small U.S. atomic bomb leveled the center city of Nagasaki on August 9, 1945. I turned 25 that August day, and this anniversary of unspeakable brutality has lived ever since in my consciousness as a rebuking reminder of the violent excesses to which war can drive the human spirit. My point of view will offend militarist Americans, but the day must come when the human race will either repudiate the insanity of violence as the way to peace or else endure the nuclear death of most of our planetary life.

Even in 1945, before the atomic bombs were dropped by decision of President Harry S. Truman, the three top American commanders warned against the action. They were General Dwight Eisenhower,

Admiral Chester Nimitz, and Air Force General Curtis LeMay. A more humane way to end the war, they reportedly contended, would have been to invite Japanese decision makers to witness an atomic bomb demonstration at sea, especially since it was known that the Japanese high command was ready to surrender that August. Harry Truman is one of my enduring personal heroes of American political leadership, but his decision to override the advice of his commanders seems to me stark evidence of the visceral madness that the long history of violence in the human odyssey continues to evoke and keep alive.

Even now, as I write 60 years later, American political leadership continues to believe in the counterfeit redemptive power of violence to secure the peace. President Bush and his advisers persuaded only Britain's Tony Blair and a few other now disengaging nations to join in devastating a small nation by using more than 200,000 troops with their tanks and high-tech weaponry to dislodge a ruthless dictator. But, as later chapters will seek to detail, world events in recent and immediate history reveal a hopeful pattern of advance in the use of active nonviolence in confronting the never-ending conflicts of the human pilgrimage from prehistory to the incendiary present. As can be forcibly shown by looking aft in history with discernment, conflict is inevitable, but violence is optional!

We surely had to mount a war of violence against the equivalent violence of Germany and Japan in World War II, but to close out that war with a radically new weapon, the use of which now threatens the survival of life on the planet, seems a dark blot on the American escutcheon. To keep adding to the stockpile of these weapons, each one many times more destructive than the atomic bombs of World War II, with an unrescinded American policy of first-strike privilege is a recipe for planetary suicide.

Of course, this will be a point of fierce debate and division long after I am gone, but I write here in vivid recollection of that fateful day in 1945 when forged orders exposed three junior officers to the unbelievable carnage wrought by the most primitive nuclear weapon in the arsenals and annals of war. The train to Nagasaki was itself an exposure to the war-induced poverty of Japan following the war. The train of a dozen or so old passenger cars was pulled by an equally old coal-fired steam locomotive. Chugging and puffing, it labored up the hills with an overload of passengers in every seat. Some riders were even standing between the cars on platforms that trembled from the clank and squeal of the iron couplings, especially when the ancient train gained speed on the downhill runs.

In stark contrast to the overcrowded cars up ahead, a last car rolled behind with no more than a handful of passengers, all of whom wore uniforms of the conquerors. The three of us, traveling on bogus orders, sat in regal isolation near the front of the near-empty car. It was equipped with old cane-upholstered seats that reminded me of the slick cane seats on the Brady Street trolley line of my boyhood in Davenport. At the top of each seat back was a handle for turning the seat in reverse direction, making passengers in the seats at each end of the car face one another knee to knee, a feature that became crucially important to me on the return trip to Sasebo later that afternoon.

We knew we were approaching Nagasaki by the first signs of war damage to the corrugated metal buildings lining the tracks. The sidewalls of the buildings remotest from the center of the city began to show damage, some with roofs entirely gone. As we rolled into the city, more buildings were badly disfigured, and some sections were blown entirely away. As the train slowed and got closer to the depot, sidewalls of buildings were entirely gone, and the supporting upright posts were increasingly bent away from the city center. Just before reaching the depot, nothing remained of the buildings except the concrete platforms that marked their foundations.

A fire-blackened concrete platform served as the depot, and a hastily erected sign in both Japanese and English announced that we were in Nagasaki. Before us were the bleak, pulverized remains of what once had been the center of a dense urban complex of 400,000 people. Nothing that I had ever seen compared to that 4- or 5-square-mile circle of brown dust. There was no rubble, only a bleak expanse of dirty ashes punctuated here and there by a standing, smoke-stained remnant of what may have been a barbershop or a small house. As vividly as if it were yesterday, I remember a white porcelain sink intact on its pedestal in the midst of all this devastation. Nothing else was identifiable. On the distant outer edges of ground zero, three tall, steel-reinforced concrete chimneys stood on one of the hills surrounding the city. Their tops were sheared off, and they were bent away from the epicenter of the blast halfway up from their foundations, like tall arms crooked at the elbow. Again I was aware of the eerie quiet of a defeated people as we beheld the unspeakable devastation.

All this forlorn ruin was the work of one tiny, primitive atomic weapon. The United States now has several thousand advanced nuclear weapons ready for immediate use, some of them as much as 80 times more destructive than the Hiroshima and Nagasaki miniatures. But in August 1945, those two tiny weapons together incinerated or rendered sick unto death more than 200,000 old men, women, and children. In Nagasaki alone, 39,000 perished instantly in a savage nuclear furnace. I did not think of it then, but I ponder a painful question now. If several thousand of the millions of Americans now living in upholstered comfort could see what nuclear warfare can do to living people and to the living earth, what would be the outcome? Would it turn enough of us to see what has become clear to some of us? If we continue to stock nuclear firepower, we are sending the quiet message to ourselves and to the world that we keep that weaponry at the ready because we reserve the right to use it. The Jesuit theologian Richard McSorley wrote:

What it is wrong to do, it is wrong to intend to do. If it is wrong
for me to kill you, it is wrong for me to plan to do it...Likewise, if
I intended to use nuclear weapons in massive retaliation, I have
already committed massive murder in my heart.
— Richard T. McSorley, SJ, in *Peacemaking: Day
by Day*, Pax Christi USA, Erie, PA, 1985, p. 32
(www.paxchristiusa.com)

The question remains. Would the sight of Nagasaki on October 25,
1945 for a million Americans move the nation to seek other ways for
dealing with the inevitable conflicts of humanity and their nation states?
Would a million of us have become pacifists, committed now to active
nonviolence? Maybe. Only maybe. If my experience is any measure,
the world would be little different than it is now — unless, unless the
people of the world across many boundaries have matured enough to
see the reality of our interconnected wholeness, unless we have matured
enough to understand that what we do to others we do to ourselves. This
sensitivity has not yet developed, so we in America are still planning to
use violence to deal with violence at astronomical cost, as if violence
were the redemptive solution to the human longing for peace. It took
me years to absorb, at my soul level, the lesson of Nagasaki. Only since
immersion in the heroic story of Mohandas Gandhi has it come home to
me, as a long-delayed learning, that violence only compounds the very
violence it seeks to subdue.

Although it took me years to understand this, the learning process
did have a quiet start 60 years ago in Nagasaki on that bright October day in 1945. It began in beholding the carnage wrought by a new
weapon and was reinforced on the return trip by train to Sasebo late
that afternoon. Again we rode in splendid isolation from the hordes up
ahead, and again the seats were arranged so that passengers at one end

or other of the car would sit knee to knee. Because I was deeply sobered by the sight of a once-thriving and now pulverized city, I sat alone at the rear of the car in one of those sets of facing seats for the return ride back to Sasebo.

Soon after departing Nagasaki, the conductor, a cheerful-looking young man, walked through the nearly empty car punching tickets. His cheeks were rosy and his countenance full of burnished Asian handsomeness. Coming to my seat, he sat down facing me. We were knee to knee. By his appearance, I judged him to be one of those very young people whom the war had pushed into the work force. He was probably 15. He wore the black uniform of the Japan National Railways. His cuffs were frayed, his jacket elbows were shiny, and the patent-leather bill of his cap was cracked. He punched my ticket but remained seated, looking intently at me and smiling broadly. He gestured with his right hand, sucked in his breath as if dragging on a cigarette, and then blew make-believe smoke. The message was clear. I held out my pack of Old Golds. He nodded in expansive politeness, taking one cigarette. Next, he hand-gestured as if lighting a match. I reached for my Zippo lighter. In the exchange of holding a lighter to a waiting cigarette, he and I were forced to come close. The open windows on a moving train pulled our faces within a few inches of each other, and, as I held the lighter, our eyes met.

We were total strangers to each other, separated by age, language, culture, race, and the remote geography of two nations locked until 12 weeks before in the rigid animosity of war. But in that moment of meeting eye to eye, all that had imprisoned two human beings in politically contrived enmity suddenly evaporated. It simply blew away in the uncontrived warmth of human giving and receiving. I remember it as an emotionally charged instant of deep sharing. It became for me another sharply remembered experience of inner transport. The war ended in mid-August of 1945, but peace came with the setting sun on October 25, 1945 when two strangers suddenly became one man.

What does this mean? Many things surely and different things to different people. To me, recently acquainted with quantum theory and immersed for many years in biblical theology, it means what both theology and postmodern science mean when we talk about the oneness of life at every level of the living cosmos. Humanity is built for oneness with the stars, with the self-renewing earth, and, preeminently, with one another. In any supernal moment of experiencing this truth, we are at one with God, the giver of all life and love. For there is no other word than *love* to encompass the ineffable riches of that instant of exchange between two total strangers made while riding a rickety, coal-fired steam train chugging up and down the green hills of the southernmost main island of Japan.

Chapter 13

Queen of the World War II Destroyer Fleet: USS *Caperton, DD-650*

After leaving the landing ship tank in Sasebo, I rode a swift destroyer escort on the last leg of the punctuated pursuit of my quarry, the sleek, armaments-heavy, no-nonsense destroyer, the USS *Caperton DD-650* of the Fletcher class. I call her "Queen" and not "King" because she was not the topmost version of a destroyer to enter the fleet during World War II. The latest destroyer type to join the 1940s navy was the Somers class, a type with heavier gun batteries and a displacement of 2200 tons. The Fletcher class displaced 2100 tons but seemed to me a sleeker ship with a more pleasing profile. She was tied to an anchor buoy at the Japanese naval base of Yokosuka in Tokyo Bay.

The dense urban sprawl of Tokyo lies at the top of Tokyo Bay. Together with its contiguous suburb of Yokohama, Tokyo at that time comprised the largest urban population in the world, something like 14 million. By the close of World War II in 1945, the Tokyo-Yokohama complex had been 85% gutted by U.S. fire bombs. In 1995, 50 years later, I made the last of six visits to Tokyo, and I felt charmed by two attributes of the great metroplex: its beauty and its relatively peaceable urban congestion. Strip-planted flowers edged all the vehicular freeways, and the pedestrian walkways in the Ginza (downtown Tokyo) were ablaze with blossoming plants. In spite of both pedestrian and vehicle density, the sound level was more akin to a hum than to the honk and drumbeat of many downtown city streets.

In comparing Tokyo with a city like New York, at least three distinctions between Japan and the United States should be kept in mind. First, Tokyo was the beneficiary of a World War II settlement that, by a new constitution, limited the Japanese military establishment to a small self-defense force. This settlement, in turn, freed lavish amounts of public funding for vigorous postwar rebuilding and beautifying. Second, gun control is the strict public norm in Japan. Only the police and the inevitable crime population have guns. The result is a minimum of violence and prison incarceration as compared with the scandalously high levels of both in the United States. We have many more people in prison per capita than any other society, and we regularly execute more people per capita. The United States is the only advanced industrial nation in the world committed to capital punishment. Third and perhaps most important, while medieval Japan was marked by warlord and samurai violence, the nation has had many more generations than the United States to develop a social maturity that has outgrown violence as the norm of personal and public protection. In recent history, the Japanese did commit armed aggression against China in the 1930s and against the United States in World War II. But the fact remains that the city of Edo (medieval Tokyo) at the head of Tokyo Bay had a population of one million at a time when the forested location of Baltimore near the top of Chesapeake Bay was only a cluster of cabins and tepees.

The United States, for all our love of country, is an adolescent society in comparison with Japan. We are a boisterous, cowboy culture devoted to guns, guts, and swagger. The American-led, preemptive war in Iraq that began in March 2003 seems a monumental case in point to many Americans and to most of the world.

At the end of a two-month pursuit involving three ships and two layovers across the Pacific, I finally found my new assignment. Riding at an anchor buoy far out in the dirty waters of Tokyo Bay was the muscular sleekness of the destroyer *Caperton*, its long silhouette the picture of power and the military victory it had helped bring to pass. A motor whaleboat took me from an untidy dock in Yokosuka to the welcoming deck of that American beauty. My journey from dock to deck was a homecoming experience. Climbing the sea ladder with my old Val-Pak, I was awed when I stepped aboard a real contemporary destroyer. The main deck was stainless steel with tidy rows of grit-coated walking pads as compared with the old and scuffed painted deck of the *Badger*. And it didn't smell of fuel oil and stack gas. It was a polished ship of the line with torpedo launchers and five 5-inch, 8-mm rifles, each in its own swivel turret — two forward, one amidships, and two pointed aft near the stern. Not much longer than the *Badger* at 310 feet, the *Caperton* was a third again as wide at the beam, and it displaced 2100 tons compared with the 1200 rated tons of the *Badger*. Turbine steam pressure on my old ship was 125 pounds per square inch, while this new seagoing power plant forced 600 psi of spin into the turbine blades, which developed 60,000 horsepower to turn the screws up to flank speeds of 35 knots per hour. Everything about the *Caperton* was superior. It was precisely like going from a Model T Ford to the newest LaSalle, and everything worked! The officer staterooms were equipped with stainless-steel washbasins and water faucets that delivered hot water, not the raw steam of the *Badger* that one had to mix with cold water for shaving.

But the very best differences were two. First was the bundle of 40 letters from home that had accumulated in two months of ship- and island-hopping. Upon arrival on board, I disappeared into my quarters to devour the news and love from home. The second great difference was the captain and his ship's morale. Will P. Starnes, Lieutenant Commander USN, skippered a happy ship. A U.S. Naval Academy graduate, Captain Starnes carried the inner mystique of command. He had come from a segment of society altogether antithetical to that of my first captain. By exterior credentials, the skipper of the *Badger* stood at 6 feet, 1 inch, held diplomas from Groton and Harvard, and had sailed the Long Island Sound from his family's private dock. By exterior contrast, Will P. Starnes stood at 5 feet, 5 inches and held diplomas from a Midwest public high school and the U.S. Naval Academy, both at taxpayer expense. But by his interior credentials, the skipper of the *Caperton* stood as the tallest man on board. The contrast between the two men led me to conclude, even then, that the navy had thousands of command assignments but many fewer commanders.

I have the same impression of my land-based institution after 56 years as a clergyperson with assignments in domestic parishes, the overseas mission field, two theological seminaries, and a diocese where I was overseer of 125 clergy. There are always more command posts than commanders! As I write, it now occurs to me that this conclusion, wrung from experience in two venerable institutions, the military and the church, explains why I chose at age 63 to retire after 12 years as bishop of the Episcopal Diocese of Atlanta to found a leadership education enterprise at Emory University.

The story of my retirement work comes later in this odyssey, but it is timely to record here that my great dream for the future of the human pilgrimage is the achievement of a social and political maturity that moves the understanding and practice of leadership from top-down command and organizational boxes to a far more productive and cheerful dynamic. The great need in our contemporary workplace is for leadership that is exercised through channels of trusting relationships and is structured more horizontally than vertically. Leadership will build great enterprises as it moves from external authority to internal spirit. That profound shift in human valuing and behavior is clearly on the horizon now. As servant leadership slowly flowers, it can bring with it achievement of the peace for which humanity longs. In a world become too small for violence, peace is achievable only as power and authority are reconceived to mean servanthood and sharing. This is not a recent personal insight. It is ancient wisdom. "The greatest among you will be your servant" (Matthew 23:11).

In spite of a unilateral war being prosecuted by the overwhelming superpower dominance of American military forces even as I write, the day of command by relational servanthood is at hand. A second superpower has emerged across all national boundaries in the millions who have risen up in peacemaking marches, vigils, and protests against the adolescent folly of using violence to counter violence. Centuries of human experience have climaxed in our time with an emerging, globally shared conviction that violence only compounds the very violence it opposes. (See Chapter 30, "Global Warming of the Second Kind.")

Besides the sterling character of the captain and my sense of pride in the robust magnificence of the ship, some keen memories of the *Caperton* abide. One of them has to do with what I have already noted about the foul water of Tokyo Bay. Urban sewer leakage from the upper bay had contaminated the estuary so severely that many officers and crew became ill with dysentery from handling boats and equipment soaking wet from bay water.

I stayed well but was happy when the captain announced a three-day training exercise at sea to clear the ship's freshwater evaporators and to wash down the topside areas with Pacific seawater. We were to cruise with the entire squadron of eight destroyers in two divisions of four ships each. The *Caperton* had the distinction of membership in division 100 of squadron 50, or maybe it was squadron 100 in division 50. Either way, the numbers seemed a good-luck designation.

The season was mid-November, and the Pacific was kicking up an Atlantic-style turbulence. One windy morning, I stood watch as senior officer of the deck while the squadron steamed in column open order, an arrangement while under way that positions the ships in a staggered, forward-moving pattern. As I remember the numbers, the vessel astern was 100 yards away at a 45-degree angle off the starboard quarter, and the vessel ahead was another 100 yards away at a 45-degree angle off the starboard bow. (These distances and angles may betray a faulty memory, but they symbolize tricky ship handling in a boisterous sea.) Station-keeping meant maintaining these distances and angles of safe separation while steaming at the standard speed of 15 knots. It took close attention to the instruments that measured distance to maintain these stations as well as frequent commands to the turbine shaft-rotation enunciators for speed adjustments to keep the ship's correct position in formation.

My post as officer of the deck that morning was on the starboard wing of the bridge where I could see fore and aft, watching our position at all times relative to the destroyers angled both ahead and astern. The seas were heaving that day. They kept pitching the ships at occasional steep angles. One pitch lifted the bow of the ship astern at so sharp an angle as to expose the keel to almost half the length of the vessel. This meant that the sonar housing below the bridge at the keel was fully out of the water for a long moment. I recall the moment vividly because I knew that I would have been hanging seasick over the bridge rail if such an exposure of the sonar housing had occurred on a similar exercise of the Atlantic squadron. But on that glorious morning in the restless Pacific, I was thrilled to be driving a 60,000-horsepower destroyer of the United States Navy.

Another and almost my final memory of the *Caperton* clusters around our departure from surveillance duty in the turbid waters of Tokyo Bay. The date was December 5, 1945. I remember it precisely as the day of departure for home. Orders to return to San Diego sent all spirits to the sky, including the captain's. He gleefully ordered all the bunting in the flag bags broken out and hoisted on the several lines that ran from the afterpart of the bridge up to both starboard and port extensions of the yardarm. (A yardarm is the sturdy horizontal member fixed high at right angles to the mainmast.) Not only that, but Captain Starnes ordered the communications shack to put a particular piece of band music on the ship's record player and, on his command, to pipe it through the ship's bullhorn at peak volume. When we cast off all lines to the anchor buoy and swung into our place in the squadron column of eight ships, the order came to play *California, Here I Come* at full amps. And it was so. Every ship of the squadron flew all their bunting as the *Caperton* sounded loud and clear our chorus of glad homecoming.

I owe so many high points of life and learning in my young adulthood to the United States Navy. Now, more than half a century later, any devotion to the military is only a memory of gratitude for the experience of learning military discipline and the skills of seagoing ship handling. I will always be thankful that I did not go directly from college to graduate studies and that service as a line officer in the navy is a proud part of my résumé. But I am no longer the naïve young man who stepped off the USS *Caperton* in San Diego. In the world's turbulent years since that afternoon of radical dismay and sorrow over the sight of Nagasaki in 1945 — and knowing that a portion of the several thousand nuclear weapons that my country keeps at the ready could incinerate the planet and all its life — I have become keenly devoted to a power diametrically different from the military with its monstrous budgets and life-menacing weaponry. Since the March on Washington in 1963, my allegiance has slowly moved to the moral art and practice of active nonviolence. I will always cherish my memories of peacemaking by the military, but later chapters will speak of my dreams of an interdependent world kept safely peaceable by a force more powerful. Slowly I have become an old progressive, stepping gradually from the ranks of a stubborn conservatism that cherishes power understood as the capacity to compel compliance. I do not think well of political and military superpower except as it can be reconceived as the truly great power of serving the absolute need of world peace by the use of power to empower others in the interwoven fabric of life.

Tying up at the dock in San Diego and having enough discharge points accumulated for sea duty and for being married (another 10 points), I qualified for immediate release to civilian status in the naval reserve. Captain Starnes signed my orders to report to the Ninth Naval District headquarters north of Chicago on Lake Michigan. The date for reporting must have been December 27 or 28, 1945 because I arrived by Santa Fe train in Kansas City at 4 a.m. on Christmas morning. Home from the war on Christmas Day! After a day and a night at home, I resumed the journey north and east to Chicago for discharge. The first news at home was that grandmother Lucy Laura Jones had died at age 74 a few hours earlier that very Christmas Eve. Burial was to be in Davenport next to grandfather Harvey Bennett Jones on the morning of December 31. This meant that, with luck, I could get to the discharge center on time and thence by train from Chicago to Davenport, 180 miles to the west.

I remember little of the homecoming in Kansas City beyond a quiet joy that overspread Christmas 1945. No details of the discharge process at the Great Lakes naval headquarters remain in memory, save for an infusing sense of happiness to be soon a civilian and home again. But recollection is keen and enduring about an incident that took place in Chicago's LaSalle Street railroad station as I waited between trains from the Great Lakes discharge station to my destination in Davenport. Wearing my naval uniform, I was standing in the rotunda of the station, a large area crowded with post-Christmas travelers. Casually I spotted another military officer coming toward me. He was wearing a naval officer's winter overcoat, a garment which I thought was the handsomest of all the uniform styles available to us. Called a bridge coat, it was dark navy-blue with epaulets of rank secured at the shoulders. I did not own one, but I remember thinking that I would surely have one made to my size if I were not now discharged. The stranger in the bridge coat kept walking toward me, looking tall and handsome. My envy grew. A bridge coat does hang low and would enhance the height of a man only 5 feet, 8 inches. I almost capitulated to the urge to order one when a light of recognition slowly began to dawn on me. The handsome man was nearly upon me before I fully realized who he was. I was face to face with my only brother! We had not seen each other in three years. Jubilation!

Edward's navy duty had him on the battleship *Tennessee*, all of it in the Pacific. Concurrently, my duty had me in the Atlantic for all but the past four months, during which the *Tennessee* was on its way through the Indian Ocean and around the Cape of Good Hope in South Africa. The *Tennessee* was headed for the Philadelphia Navy Yard, from whence Edward had departed that morning on his way to Davenport for Grandmother's burial. We were both changing trains at the LaSalle Street station. There we were, suddenly reunited after three full years. It can be imagined how two brothers whooped it up, oblivious of the crowded rotunda. We hugged, pounding each other's backs, probably accompanied by yips of glee. We must have made a noisy scene. When we broke from our embrace and stepped back, I noticed that a small circle of travelers had gathered around us, all smiling broadly, one of them applauding, another quietly wiping tears.

With the return of our composure, we discovered that we were ticketed on different trains from Chicago to Davenport. This would never do! Edward, always the more aggressive of the two of us, insisted on taking my ticket to the Rock Island window for exchange to the train on which he was booked to ride. He soon rejoined me in the rotunda, holding reserved seats for two in the club car of the next departing train for Davenport. The beauty of those old club cars was that they were outfitted with upholstered swivel armchairs at each row of windows.

We boarded the train, found our seats, swiveled toward each other, and were instantly lost in an exchange of intensive chatter. It was life's happiest and swiftest travel experience that either of us remembers. Three hours of rail time in Illinois felt like four minutes of soul time in postwar catch-up.

Chapter 14

Princeton Theological Seminary:
Feast and Fast

Back in Kansas City in January 1946, I was overjoyed to have been part of my country's military victory and proud to have served in the destroyer navy. But I wanted no more of the uniform of a lieutenant junior grade. I found my old college togs reassuring and deliciously comfortable. My immediate business was to apply for admission to Princeton Theological Seminary. Since I prized sturdy memories of the First Presbyterian Church of Davenport and the Friendly Indians, nothing seemed more sensible than to go for what many Presbyterians regard as their finest seminary.

Bea was supportive of my hope to make the ministry my lifework, but my parents were ambivalent. I sensed that they both hoped I would choose a getting rather than giving kind of career. In one side of their hearts, they must have been pleased that the firstborn of two Sunday school teachers should make a run at a low rung on the professional ladder. But in the other side of their hearts, they waffled. My mother had always encouraged my adolescent hope to become a medical doctor, a high rung on the ladder. My father, it seemed, was hoping that one of his sons would go for some kind of successful entrepreneurship, perhaps as a corrective to his own sense of unsatisfying vocational achievement.

Over time, however, both parents grew warmly appreciative of their sons' selection of impecunious careers. (Our choices hardly turned out to be impecunious. In vocational retirement now, both Edward and I are astounded to have such well-furnished lives. Each of us owns a home, and retirement incomes keep us solidly in the middle class.) Edward's choice of the ministry came later than mine by a year. In early 1946, he was still on active duty aboard the USS *Tennessee*. Since he was not married, he had to wait for an adequate accumulation of discharge points before he was free to choose a civilian career. Edward's choice came after a tentative approach to Harvard Law School. No doubt his keen intellect and aggressive personality would have netted him a great career of wealth and satisfaction as a lawyer. But this was not to be. The Spirit spoke forcibly to Edward during the months of his frequent visits with Bea and me in Princeton while he was stationed only an hour away by train in Philadelphia.

While my father later came to embrace the career choices of his two sons, he was offended by the next piece of business I attended to and never approved. Always a nut about cars, I must have taken days to shop the ill-furnished auto dealerships in Kansas City. I had the money, but the dealers had almost no cars. There hadn't been an automobile built in the United States since early 1942, and now it was four years later. Almost all the industrial manufacturers had turned to the war effort, making tanks and guns and airplanes and even canned meat for fighting a two-theater war. Consequently, only used cars were available in January 1946. Most were very used, and all were overpriced in a sellers' market. I finally settled on a blue Chevrolet convertible that was built in 1940 and had an odometer reading of 40,000 miles. When I brought the car home to my parents' house and answered truthfully my father's question about how much I had paid for the old ragtop, he exploded and never cooled. He was thinking (and I was, too) that he had bought a shiny new Oldsmobile of the same 1940 model year and paid only $200 more than I had to shell out for my very used old convertible. We baptized the 85-horsepower, six-cylinder, overhead-valve ragtop "Huckabuck." Where the name came from is a mystery, but it had a jolly ring. After a day of elbow grease and polishing rags, the old car took on a semblance of class. Not only did the top retract and fit nicely into the well behind the small rear seat, but the steering wheel was fitted with what we called a built-in necker's knob in college circles, a smoothly rotating device that enabled the driver to steer deftly with the left hand while keeping the right hand free for better things.

On a frosty morning in February 1946, Bea and I loaded Huckabuck with a few worldly goods, mostly clothes and knickknacks, and started for Princeton without having heard a word from the registration office in response to my letter of inquiry regarding admission as a student. Apparently, my belief in luck was very strong, and it never occurred to me that Princeton would not be happy to welcome me. The Yiddish word for this is *chutzpah*, which translates as colossal nerve! The long trip took five days of driving on two-lane, war-neglected highways, some of them brick, some concrete or macadam, and a few humpback gravel. We crossed Missouri, Illinois, Indiana, Ohio, and West Virginia and then headed north into Virginia, Maryland, a tip of Pennsylvania, and finally New Jersey. The two most memorable parts of the trip involved backing blindly into a telephone pole in Illinois and later working our way through Baltimore on the city portions of old U.S. Highway 40.

In Illinois, we had stopped at some small-town café for lunch, parking at a slightly right angle to the curb. Huckabuck, loaded to the canvas top with gear for starting a stripped-down household, disallowed much in the way of rear viewing except by craning out the side windows. I had apparently neglected to notice our proximity to a utility pole when parking. To regain the street from an angle-in parking place, I had to turn slightly left and back swiftly after spotting an opening in the small-town, main-street traffic. Bea had learned some of my navy jargon and was charmed by a particular maneuvering command to the engine room telegraph. I am not clear about the details, but other drivers must have parked their cars in such a way as to require of Huckabuck a sharp turn in backing away from the curb. As navigator, Bea spotted a traffic opening and hollered proudly, "All engines back full!" Blindly, I tromped on the accelerator and within an instant caught the immovable telephone pole hard in the rear bumper. Small towns in the Midwest are famous for benches in front of cafés, pool halls, and hardware stores. These benches are regularly occupied at noon, even in February, by leisurely lookers from the farms around, generally wearing wool caps, sheepskin coats, and bib overalls. I remember hearing some amused hoots as I examined the now-undulating rear bumper in embarrassment.

In February 1946, Baltimore routed U.S. Highway 40 directly through the center of the city, using Mulberry Street for one-way traffic eastbound and Lexington Street, a block to the south, for one-way traffic westbound. Only years later came the circumferentials that skirt big cities with multiple-lane accommodations. Worst of all, there had been no time for repairs to blacktopped city streets in the months immediately on the heels of World War II, and the necker's knob came in handy as we dodged potholes.

Halfway through Baltimore on Mulberry Street where it crosses North Charles Street, I turned to Bea with a solemn promise. "I have no idea where in the world the church's ministry will take us, but you can count on my determination that it will never be Baltimore." By the most providential irony, my first parish assignment upon graduation, as you can probably guess, was Baltimore — and on North Charles Street! My assignment to a church on Charles Street was not at the corner of Mulberry, God be praised. The Episcopal Church of the Redeemer is located miles north in a pleasing residential section of the noble city. Baltimore became home for 16 happy years among beloved people, and two of our three children claim Baltimore as their birthplace.

Despite or perhaps because of my colossal nerve, I went to the admissions office on arrival at the seminary and found Dean Roberts politely cordial but cautious. I had no college transcript to offer. And even if I had one to present, it would hardly have been impressive except for my grades from Hiram Weld. The dean was probably noncommittal, but he did say that the seminary was prepared to give returning veterans preferential regard and that the seminary had set aside an old dorm on campus to accommodate returning service personnel who were married. My chutzpah paid off. I was accepted! Hodge Hall, which was built nearly a century before, came to be our abiding place for awhile.

In March 1946, I started classes in the third semester of a three-semester schedule and set to studying at an old oak desk in our single room. Having no kitchen or bathroom, we took our first meals at one of the student eating clubs. For plumbing facilities, the men went to a bathroom on the floor above and the women to another bathroom on our floor. It was all very spartan and quite Presbyterian. Our eating club was named for the founder of the Presbyterian reformed tradition, the brilliant, frosty, and forbidding formulator of the doctrine of double predestination, John Calvin. The Calvin Club was such a cheerless place that we turned to taking breakfast and lunch at Hodge Hall. Dry cereal and buns were stored in a bureau drawer, and the broad outside stone windowsills were perfect for milk and cheese in the cold of February and March. For evening meals, it was mostly the inexpensive Balt and occasionally Renwick's, then on Nassau Street downtown.

The great surprise at Princeton Theological Seminary was my discovery that I had a lively relish for the work of learning. The classes were all stimulating, New Testament Greek most of all. I aced that language course under the renowned scholar Bruce M. Metzger, a youngish Ph.D. and son-in-law to the seminary president. Dr. Metzger called me

Burnet the whole semester (facility in scholarly Greek does not translate to accuracy in classroom English), but he did redeem himself by awarding me some A-pluses on my blue-book quizzes. Princeton was the locus of two greatly significant events: (1) my decision to seek ordination in the Episcopal Church and (2) the birth of our first child.

My academic satisfaction at the seminary was in sharp contrast to a growing disenchantment with the ecclesiastical context of the Presbyterian tradition. Although I greatly esteemed my professors and loved the learning experience, I slowly grew aware of a profound discomfort with the prospect of years and years as a Calvinist minister.

More and more, it became clear that I did not fit what seemed to me a grim personal and ecclesiastical box. Maybe I was the only one for whom this was true, but the somber sobriety of the seminary seemed to me to contradict the opening declaration of the Westminster Confession. It begins with a question and its answer: "What is the chief end of man? The chief end of man is to glorify God and enjoy him forever." No grimness there, only a kind of Buddhist buoyancy with its accent on inward and outward joy. This answer sharply contradicted the frosty gloom of the Calvin Club and the white, antiseptic severity of the seminary chapel.

One Sunday morning in what must have been the autumn of 1946, Bea and I visited the late morning service at Trinity Episcopal Church across Stockton Street from the seminary. I knew instantly that I was at home in the gladness of God. The Anglican tradition shares all the flaws of institutional religion, but it was not born full-blown from the fierce fires of the sixteenth-century Reformation. Its ecclesial roots go deep in Christian history. At Trinity Church that memorable morning, I felt warmed and embraced by the vaulting twelfth-century Gothic idioms of its architecture, the mildly medieval accents of its liturgical music, the high Shakespearian cadences of *The Book of Common Prayer*, and most of all the warmth and ardent humanity of the rector and his preaching.

There was nothing forbidding in his theology or pompous in his delivery. Arthur Lee Kinsolving was an authentic human being who communicated his own experience of suffering and the lifting power of love. Bea's response to the service was the same as mine, and not long afterward we affiliated at Trinity and were confirmed in the Episcopal Church.

Our first child was not expected until mid-February 1947, a full year after arriving in Princeton. On New Year's Eve of 1946, Bea and I were making proper Christian whoopee with a dozen other married seminarians when she began to feel labor pains. Huckabuck took us swiftly to the hospital, where Laura was born seven weeks premature and the first girl child of 1947 in Princeton, New Jersey. Through the nursery glass, I first saw Laura at three pounds, fifteen ounces. She was fully formed with all parts perfectly in place, but she looked like a wizened, overripe tomato, all splotched red and wrinkled. She spent more than a month in a heated crib at the hospital, a painful time, especially for the mother of a first-born child. When Laura came home to a tiny crib at the foot of the bed, she had blossomed into a five-pound human being. We went all out celebrating. Of all the remembered incidents of Laura's infancy and little girlhood, I fix first on a precious moment of cuddling that tiny child to my chest as I lay on my right side in the bed, marveling that this warm and fully functioning miniature human, made in the image of God, was really alive. She was my daughter to cherish, protect, and provide for. Not until that moment did the miracle and gift of parenthood come home to me. And it needs to be said that Laura, now age 59 and a gracious mother herself, has given her parents only mounting joy in her remarkably developing wholeness, high talent, and personal beauty.

A theological education does not guarantee immunity to heresy, but it does open the doors to orthodoxy. In simplest terms, *heresy* means crooked thinking. By contrast, *orthodoxy* means the opposite, straight thinking. One of the most insidious heresies conjured by a competitive culture is the idea that each of us must strive to be more than we are. So we have baseball players who are already great athletes sneaking steroids in order to be greater than they are. And all the rest of us are easy prey to the seductions of a culture addicted to competition for perfection and material trophies. The problem is that competition for perfection never lets us get there.

By contrast, the straight thinking of orthodoxy is quietly gracious, urging that we see ourselves as already there. Orthodoxy gently urges you to be glad that you are you, accepting yourself in every moment because, in Christian terms, the message comes to you with a blessed assurance that you are valued just as you are. This must be the grand truth of life, or else the words and work of Jesus and Paul are perennial nonsense. Everyone is free to make a choice about Jesus. Did he or did he not, in the agony of his own bloody dying, murmur the world's best gift, "Father, forgive them; for they know not what they do" (Luke 23:34, KJV)? And if he did murmur this mercy, then forgiveness or love for you, both at your worst and your most ordinary, is present and powerful long before you ask. This exalting assurance of acceptance never waits for human worthiness, never needs to be summoned from afar, is never even contingent on penitence. Penitence is seeking love's favor knowing that you have no right to claim it and knowing, too, that penitence does not create the mercy it pleads for. Grace is built into the fabric of creation and will bestow its gift even long before penitence opens the heart to receive it and be set free to enjoy the gift of life in all its incompleteness.

Perhaps some may object that there would be little or no achievement if there were no compulsion to be more than we are, no drive to compete. Maybe so. I am not sure, never having lived in a noncompetitive context. But, marvelously, when the orthodoxy of grace takes hold of one's heart, the restless anxiety that usually propels human effort begins to give way to a new measure of confidence and peace. All of this is to embrace the truth that acceptance of one's self comes more easily in yielding to grace, and love of others begins to enlarge. In my struggle for maturity, this truth has more and more laid hold of me. It tells me that the whole human species is a work in progress. God is not finished with anyone because we are living components of a living cosmos still in the making, and love is every life's most girding gift from the first heartbeat of creation.

This supernal assurance of forgiveness may be the most difficult of all the good news in the world to accept because a powerful, pervasive, and acquisitive culture denies its truth and uses its seductions to keep us captive to anxiety, bad conscience, consumerism, and unbelief in the grace of God. But down deep, after an excruciating bout with despondency, the leading edge of this cosmic good news is what I discovered that evening on the beach at Waikiki in September 1945.

Chapter 15

Virginia Theological Seminary: Altogether a Feast

Between student life at the Princeton and Virginia seminaries, our little family of three spent the middle months of 1947 in a rural ministry. We occupied the manse of a lakeside summer chapel bearing the misleading name of Silver Lake Presbyterian Church. Silver Lake resembled the color silver about as faithfully as an elephant hide resembles a bright summer sky. The misnamed lake, maybe two miles long, was formed by an earthen dam on a muddy creek in the green hills of northern Pennsylvania. The manse, a vintage frame house of one story, probably had 60 years to settle on stone pillars at the perimeter plus one pillar at the center. The living room floor, supported by the weary center pillar, sagged perceptibly under the weight of a big wood stove that was the only heat source. For plumbing, we had a well pump with a great curving handle at the kitchen sink and a two-hole privy up a slight rise and in deep weeds at the back. But the people were a heart-warming introduction to the quality of congregational life at its worthiest, even though one plump layman introduced me to a humbling experience by falling asleep with fair regularity during sermons on which I had beaten my

125

brains to make worthy of rapt attention. At one point in the middle of that long summer, I wanted nothing more of the ministry. Give me a Kenworth 18-wheeler, a smooth interstate, and a load of cabbages for California and I could be King of the Road.

Immediately after my 15th arduously prepared sermon, we stuffed Huckabuck with Laura's crib, our luggage, and a diaper bucket behind the passenger seat and took off for Alexandria. Virginia Theological Seminary had arranged for a one-bedroom apartment in an upscale development called Parkfairfax. We drove up to our garden apartment at 3260 Martha Custis Drive and parked. What a contrast to our summer home! Our apartment had parquet floors and a modern kitchen and bath, all in a tidy, landscaped setting of flowering shrubs and mowed lawns.

Almost the first thing I noticed was a familiar face from the recent past. He was walking from his parked car three or four spaces from ours and heading for the building directly across the courtyard from 3260. He was wearing the khaki shirt and trousers of the navy summer uniform, and I knew that I had seen him before. But where? Suddenly it dawned on me, but only after he had turned away and was headed for his apartment. I was looking at the back of the handsome man who had told me of his intention to enter the ministry and with whom I had first shared my intention to do the same when we sat for hours on the narrow balcony of a navy barracks barge in the Eniwetok lagoon under a wheeling spangle of stars. He was none other than retired Lieutenant USN James M. Reeves. Here we were, two years almost to the day later and half a world away from the South Pacific, living across a courtyard from each other and enrolled as classmates at Virginia Theological Seminary. Jim and I occasionally drilled each other for exams for two years until graduation in 1949 when he went to Charleston, West Virginia and I to Baltimore. Jim died a few years ago, but we had a lunchtime reunion in Phoenix, Arizona when the General Convention of the Episcopal Church met there in 1990.

My first impression of the Virginia campus was that fortune had smiled again. I was at home. The seminary was located on a 90-acre tract dominated by rolling lawns that led up to a plateau of high ground topped by vintage brick buildings and a great oak grove beyond. The whole scene struck me as an embrace of welcome. Virginia Theological Seminary was founded in 1823 by Church of England clergy and laity of the newly created Protestant Episcopal Church in America. The new church used the English *Book of Common Prayer* with only the modifications that would make it fit a newly formed Church of England independent of the King and Queen. Among the founders was Francis Scott Key, composer of the *Star Spangled Banner* from his battle observation post as he beheld the British assault on Fort McHenry in the Baltimore harbor during the War of 1812. The seminary was first housed near the Potomac River in downtown Alexandria where it would be geographically close to the founding dioceses of Maryland and Virginia. But the school grew, and it was moved to its present 90-acre tract some miles into the countryside in 1843.

At the center of the campus stood Aspinwall Hall sporting a tiered, cupola-like tower that faintly resembled an Asian Buddhist pagoda. Later, students named it the "Chinese Revenge" in mock honor of the many seminarians who had gone forth over the years as missionaries to the Far East. Clustered at its haunches and extending away on both sides from Aspinwall were old brick dorms, classrooms, and faculty offices. Across a narrow, interior blacktop road stood the balconied brick Victorian chapel of oddly reminiscent Gothic design. Less than 20 years after the seminary moved in 1843 to a more expansive campus, the Civil War erupted, and the school was commandeered as a military hospital by the Confederacy in 1860. It was returned to the trustees in 1865, much bruised and battered. By 1947 when I enrolled, the school was tidy but tired, a genteel weariness having overtaken her. Successful fund-raising has since added splendid colonial-motif dormitories and a refectory across a large grassy expanse to fashion an expansive kind of quadrangle. New faculty housing and offices came later, along with a gymnasium, a fine library, and a handsome academic building for additional classrooms, seminar space, and a modern bookstore.

While I was a student in the late 1940s, the great oaks were food and housing for hundreds of bushy-tailed tree dwellers. I remember thinking that the population of Virginia Seminary was 10 faculty, 100 students, and 1000 squirrels. The faculty and student population must be twice that size now, with squirrels still vastly outnumbering everyone else. In my student days, the seminary was a place of serene simplicity and the spirit of the faculty humanely liberal. Coming from a conservative Calvinist seminary, Virginia suited me in every important way. The most significant difference between Princeton and Virginia was the broad sense of history that informed the teaching at Virginia as compared with the far narrower historical framework that marked the scholarship at Princeton. Both schools were deeply grounded in the Hebrew and Christian scriptures. However, the Reformation of the sixteenth century was the linchpin of the defining doctrine and history at Princeton, while there seemed to be a seamless embrace of the whole timeline of the church's origin and contemporary life at Virginia. In simplest terms, I understood this distinction to be the difference between the Catholic and Protestant traditions. The Episcopal Church in the United States is the American expression of the Catholic tradition found in the Anglican line of churches around the world, a tradition in which a wholesome blend of Catholic and Protestant memory and practice exists.

Following World War II, Episcopalians boasted high-church and low-church identities at seminary, diocesan, and parish levels. High-church practice embodied the Catholic tradition, while low-church practice honored the dynamic of the Reformation in its simpler expressions of worship and discipline. Virginia Theological Seminary was decidedly low church at that time and today remains tilted in that direction. Since my seminary days, the whole ethos of the Episcopal Church has moved to recover more of its own historic catholicity in its worship and theology, and Virginia has shared in this recovery of historic wholeness. But on a scale of high and low, my cherished old seminary continues to lean low. It was so low in my day that we had no candles on the chapel altar, and I graduated not having a clue about how to wear Eucharistic vestments. I suffered a nightmare early in my ministry that put me in the sacristy of a high-church parish having to celebrate the Holy Communion. I anguished in total bewilderment about how to wiggle a large, white napkin as a collar under a long, white skirt tied with cinctures and covered by an ornate poncho (called a chasuble) that had to be tossed adroitly over one's head. The subsequent years have instructed all of us clergy in the sartorial secrets of high-church haberdashery.

Of greatest importance to me as a student at Virginia was the relaxed liberal spirit of the faculty. Good humor was everywhere balanced by a serious devotion to the pursuit of sound learning and discipleship to the Christ of the Bible. Daily worship was central to the rhythms of the seminary with a special accent on the foreign missionary tradition of the school. From the academic class of 1950, the class that followed mine, no fewer than six men chose the foreign field following graduation, two going to Japan. Over the great east window behind and above the chapel altar and painted in arching Gothic letters were the words, "Go Ye into All the World and Preach the Gospel." Although foreign missions no longer command the special devotion of the contemporary church, those words remain bold above the window.

Over more than 50 years since my student days, the world has become more and more an interfaith phenomenon. The United States is now more a receiver of non-Christian mission than a sender of

Christian missionaries. Practicing Muslims in America now outnumber all Episcopalians and Presbyterians combined. This has forced a serious rethinking and redoing of our missionary praxis. The most serious mission challenge to all the world's religions is to recognize and gear up for a liberal outreach to one another in a world become too interwoven for business as usual. The good news is that a chorus of religious voices now call for an unprecedented interfaith spiritual revolution. Contempt of other religions is still alive and blooming in fundamentalist circles, but a new wind of interfaith respect and exchange now blows. There will be more about this in later chapters.

Part of my joy as a student at Virginia was that little or no attention was paid to the behavioral moralities of smoking, drinking, and dancing. That is not to say that moral laxity was tolerated, but the goals of the faculty seemed to be building a strong personal and pastoral character in each student as well as providing as much intellectual enrichment as a student could absorb. The motto of the seminary rose from the writings of an earlier dean, William Sparrow: "Seek the truth, come whence it may, cost what it will." This expansive summons translated into a political liberality among most of the faculty that challenged my then-unexamined political conservatism. Although real change required years to be wrought, I am sure that the strong prophetic accents in the teaching of historian Kenneth Heim and ethicist Albert Mollegen were secret seeds in my soul. They began to blossom into modest liberal flowers by 1958 when a severe architectural challenge accompanied the building of a new church in my first parish. More of that convulsive story is reserved for later chapters.

In seminary at Virginia, I had started down the liberal road. Still, a moral conservatism hung heavily around the issue of homosexuality. One of the members of my class, a man in the dorm, was suddenly not a part of the community. I remember being confused and saddened when whispers went around that his expulsion came because he betrayed homosexual tendencies. This issue remains today the most divisive force in the life of all the churches, but I am pleased and proud that Virginia Theological Seminary, at the cost of losing a trustee or two, has removed any mention of sexual identity or preference from its enrollment requirements. No doubt the justice-serving vote at the 2003 General Convention to confirm the election of an openly gay priest as bishop of New Hampshire had some of its roots in the progressive social teaching of the Virginia Seminary. My old school sends more priests and bishops into the ranks of the ordained ministry of the Episcopal Church than any of the other 10 or 11 seminaries of our denomination.

The class of 1949 was made up overwhelmingly of returning veterans of World War II. Of the 36 of us, all but 3 or 4 were supported by the GI Bill with allowances for housing, tuition, and books. Although Bea and I lived off campus, our lifelong friends were not from the off-campus neighborhood. Among our dorm-dweller friends was Gordon T. Charlton, Jr. of Texas, later a missionary to both Alaska and Mexico and later still a seminary professor and dean and finally a bishop in Texas. Gordon and I played occasional hooky from classes in favor of golf. Later, when we were both on the faculty of the seminary, we fished from his boat in the lovely Shenandoah River some miles from Alexandria. Two other special 1949 friends from the dorms were Philip Alan Smith, later bishop of New Hampshire, and Charles Philip Price, our class star and later preacher to the University at Harvard. All four of us were to become teachers at Virginia Seminary, and all of us have kept in personal touch. At this writing, Gordon's wife Cutler has died, and Betty Price is a widow. Both Cutler and Charlie were victims of cancer, and both are buried in the old seminary burial ground.

Of special memory in the Alexandria days is the long summer between my second and final academic years. As middlers, we could exercise some freedom in our choice of guided program in the summer before our third year. Most of my classmates wisely chose some form of clinical pastoral training under close supervision and frequent seminar work in one of several hospital settings around the country. I say wisely because my choice of town-and-country ministry training in rural Missouri did not equip me for anything except the insight that I was not fitted for any ministerial setting other than a city parish with modern housing. After a few weeks of small-town and rural-Bible-school play-acting with small children and helping local farmers with plowing and planting, my supervisor concluded that the nearest I should come to a country ministry was a golf course not too far from a posh parish. He spoke prophetically. The first parish of which I became rector was in the fine suburbs of Baltimore with a rectory only four blocks from the most exclusive golf and social circle in all of Maryland, the Elkridge Hunt Club.

I ought to have known better than to choose a summer of town-and-country ministry training. I had had my fill of it in the summer of 1947 as preaching pastor of the very rural Silver Lake Presbyterian Church. But there was a method in my madness. The location of the summer 1948 training was Park College, just a few miles from home in Kansas City where we could sneak away in Huckabuck for frequent family visits and occasional golf. All this may reveal ambitions quite disillusioning to distant observers of seminary students. Are not such people supposed to be disinterested in worldly pursuits such as family frivolity, fancy blue convertibles, and golf? Maybe so, in some pinched and prudish circles, but not unless a clergyperson is prepared to deny his or her created humanity. The authenticity of humanity was central to the theology of the Virginia Seminary, and that became the benchmark of our training in ministry. In all my theological research and thinking since, Jesus of Nazareth revealed so robust and profoundly illumining a humanity that the fullness of his personhood, up to and including his death and resurrection, persuaded those who knew him best that they had walked with the finest specimen of humanity available to human encounter, a humanity that mirrored the very nature of divinity. "'But who do you say that I am?' Peter answered, 'The Messiah of God'" (Luke 9:20).

The summer ended, and we returned to Alexandria in our ragtop, anticipating a fine concluding year at the Virginia Seminary, which indeed we had. The year was so good that I felt deeply ambivalent when it came time to graduate even though I was weary of papers and exams. In a movie that was popular at the time, Jimmie Durante stood at a piano and belted out a gravel-voice ditty: "Did you ever have the feelin' that you wanted to go, yet still you had the feelin' that you wanted to stay?" That became my private commencement music.

No doubt the best thing that marked my senior year at Virginia was an invitation to interview for a weekend job in a parish church. Along with five other seniors, I was recommended by the dean to interview with the rector of the Episcopal Church of the Redeemer in Baltimore and his director of education, Miss Frances Young. The interviews were scheduled for the morning. However, I had no break that day in my morning schedule of classes and was a left-over interviewee for an afternoon meeting with Frances. She told me two things: (1) the weekend task in Baltimore was to help with the growing Sunday church school and to take charge of the young peoples' Sunday evening meeting; and (2) the rector, Richard H. Baker, could not be present for my interview because he had to return to his parish at the end of the morning. Concluding our talk, Frances asked if I could come to Baltimore the next weekend to meet Mr. Baker. She could not make a hiring decision; that was the rector's privilege. So I went to Baltimore. Meeting Dick Baker and his staff was an immersion in hospitality and an approach to the work of ministry that fit my education and my hopes. I felt at home. The spirit of the rector and his team was emblematic of the cheerful humanity of Virginia Theological Seminary. If I were the one chosen among the six of us interviewed, it would be a seamless transition from seminary to parish church. Providence smiled. I got the job and spent every weekend of my senior seminary year in Baltimore. Better still, upon graduation from Virginia, I was asked by the rector to join the Redeemer staff full time as his curate.

Chapter 16

Episcopal Church of the Redeemer, Baltimore: Architectural Trauma — "You Can Still Go to Hell"

Charlie Price, a classmate at Virginia Theological Seminary, graduated at the top of our 1949 group, taking most of the honors and going later to Union Theological Seminary in New York for a doctorate in theology. All the rest of us 49ers went to parishes as curates (assistant ministers) or to small mission churches as vicars. As a deacon at the Episcopal Church of the Redeemer, I earned $3600 a year plus an apartment. Today this seems a ridiculous sum, but in 1949 it was the highest salary of any in the class. Our brand-new apartment was in a development near the church called Drumcastle. We took up residence when construction and earthmoving were yet incomplete, and malodorous manure was being plowed into the fill dirt beneath our windows in preparation for seeding. When asked by members of the congregation how we liked the apartment and its setting, I joked that it was fine inside but misnamed outside. Its real name should not be Drumcastle, but Dirtcastle or Manure Manor. I should have kept quiet. It got around that the new deacon didn't like his housing, a lesson in how quickly a clergyperson can arouse parish gossip.

Richard Baker as rector and Frances Young as director of education could not have been more helpful as colleagues for the break-in of a young deacon. Other welcoming staff people included a comptroller, two secretaries, and a frosty-tempered sexton plus his helper William Williams. All were very kind. However, Sexton Robert Lee Owings kept me at a distance. When I became rector 18 months later, it quickly became clear that I was not going to take Dick Baker's place with Lee Owings. In a subtly officious way, Mr. Owings, who was in his mid-50s at that time, communicated a proprietary air. He was omnipresent and very capable. The great nine acres, along with its trees and plantings and its several buildings (except the stone rectory), belonged to him. No one could have been a prouder and more efficient overseer. He and his wife Katherine and their upper-teenage daughter Dolores occupied a two-story frame house at the rear of the property. Living on the grounds must have given him an additional sense of ownership. After we moved into the old 1863 rectory in 1951, we discovered just how widely the sexton's proprietorship was communicated. We were at the dinner table one evening and engaged in characteristic family talk about the church. The children were probably three, six, and nine. Expecting a proper theological answer, I asked the children a Sunday school question: "Whose church is that across the driveway?" The answer came instantly and almost in unison: "Mr. Owings."

The Church of the Redeemer was founded in 1855 by the Perine family whose grand country estate was named Homeland. The family had deeded the high ground of the northwest, nine-acre corner of their large holding to be occupied and owned by the vestry of a Protestant Episcopal Church parish in the Diocese of Maryland. It was never to be a funded mission but always a self-supporting parish. The church building came along in 1858 as a simple rectangular worship space with a steep, Gothic-like interior ceiling and a slave balcony at the back above the entrance door. Five years later, the three-story stone rectory was added some distance north of the church but located on the same expansive nine acres. The rectory, of a design called cottage Gothic, went up in the midst of the Civil War at the war-inflated cost of $5000. In 1879, the great steeple was added with gold Roman numerals on the four-sided, chime-striking clock halfway to the gold cross fixed at the pinnacle. The steeple remains a landmark on a gentle rise of North Charles Street. The steeple construction was apparently accompanied by the addition of the shallow transepts and chancel. These interior expansions increased the seating capacity by a little and gave the building a pleasing cruciform shape. All was in native stone quarried from only blocks away. The site of the old quarry is still visible as a yawning depression at the present corner of Northern Parkway and North Charles Street.

Old Baltimore grew in all directions from the harbor, but the northern sections became home to the finest neighborhood developments. Roland Park, slightly to the northwest along Roland Avenue, came first, around 1900. Then in the 1930s and 40s, Homeland was developed in the old Perine estate directly north of the city on what was earlier called Charles Street Avenue and then Charles Street Avenue Extended. The street name was finally simplified, and the address of the Episcopal Church of the Redeemer is now 5603 North Charles Street.

The parish grew apace with the city's growth. A parish house was built in the space between the church and the rectory in 1928, and that small building was expanded to three times its 1928 dimensions in 1949. This grand addition was built precisely between the time that I arrived as a deacon in May of 1949 and the time that Dick left to become a bishop in 1951 when I became his successor. Housing growth in the years after World War II gave rise to an explosion in the church-going suburban culture of the 1950s and 60s, and we had to multiply services until Sunday morning kept the little church busy at 7:30, 9:00, 10:30, and noon. Attendance and activities continued to increase. We knew we would have to do something substantial soon.

We called in the architect who had designed the parish house addition, Harold Waggoner. He demolished our high sense of accomplishment with one leveling statement. He explained our phenomenal expansion by saying that Redeemer had three qualities that made it advance so rapidly: location, location, and location. I think we all forgave him that utterly tasteless remark because we knew that the Perine family's gift and the city's loveliest suburban expansion had situated the Redeemer precisely in the path of institutional church prosperity. Harold designed a useful one-story expansion of the north transept that would link the church to the older section of the parish house and give us another 150 church seats, all in a roughly compatible neo-Gothic idiom. This was 1955, four years after I had become rector. Accordingly, the schedule for services was restored to the earlier timetable of 8:00, 9:00, and 11:00. But within two years, we were back to four services on Sunday. We could temporize no longer. We needed a greatly expanded church or an entirely new one.

Meanwhile a youngish architect in the parish with fine credentials had been elected to the vestry. Although in practice locally, Alexander Smith Cochran was a frequent lecturer at Harvard and other Ivy League architectural schools. Alex put forth two ideas regarding a new church. First, he would personally decline to become the architect for any new building project the vestry might undertake. Second, the vestry, using him as a consultant, would create a select architectural committee of the vestry and other membership with a vestryman as chair. This was agreed to, although some surely must have hoped that Alex's well-known contemporary flair would not unduly influence the committee. Alex and his wife Cally had built and were occupying the raciest modern home in Baltimore, only blocks from Redeemer. The style of their house had scared the daylights out of many in that staid neighborhood, and the offended neighbors included one of our own vestrymen.

But sometimes the mystery of Providence intercedes in ordinary human affairs to produce results beyond imagining. The initial magic of Providence produced Edward E. Yaggy, Jr. as committee chair. Ed was president of a large manufacturing company in Baltimore and a man of great executive skills and imagination. Ed gathered a representative committee but was careful to include a fair number of those who shared his imagination and energy, both women and men. His first task was to produce a document that would describe the parish history, its prime location, and current heavy challenges. With help from his committee and key input from Alex Cochran, he created multiple copies of a 20-page booklet that related the parish history, outlined our present problems, and carried both ground-level and aerial photographs of the nine-acre property. Alex's principal contribution was to make sure that the booklet would solicit architectural competition and that it would be sent to a representative group of architects, both the world-renowned and the lesser known.

Among the best-known architects were Eero Saarinen, Marcel Breuer, and Pietro Belluschi. Among the local and lesser known was the Annapolis firm of Rogers and Taliaferro. A total of 15 architects from here and there were invited to see the property and to be interviewed by the committee. As rector, I was included in the interviews. All but 4 of the 15 accepted the invitation and were interviewed on site. Of the renowned, only Eero Saarinen could not come. He wrote that he was covered up with commissions at the time and could not add one more. Strange to say, I remember only three of those who did come: Marcel Breuer, Rogers and Taliaferro (pronounced *Tolliver*), and Pietro Belluschi (pronounced *Bellooskee*). I may not remember the others because I did not participate in all the interviews or because only those three made a strong impression. Marcel Breuer was very impressive, but he seemed a little scornful of the buildings already on our campus. Rogers and Taliaferro were of my generation, in their 30s and shortly out of graduate school. They had only a splendidly rustic Girl Scout encampment headquarters in their portfolio. Still, they liked Redeemer, and all of us liked them. Pietro Belluschi, then dean of architecture at the Massachusetts Institute of Technology and the very first to come for an interview, won us completely. He was the committee's glad, unanimous choice.

Looking back, I believe that two primary attributes won Pietro our high confidence. First was his evident respect for the 1858 church and its tall 1879 steeple. If we decided to build an entirely new church and related buildings, he told us, everything that was added must use the existing church as the commanding architectural message. Most of all, nothing must overshadow the old steeple. That landmark must remain the exterior climax of any composition of new and old structures. That insistence squared with everyone's deeply held sentiment. Second, he looked like one of the vestry. Impeccably dressed, strikingly handsome, and graciously articulate, he had all the appearance and personal bearing of a leader in the Church of the Redeemer! The only limitation he placed on his availability was that, as a professor and graduate school administrator, he had no drafting office or the time to do such important work. He would need a local firm as his on-site drafting and engineering colleagues. Instantly, I hoped that Archibald Rogers and Francis Taliaferro of Annapolis would be willing to undertake the local end of things and that Mr. Belluschi would find them acceptable. And so it was! Everyone agreed, and the second great piece of magic was wrought by the Holy Spirit, which for many of us is the proper and personal name for Providence.

Pietro's winsome respect for our fieldstone Gothic church must have suggested to all of us that he would design a kind of big brother in the traditional idiom. All of us, including me, apparently forgot his insistence that a new and larger church must not diminish the exterior climax of the old steeple. It never occurred to me that a big brother Gothic structure must necessarily carry a strong exterior verticality to qualify as representing the Gothic pattern. Still, we needed not only a new church but a very large helping of money. Ed Yaggy was a canny leader. He knew that a conservative congregation would not be charmed by any contemporary design for a new church, but he also knew that we would need a vigorous campaign to build anything as well as some kind of artistic representation of a new building for a fetching fund-raising brochure. So with only the line drawing submitted by Belluschi, Rogers, and Taliaferro of the soaring interior of a new church suspended from great Gothic arches of laminated wood, the committee prepared a compelling brochure, and we proceeded in high spirits to raise the money. The vestry agreed to a monstrous amount late in 1956, something in round numbers like $750,000. Three large gifts of $25,000 each got us off to happy start, and we had exceeded the goal by the time the final pledge was counted. The Spirit thus worked a third great piece of magic: the money was raised before any truly revealing pictures were available.

But a backlash was lurking. Pietro came to be with us during Lent of 1957 to present and explain his astonishing design for a complex of buildings and courtyards. The design multiplied our worship space by more than twice but included no spire. Pietro's grand design included a flowing-water, outdoor baptismal fountain in an entrance courtyard on an axis with a free-standing, white marble altar in a church with only horizontal windows. The congregation surrounded a bold, out-thrust chancel platform on three sides in a great nave and two deep transepts. Pietro said that we could have any color of carpet in the aisles and on the altar platform as long as it was a light shade of purple. That evening in February was known thereafter as Black Tuesday.

The shock-and-awe experience actually involved two back-to-back evenings to accommodate the large congregation in the parish house. By the second evening, there had been time for the congregation to catch its breath and marshal resisting forces. One prominent lawyer in the congregation had met the bishop of Maryland at his club and shared his distress over the design for the new Church of the Redeemer. Bishop Powell was negative about the plans for the new church, and he had apparently failed to insist that his comments be kept confidential. Following Pietro's talk and slide presentation on the second evening, the lawyer rose, asked for the floor, and strode to the front. Respectfully challenging the architect, he delivered a resounding negative from a group of parishioners whom he had canvassed after the previous evening. In addition, he repeated Bishop Powell's negative response to his description of the new design.

By decided contrast, I myself was charmed and totally persuaded by Pietro's lecture and historical presentation. I was actually surprised at myself. The design was antithetical to my young lifetime of conservative training and preferences. As the objecting lawyer told of his and others' resistance to Mr. Belluschi's design, I found myself fuming inside. I had bought the architect's sensitive blend of tradition and modernity with enthusiasm. I felt that we had been handed a work of genius and wanted with all my heart to proceed with the project. I deeply resented Bishop Powell's scornful rejection of the new design and his talking to a member of the parish behind our backs, as it were. So, with as much composure as I could muster, I asked Ed Yaggy, who was presiding that evening, for the floor. I remembered a story about a certain rector's response to his bishop's visit, and without any preamble I simply began the story.

At his annual visitation to a parish of his diocese, the bishop noticed with evident disappointment that the building and grounds betrayed much neglect. And his eye caught the unkempt vestments of the choir and clergy. The organist hit some wrong keys, and both the choir and the congregation were desultory in singing. At their oral examination by the bishop, the confirmands seemed grossly unprepared. Time came for the bishop's sermon, and he gave the confirmands, the congregation, and especially the rector a series of withering rebukes for their poor performances and overall churchmanship. Following the bishop's demolishing sermon, it was the rector's turn to speak. From the chancel steps, he offered a brief commencement address to his confirmands. He cleared his throat and began.

"Children and mothers and fathers, you must remember that just because you have been baptized and confirmed, these sacraments represent no guarantee of heaven. Good and godly behavior is all the more expected of you. And I myself must remember the same, for ordination to the priesthood is no guarantee of a heavenly outcome for me. As a matter of fact, though the bishop is recipient of the highest status that the church can bestow, he too must live a life in accordance with the demands of the gospel. So I leave all of you with this solemn warning: you can still go to hell, and so can the bishop!"

There was laughter, some it embarrassed no doubt. When the meeting adjourned, an incensed prominent member of the altar guild assaulted me in a rage, saying that she would report this to the bishop of Maryland and recommend my immediate dismissal from the ministry of the Episcopal Church. At my initiative, I saw Bishop Powell the very next day, and we both had a laugh, although he did admit that he was not convinced of the new architecture of the largest parish in his diocese — that is, not until later when he found it so pleasing that he and his wife Mary became frequent worshippers at Redeemer after his retirement.

Still later, long after the new church was in place and booming, it was my privilege to officiate at the burial of that outraged woman from the

altar guild. Going through her treasured mementos one day, her oldest
son came across her well-used, leather-bound Bible. She had marked a
favorite passage in the eighth chapter of the Epistle of Paul the Apostle
to the Romans, which includes a recital of all the earthly and celestial
things that cannot separate the believer from God: "Nor height, nor
depth, nor any other creature, shall be able to separate us from the love
of God, which is in Christ Jesus our Lord" (Romans 8:39, KJV). In the
margin was a privately penned notation: "Nor Bennett Sims"!

Chapter 17

Episcopal Church of the Redeemer, Baltimore: Architectural Triumph — "The Scale Is Perfect"

As chair of the architectural committee at the Episcopal Church of the Redeemer, Edward Yaggy knew that something had to be done to rescue Black Tuesday from any further disaster. All of us on the vestry felt the power of the negative reaction to Pietro Belluschi's presentation. Even though that reaction seemed to be confined to a strident vocal minority, Ed countered with a brilliant pictorial idea. From designs to be submitted by Mr. Belluschi's local collaborators Rogers and Taliaferro, he would have the model makers at his manufacturing plant design and build a large-scale model of the new church and related buildings on the nine acres. The model would occupy a prominent place in the parish house on a sturdy pedestal and would rotate slowly at waist level using an electric motor and reduction gears concealed behind pleated green hangings suspended to the floor from the model platform.

When the model was installed about a month later, it was a smash! All the trees were in fetching fall colors, the six courtyards connecting the several buildings were landscaped in miniature, and the great steeple of the original church dominated the scene. For at least three months, the model rotated after every Sunday and weekday service and drew crowds that reached three or four deep around the model platform. Lee Owings, the sexton, would happily throw the switch on the motor for anyone who wandered through the parish house at odd hours and wanted to see the model rotate.

During this interlude, the architects polished their plans and specifications even though grave doubt prevailed in both the vestry and the congregation that the Belluschi buildings would ever be built. Controversy continued to divide every group in the parish. Division was especially sharp in the vestry, where it was clear in every monthly meeting that many did not favor the Belluschi Church, as it came to be called with scorn. There is a peculiarity about the canons of governance in churches of the Episcopal Diocese of Maryland that dates back to the colonial era. The so-called Vestry Act was put into place when the Church of England governed the churches of the colonies, and that legislation was never abrogated when the colony in Maryland became the state of Maryland in 1789. The Vestry Act designated each vestry as "Corporation Sole." Ownership of the church and its property was vested in the governing body of lay members of each congregation, appointed or elected. This further meant that all decisions touching on the property and its buildings were the sole prerogative of the vestry, the vestry having no legal accountability to the congregation.

Thus it would be up to the sharply divided 1957 vestry of the Church of the Redeemer, and not the congregation, to decide on the new church. Most assuredly it was not the rector's prerogative to decide such an issue, although the incumbent in 1957 was hardly silent in sermons and conversations. My outspokenness was hardly pleasing to many members. One Sunday morning following the early service, a prominent banker in the congregation who had led the greatly successful fund-raising took me aside and said, kindly but forcibly, that I was out of order in using the pulpit to influence decision making about the new church.

Robert Merrick's rebuke probably muted me a little but not entirely because my personal fever ran high. I passionately believed that, having the choice to build, we must build in terms that bespoke the ever-new contemporaneity of the living God. To revert to an architectural idiom of an earlier era, as cherished and legitimately historic as it might be, would suggest that we were erecting a monument to the memory of God. Pietro Belluschi had opened my mind and heart to the symbolic truth of architecture when, in his address to the congregation on Black Tuesday, he said something like this (allowing for some partisan dash from me):

> You must not place on this lovely corner in Baltimore a salute to an absent God of another era. If it is given me to be your architect, we must build an evangel, a winsome invitation to worship the God of the whole spectrum of time past, present, and future, and especially of Jesus whose invitation in the gospels is never to join him at some convenient spot but always to follow him on a journey of discipleship. Whatever is built on these acres of beauty-favored land, let it be a ringing sermon in wood and stone and stained glass.

Ignoring the privilege of cloistered decision making accorded the vestry by the seventeenth-century colonial legislation, our noble governing body of friends, 16 men in those days, decided to settle the issue by congregational plebiscite. At that time, the parish numbered 1700 families, and a simple mail-in ballot was sent to every household. The ballot gave church members two choices and requested that one or the other be checked: (1) we should proceed to build the Belluschi design; (2) the vestry should engage another architect. The tally was kept confidential by the treasurer's office, and no result would be available to anyone, including the vestry, until a fair amount of time was given every household to reply. Probably two months later, the vestry was informed of the result in a solemn meeting. That meeting is riveted in my memory for its exceeding gravity. About 1000 ballots had been returned, and the tally kept by the treasurer was 77% in favor of the Belluschi design and 23% in favor of seeking an alternative solution.

The scariness of that evening meeting was deepened when it became an open secret during the course of the meeting that the votes of the vestry and their wives were almost the precise reverse of the votes of the congregation. I had only recently been placed on blood pressure medicine, and my own mixture of delight and foreboding must have pushed my blood pressure to new highs. At 37 years old, I was by far the youngest member of the circle and was presiding over the vestry of my very first parish. Of the 16 men on the vestry, 12 voted to contract with another architect, leaving only 4 who agreed with the majority of the congregation. The vestry was split 75% against the Belluschi design and 25% in favor. Had the Vestry Act been invoked, there would have been no doubt of the outcome. Even if the vestry had done what was in their just power to do and insisted on delaying a decision until another architectural solution could be presented for a plebiscite, it was clearly doubtful that another proposal could have unified the congregation. The plebiscite, as it stood, was too overwhelming to be ignored. The tension in the room stood at the top of any imaginable scale.

Following a painful discussion of maybe half an hour, the most widely respected vestryman stood up and asked for the floor. At 59, Charles Garland, a graduate of Yale in the class of 1922, was handsome, wealthy, urbane, and articulate. Here is what he said, as clearly as I can reconstruct it:

Most of you know Aurelia's and my position on this thorny issue. She and I regard it a privilege to have pledged a substantial gift for any new church, but we are firmly against the Belluschi proposal. It seems to us entirely out of order, and we are joined in this conviction by most of our Redeemer friends. However, what most of you probably do not know is that we have children and grandchildren in this congregation, and all of them ardently favor the Belluschi design. Of the Garland clan, our young people will be here to love their church far longer than Aurelia and I. Fairness dictates that we vote with them on the setting for our worship of God. I therefore move that we accept the clearly declared wishes of the congregation and proceed to build what our architects have proposed.

One of the four in favor of the architects' proposal swiftly seconded the motion. Then silence. Prolonged silence. Finally someone in the circle solemnly called for the question. In the chair as rector, I asked for discussion before a vote was taken. I well knew the heat of objections to the Belluschi design in that circle of powerful men. Many had voiced their stiff opposition to me privately in the preceding weeks. Still silence. I then asked if they were ready to vote. "Question," came a quiet reply from someone. I remember putting my head down and looking into my lap: "All in favor please say 'aye.'" There were more *ayes* than I anticipated. "All against please say 'nay.'" More silence. Prolonged silence. I was stunned, but I managed to ask if anyone wished to be recorded as abstaining. Still more silence. From somewhere in the circle, a voice said, "Bennett, it seems time for a closing prayer." The undeniable fifth great gift of the Holy Spirit had been handed us. I must have stumbled through an unprepared offering of thanks and a benediction.

The place of every vestry meeting was an upper room in the parish house — a glass-windowed balcony space overlooking the large assembly hall one floor below. Against one wall in the room was a large, open fireplace framed in cut limestone and a heavy hewn oak lintel. Hung from the lintel was a real ox yoke taken from a Maryland farm, and into the lintel were carved the words of Jesus, "Take my yoke upon you" (Matthew 11:29). In all the years of meetings in that lovely room, I cannot imagine a more spirit-filled moment than the one on that fateful night in 1957 when we said yes to the wishes of the large majority of the congregation. Following grateful farewells that night, especially to Chuck Garland, I walked, high-hearted, to the old stone rectory of 1863. By decision that night, it would be dismantled and its weathered stone reclaimed for the interior and exterior walls in the great new church shown in the rotating model. The Belluschi design called for the new church to occupy precisely the ground of the old rectory, and, with connecting courtyards and a welcoming entrance atrium open to the sky, it would become the anchor for a composite of native stone and slate-roofed buildings to beckon spiritual seekers for generations.

It must have taken another year or more for the new buildings and courtyards to be completed. Meanwhile, we lost two families, just two. No one from the vestry left, but many in the congregation openly cooled. During the construction, some congregants vowed never to set foot in the new church, calling it a Miami nightclub for its purple carpet in the aisles and on the altar platform. The new church was designed to hold 850 worshipers in duplicate Sunday services. As a chapel, the old church would be used for early Sunday and small weekday services.

A fine professional quartet and a faithful elderly organist who had been at the instrument for many years led the music in the old church. The organist, Chester LaRue Mahl, was so close a friend of the rectory family that we had invited him to be a godparent to David Lewis Sims, our third and final child. The new church would have a splendid, 45-rank Austin organ and a large choir, and Chester recognized, with all of us, that a professional choirmaster would be required. I am not clear just when Chester did retire, but it fell to me to ask him for his resignation. No one could have been more gracious than he in agreeing to step down after years and years at the ancient 10-rank Estey organ in the chapel. The vestry awarded him a fine pension with ardent thanks.

A search was instituted for a new organist-choirmaster. I asked one of my two priest assistants, the Reverend Charles Griswold, to head a committee commissioned by the vestry to find the best musician we could persuade to come to Redeemer. The search homed in on Arthur Rhea, greatly esteemed as organist-choirmaster of the famous Bruton Parish Episcopal Church in Williamsburg, Virginia. Arthur did come to us, and, with his wife Dolly and their three young sons, he fitted hand in glove in the challenging new setting. He and I discovered a deep personal kinship. We shared ecclesial, liturgical, musical, and theological passion and even kindred political convictions. We became fast friends and remain so today. Arthur is 86 as I write and in unfailingly good cheer.

The organ console in the new church is situated at floor level just below the clergy stations, which are two steps above on the altar platform. The choir occupies the first rows of the north transept, where Arthur directed them with gestures to his left as he labored away on the great console and its pedals. I have a favorite recollection of the new church on Sunday mornings. Processing up the main aisle behind the choir and the other clergy, I mount to the clergy pews above Arthur, catching his smile and sparkling eyes. All the while, he is levering the foot pedals and pounding the keys with his right hand while vigorously waving a practiced left arm to command his large and obedient choir. No exchange of comradeship in the gospel could better symbolize the climax of my first major deliverance from the ruts of convention to the high road of transformation. The great new Church of the Redeemer is permanently emblematic of the gradual shift in the inner life of an early conservative.

Before the new church was ready for use, it was visited by both Pietro Belluschi and a colleague at the Massachusetts Institute of Technology, Gregory Kepys. Professor Kepys was the Czech designer of the great altar screen made of fist-size chunks of stained glass, and he oversaw its casting in the French cathedral city of Chartres. I had the privilege of being with both great men of art on separate occasions.

Professor Kepys's visit came first. He was there to make an inspection of the altar screen immediately after its installation. It rose from the floor of the altar area to the apex of the high, laminated wood arch that framed the cross-hatched steel support structure for the two-foot-square sections of concrete and glass. Embedded into every one of the more than 130 sections were faceted stained-glass pieces of both sharp and shaded colors in 127 different hues. The sections of stained glass were arranged so as to trace an enormous and deeply muted cross at the center of the screen. The arrangement of lighter colors was so ingenious that the great cross was not immediately apparent, despite the fact that the vertical axis stretched from top to bottom and horizontally from side to side, something like 40 feet up and 25 feet across. Strategically lighted from behind, it was relatively immune to outdoor variations in brightness and shadow, although it glowed best in the late afternoon of a sunny day since the altar end of the church faced due west.

During a conversation with Professor Kepys, I thanked him for the spectacular beauty of the altar screen but confessed my disappointment that the great cross at its center was so muted as to be almost disguised. I asked, "Why must we appear so restrained, even apologetic, in setting forth the central emblem of the Christian faith?" He answered with polite scorn. What follows is his answer transposed into my instructed understanding, seasoned by nearly half a century of grateful recollection:

Good priest, you give yourself away as a typical American with a shallow sense of the symbolic. In this country, everything must be so boorishly apparent. You seem not to grasp the profound distinction between a sign and a symbol, between a Coca-Cola advertisement and the sound of great music. People grasp instantly any old sign, but a symbol grasps you! A sign comes and goes, leaving nothing but information. But a symbol asks for your undivided attention and, while eluding immediate appreciation, will instruct and nourish you increasingly with repeated exposure. A symbol is not for information but for infusion, for inspiration. The altar screen is not intended to be instantly appreciated nor its message immediately appropriated. It is designed to be symbolic, symphonic, stimulating, and refreshing to your soul with every repeated encounter.

Ah so, Mr. Kepys!

Pietro Belluschi came late in the afternoon of the day before the dedication of the new church in November 1958. The day was darkening when he and I entered the church through the courtyard and east doors. Slowly Pietro began walking up the main aisle toward the altar, while I trailed behind him a step or two. He kept glancing right and left and upward while he walked, keeping very quiet. Finally, on reaching the altar steps and without turning to me, he spoke in a whisper as to the building itself: "The scale is perfect, miraculously perfect." That was all he said. Bewildered both by his solemnity and his words, I asked what he meant by scale. I cannot do justice to his answer, but it needs recording even though it may not be quite accurate architecturally:

Scale is the mystic relationship between three elements of design: the width of the building between its interior walls, the height of the ceiling above the people who are to occupy it, and the function

of the building. In a church, the width must be such as to combine a generosity of space with the intimacy of an
embrace of the congregation. The height of the interior must
combine transcendence and immanence, suggesting the basic
theological attributes of the Christian God. And the building
must have a focus that conveys the purpose and function of the
structure as a place of worship. The mystique in this set of relationships is that there is no way to compute these dimensions and
relationships in advance, either on a slide rule or by means of a
computer model. You just have to guess with the help of the Holy
Spirit. The miracle here is that, in my judgment, we architects
have been so assisted by the oversight and goodness of God.

The great building and related facilities were dedicated with appropriate flourishes and fanfare. Not all the congregation participated,
although it was a stirring morning with full churches at 9:30 and 11:15.
In the weeks that followed, professional architectural photographers
spent two days on the property. Many months later, *Time* magazine fea-
tured the Church of the Redeemer as a centerpiece photo in its Christmas issue. It is amazing how popular applause can alter firmly held
feelings and perceptions. That Christmas week, church members who
had vowed never to worship anywhere on the property but in the old
chapel were seen escorting friends and family from Cleveland and California through the new church and exclaiming how they had helped create this splendid outcome.

Chapter 18

Tokyo and Around the World

Looking back on my young adulthood, I confess with regret that work always came first in my assignment of priorities. My lovely wife and three stunning children came in second to the demands of a booming parish church with its staff of 22 women and men. At least two powerful and largely unconscious factors, I believe, were at work in this regrettable ordering.

First was my fierce personal motivation that rose from competitiveness with my father. Because he failed in high worldly accomplishment, I was driven to succeed. Second, most men of my generation who had been reared on hero stories and gone to war came to adulthood with an unexamined sense that care of the home and family was the responsibility of wives and mothers. Our job, whether we succeeded or not, was to provide the financial wherewithal and quality of manhood in which our wives and children could be secure. While I loved my father, my feelings for him were severely conditioned by a sense of shame that my worldly status was, for the most part, gravely inferior to my friends. Nearly all of them were in finer homes and owned cars when we had none, and many of them had country-club privileges.

But hindsight for everyone is only selectively comfortable. Full retrospection must give everybody the willies. That is what makes the healing work of counseling and psychiatry so significant. For me, effective psychotherapy has healed many memories and has helped me accept with gratitude my personal and family past — all in an embrace of reality that allows for the whole range of the lights and shadows of recollection. What must be at work in this gracious transaction is the life-giving wholeness of self-acceptance and self-forgiveness, transactions made possible by the love of God and family.

So it is time in this chronicle to recollect the highlights of the great adventure that thrilled and enriched our little family fivesome of Bea at 41, Laura at 12, Grayson at 9, David at 6, and Bennett at 42. We circled the globe together by air, ship, and rail. All of us were agog to be so privileged.

Our odyssey began early in 1961 with receipt of a letter from Japan by a former professor at Virginia Theological Seminary. It came from the Reverend Dr. Kenneth Heim, a professor of history and missions who was at that time posted as the senior American missionary to Japan for the Episcopal Church in the United States. Ken invited me to substitute for six months as interim priest in the English-speaking congregation of St. Alban's Anglican-Episcopal Church in the heart of Tokyo. The resident American missionary was due a sabbatical leave for study and rest in the United States. Would I accept an appointment as priest in charge of St. Alban's from January to July 1962? Man alive! What a chance at adventure. Bea and all the children shared my instant enthusiasm.

The only serious potential impediment might be an unwillingness on the part of my vestry at the Church of the Redeemer to grant me such an extended leave of absence. Providentially, the invitation arrived coincident with my 10th anniversary as rector, and the impediment vanished when I shared Ken's letter with the vestry. Not only did they agree to a mission leave for me, but they also elected to award me a full salary for the 10 months as a gesture of salute for my 10 years as well as a gesture of support for the foreign missions section of the 1962 budget of our national church. And so it came to be.

Close friends in the parish drove us in two cars to the Baltimore-Washington airport in late December 1961. It took that many cars and drivers to get the five of us and 14 pieces of luggage to the ticket counter. As can be imagined, five Americans who were going to live for 10 months in a foreign country and then take a trip around the world required nearly as much luggage as the suitcase section of a department store, including a separate shoulder bag for each child. Even so, we sent ahead a footlocker containing books for me and summer togs for all. We did leave enough space in the trunk for the mementos we hoped to collect in our travels.

When our plane landed in California, my widowed cousin Lucile Douglass gave us overnight hospitality. The next day, she drove us and our huge baggage collection to the SS *President Cleveland*, docked at a San Francisco wharf with gangways rigged fore and aft for first- and second-class passengers. Lucile, in her big Cadillac, drove to the first-class gangway, where we were told that our tickets had us located in the aftersection of the ship below decks and above the propeller shafts. Lucile was visibly taken aback, but we were so excited that it scarcely mattered. By the time the ship got underway, we had seen many of the passengers billeted with us in the second-class section, and it became clear that only missionaries, student adventurers, and Asian deportees rode the rear of the *President Cleveland*. Still, we were pumped up with wonder and joy as the ship plowed its way to a first stop in Hawaii a few days later.

Claude DuTeil, a classmate from Virginia Theological Seminary, and his family met us in Honolulu. They festooned us with leis and took us on a tour of the island. In the course of the tour, we had lunch with Richard Kirkhoffer, another seminary friend, and his family. Both men were posted at the time as priests in the Episcopal Church's missionary district of Hawaii. In midafternoon at one of the mission churches, I baptized the newest baby of a young couple who had attended the Church of the Redeemer as teenagers and were now in the military and posted to Honolulu. On the island of Oahu, we saw more pineapple fields than I imagined were in the world, and we were struck by the sharp volcanic lay of the land. All the Hawaiian Islands are the tips of volcanoes that erupted from the ocean floor eons ago and subsequently have been in the process of being sculpted by storms and tropical rain. By nightfall, we were back on the ship, happy, weary, and ready for our bunks.

On the final day of the weeklong ride from Honolulu to Yokohama, a crisp storm tossed the ship for hours. As a seasoned destroyer sailor in World War II, I felt at home in the tumbling sea. Bea and I rode the storm out in soft chairs, while our children played ping-pong and cards with the other missionary children in second class. The young crowd included Asian teenagers, many of whom spoke English. The next day we entered Tokyo Bay and headed north for the great docks of Yokohama, the smaller port city to great Tokyo, contiguous at the top of the bay.

The day was January 10, 1962. The weather had cleared so that all the usual limits to seeing great distances had disappeared. The morning at sunrise was crystalline-beautiful. All five of us were on deck to see what we could see, like the bear who went over the mountain. What we saw 50 miles to the west was the breathtaking, snow-capped volcanic cone of Mount Fuji, rose-colored in the dawning light and rising to 12,388 feet in almost perfect symmetry. I had been in Tokyo Bay for several weeks on the USS *Caperton, DD-650* 17 years before but was never lucky enough to see Fuji. It last erupted in 1707 CE and has five lakes at its northern foot. I could scarcely take in the high privilege it was to behold the great mountain with my family. We were now 10,000 miles from home and headed for an adventure of living in the world's largest city for six months followed by a journey of some 30,000 total miles around the globe.

Kenneth Heim, Verne Stolle, and Verne's wife Elva met us at the dock. Verne was an American business executive living in Tokyo and the senior warden of St. Alban's Church. Again, there were two cars to take us and our piles of luggage to the rectory near the Juban shopping street in the embassy district, maybe 25 congested, honking miles into Tokyo from the Yokohama wharves. Words to describe the sensations of this fantastic arrival cannot match the exquisite sense of adventure that overtook me and, I believe, all five of us. There is no way to articulate the enduring thrill of that fabulous morning. Our Japanese maid and housekeeper Namiko-san, a smallish young woman of bland but smiling face, met us at the rectory door. Immediately she asked us to remove our shoes, a very practical housekeeping maneuver characteristic of all Japanese homes. Tokyo, which is situated longitudinally on a line with Norfolk, Virginia, can be bitterly cold in January, and the rectory had no central heat. Namiko-san had the kerosene space heaters going, but they warmed the two-story house only partially, making us all glad to have carpet slippers supplied at the door.

In the course of our six-month residence in Tokyo, we went from winter to summer and saw the blossoming plum trees and all the other signs of spring. The children were enrolled in the American School in Japan at some distance from the rectory and learned to ride the streetcars. They stayed in Tokyo under the devoted care of Namiko-san while Bea and I toured the main island of Honshu by bullet train, local rails, and taxi. In Kyoto, we relished our stay in an authentically reproduced medieval Japanese inn, sleeping on traditional futons placed on the tatami, or straw matting used as a floor covering. For me, those six months in Japan as interim priest in a congregation of 100 members was an experience of total relief from the arduous role of heading up a suburban American parish of 3000 baptized members and a staff of 22 clergy and laity. Our adventure felt akin to what release from jail must mean to inmates, and my spirits soared. With the children, we visited the parks and temple gardens all over Tokyo and beyond. One of these tours took us to the elaborate shrine city of Nikko, a baroque architectural memorial to the Tokugawa shogunate an hour's train ride north of Tokyo. We were with Ken Heim as our host and guide, and all of us stayed in a large old missionary house complete with a deep wooden hot bathtub.

St. Alban's Church is located only a block from the great Tokyo Tower in Shiba Park. The tower is an open steel structure painted red-orange that celebrates the rebuilding of Tokyo after it was almost totally incinerated by United States fire bombs in World War II. Completed in 1958, it is taller than the Eiffel Tower in Paris and boasts high-speed elevators, souvenir shops on two observation decks, and television transmission facilities. St. Alban's Church, nestled across the street at the tower's haunches, was designed in rustic Japanese style to seat 100 worshippers in open-back pews of polished pine. The altar was fashioned in congenial rusticity and stands beneath a heavy, polished pine cross. The vestry and altar guild reflected the international composition of the congregation. We were Americans, British, Canadians, Australians, Japanese, Chinese, Sri Lankans, Indians, and a steady stream of visitors from greater Europe and Africa. I had the privilege of baptizing and presenting for confirmation a young faculty member of Keio University along with a young woman who was a high school student, both of whom had converted from Buddhism. They were Professor Hajima Kodama and Miss Mihoko…her last name escapes me. But there is no forgetting Mihoko's excuse for missing one of the confirmation classes held weekly in the rectory. Holding her jaw and frowning, she told me that she was sorry to miss the class, but the week before she had suffered a bad toothquake!

All of us in the rectory developed a relish for Japanese food. In the home of another missionary, we first tasted the special delight of a sukiyaki dinner prepared in a large iron skillet placed in the center of a circle of hungry people and fired from a hibachi below. In restaurants, a kimono-clad Japanese server would do the honors, using thin-sliced beef, onions, tiny round transparent noodles, Asian peas in their pods, and other ingredients of culinary delight, all cooked in a delicious sauce while the impatient guests watered at the mouth in response to the aroma of the sizzling skillet. Into a small ceramic bowl placed before each guest, the server might crack a fresh egg to be used for dipping chopstick-lifted morsels of sukiyaki delight. And always there would be a large bowl of steamed rice at the side of each dinner plate.

We learned a little Japanese for emergency use. One of these emergency requests in Japanese was "Benjo wa doko deska?" ("Where is the toilet?") We also learned the words for right, left, and stop, along with Rippongi, the Japanese name for the large intersection of several main streets nearest the rectory. Getting into a taxi on the Ginza (downtown shopping district), we would say, with as much foreigner flair as possible, "Rippongi-des kudasai" ("Rippongi, please"), to which request the little taxi would take off honking. Reaching the grand intersection, we would order "Hidari-des kudasai" ("Left, please"), and down the Juban street we would dash. Getting to a nearby small intersection in the Juban, we would order "Migi-des kudasai" ("Right, please"). Up a steep, curving street between high stone walls we would drive, and, upon getting to the top, we would say again "Migi-des." Going one more block to where the rectory stood, we would say "Tamate-des kudasai" ("Stop, please"). Paying the taxi in yen (360 yen to the American dollar in 1962), we would hop out at 35 Honmura cho, Shiba ku, our rectory address. Just once I tried using simply the house number and Honmura cho, and the poor taxi driver shook his head, uncomprehending.

Of course, everyone acquired some Japanese things to take home before departing Tokyo: a blue and white wool kimono for Bea; scarves, banners, and unremembered items for the children; and a Canon camera for Dad. Finally it was July and time to go. We had learned by then to travel a bit lighter, but it still took a couple of cars to get us to the docks in Yokohama. We had made many close friends in six months. Several of them saw us off, including the Honorable Laurence McIntyre, ambassador to Japan from Australia and the junior warden at St. Alban's.

From Tokyo, we sailed on the British ship SS *Oronsay*, departing for Hong Kong, Manila, Singapore, Colomba in Ceylon (now Sri Lanka), Bombay, Aden, and the Suez Canal. We disembarked at Naples, where we were entrained for three days as delighted tourists in Rome. We traveled by train for three more days to Paris and Chartres and thence by rail and channel boat for a week in London where we were guests of the provost of Southwark Cathedral across the Thames from the dome of St. Paul's Cathedral. In all this time, both in Japan and while touring Asia and Europe, we stayed well except for a brief stomach upset in Rome that nine-year-old David Sims experienced. We went from London to Southampton by train and then rode the old Queen Elizabeth in tourist class.

When we landed in New York, we were met by the administrator of the Church of the Redeemer, Henry Albert, Jr. He drove us happily to Baltimore for an after-dark arrival. When I awoke the next morning and looked around at our home and ample grounds, I could not believe how extensive and uncluttered our suburban privileges were in America. Everywhere in the busy world we had visited, all the streets and neighborhoods were crowded, the houses packed close, and all the avenues choked with traffic, especially in Japan and Hong Kong. At home, we had an immensity of grass to cut, but it was easy to negotiate the limited traffic on North Charles Street.

The details of life in Japan and around the world have dimmed after 43 years, but the supernal shine of our nine-month enchantment continues to cast a warm glow. Of special delight is the memory of so much family time. In retrospect, there seems to have been so little family time on the job in Baltimore and elsewhere in the United States. "Too soon old and too late schmart." But we were blessed with time to be smart when the Episcopal Church bestowed the incomparable gift of family time for seeing the world in 1962.

A special memory is family time on a bright February morning when the five of us left from the Shinjuku station in Tokyo for two connecting train rides for ice-skating at the foot of snow-mantled Mount Fuji. The public rink, named Fuji Kogen, offered rented skates in all sizes at the gate. Ankle-sore at the day's end, all five of us sped and spilled our way around the huge frozen pond. We were conspicuous as the only *gaijin* on the ice, the only foreigners in a mob of smiling Japanese, young and old. They seemed to hold us in some strange esteem until several young people made bold to halt our skating to tell us how proud they were of John Glenn, whom they pronounced Gren. Only days before, on February 20, 1962, he had rounded the earth three times in a space capsule. Not only were they keen about the American astronaut but proud that he had used a Japanese Minolta camera to shoot the planet beneath him for personal snapshots never before seen. "Ah so!" was the invocation for the occasion. They and we repeated it over and over that day, and we still revert to it now and then in happy conversations in our family circles.

Chapter 19

"I Have a Dream": The March on Washington, August 1963

A single moment can be pivotal in a person's life. Such a moment can cancel an old way of seeing the world and start an inner pilgrimage that moves life in a new direction. This happened to me on August 28, 1963 in the nation's Capitol. The decade that cradles this date was pivotal for hosts of Americans, blacks certainly and whites as well, and it acted like a long heat wave.

Just as the sun melts ice but stiffens clay, some hearts were warmed by the events of the 1960s, while other hearts were hardened. The reason for this difference is suggested by the fact that the sun's action is conditioned by the substance of the material acted upon. This same principle must apply to hearts as well, so that the heat of social convulsion creates different outcomes in people depending on the innerness of the human heart. We seem to respond according to the two commanding psychic forces in human experience, namely fear and love. I know keenly the power of these terrific energies. I have been melted by love and benumbed by fear. But on that pivotal day in Washington, I was transported. I was warmed, even heated, by the welling up of a personal compassion that I did not know was inside me. To me, the best and simplest definition of *compassion* is *feeling from the other side*. Literally, *compassion*, which comes from the Greek, means *feeling with*. "Walking in another person's shoes" says much the same thing.

Events leading to my pivotal moment all started when a friend in the Episcopal Diocese of Maryland asked me to allow two busloads of pilgrims to meet for early morning worship in the chapel at the Church of the Redeemer and to be served a simple breakfast before they rode together to Washington, DC as participants in a mass protest of racial injustice under the leadership of the Reverend Dr. Martin Luther King, Jr. As planned, 80 people from the Baltimore area gathered at Redeemer for worship and the ride to Washington. The opening service of the Eucharist was celebrated by the bishop suffragan of Maryland. Our special intention was to offer the day's event for God's blessing and ask that it be used to advance the Kingdom on Earth — for which the church routinely (and to a large extent thoughtlessly) presses heaven to install. Bishop Harry Lee Doll prayed that the day would be so presided over by God's spirit that it would bring credit to the cause of social justice, move the hearts of many, and keep those of us who participated from judging those who ignored or resisted the event.

After breakfast, whites and blacks together boarded our two waiting buses. I recall with sorrow that Harry Lee Doll did not board with us. He was moved by his sense of loyalty to his superior, the bishop of Maryland, who did not approve of the March on Washington, as perhaps most of his constituents in the diocese did not. Present in addition to the waiting buses were two police patrol cars summoned to surveillance duty by a scowling man from another waiting car. With an equally scowling friend, he stood at the doors of the buses and handed to each boarding passenger a strongly worded flier of protest urging us in the name of God to desist from this action of rebellion against the peace of God and the ordained social order.

Ignoring the fliers, we boarded the behemoths and drove to the Baltimore-Washington Parkway. Traffic began to thicken on the parkway about 10 miles above the district line. We were passed by several other silver monsters, all bearing bright banners tied below the bus windows. One of them read, "Pilgrim Baptist Church, Brooklyn, New York, March on Washington." They had left their homes before dawn.

By the time we entered the city from the northeast, the buses had clustered four abreast, using both the inbound and outbound lanes. Police preparation had cleared New York Avenue of all traffic. The buses were a tidal wave of thundering vehicles churning bumper to bumper through the black residential area. A strange silence had settled over the neighborhood, broken only by the diesel growl of the buses. I had felt the same threatening explosiveness of tense public silence as a street-side observer of two Communist-led demonstrations in Tokyo in 1962. By sharp contrast, the midmorning hush along the crowded avenue that day seemed like an expectant reverence. Scattered in clusters along the curbs were hosts of black children, all of them waving a welcome. Under the rules of the march, children under 14 were excluded, so they participated as jubilant greeters. Some even danced, the white flounces of the little girls' dresses bouncing in the sun. Their faces were aglow, like the shining faces of children everywhere when transfigured by an uncomprehending joy.

The caravan swung half-left into 4th Street NW so as to pass in front of the Capitol on its way to large parking areas near the National Mall. As our bus rounded the corner at 4th Street, it grazed the curb in making the turn. There, not 10 feet from the right-side bus window against which I was pressed, stood a large black woman of middle years. The picture she made remains as vivid in memory as if all my days were that day in 1963. She had her feet planted wide, her arms raised up and out in an expansive gesture of welcome, her head thrown back, her cheeks awash in tears, her face radiant in the noon sun. In that instant, I saw a living soul in all its majesty, in all its beauty of suffering, forbearance, and longing, a fully human soul like my own.

In that instant, I knew that all the noble words we use in religion and the defining documents of American freedom — all the careful, cloistered words of resolution, all the faithful Christian words about the equality and worth of every human person — in that instant, I knew the words were true. Best of all, I believed them. And I was thrilled to be on that bus, ashamed of my complicity in that woman's humiliation, transported by the joy of deliverance from a smothering prejudice that had imprisoned and stunted my soul for 43 years. As a society, we are imprisoned still, although less so today, I believe, and with "miles to go before [we] sleep" (Robert Frost, "Stopping by the Woods on a Snowy Evening," 1923). The secret of my release from prejudicial bondage lay in the unbidden moment of seeing deeply into another's soul. That black woman and I shared a transport. We were one.

When we Baltimoreans had found a grassy spot for our picnic lunch near the Lincoln Memorial, I knew this was to be a momentous confirmation of my noonday exultation. Estimates were that 250,000 black and white Americans lined the reflecting pool on both sides and stretched back from the Lincoln Memorial to the Washington Monument. We heard amplified speeches from A. Philip Randolph of the Railway Workers Union, Walter Reuther of the UAW-CIO, and one or two members of Congress. Mahalia Jackson sang a plaintiff spiritual, and then the Reverend Dr. Martin Luther King, Jr. stepped to the microphone. What followed was one of history's great orations. About a third of the way back from the steps from which he spoke, I heard Dr. King deliver his momentous "I Have a Dream" address. That vivid event marks another major influence that moved me from cultural conservatism to the bracing liberation of a progressive freedom.

The week before the March on Washington, I sent a pastoral letter to all the families on our parish mailing roster. In the letter, I said that I planned to attend the controversial March on Washington, asked for their prayerful support, and promised to speak from the pulpit the next Sunday if the event warranted it. (Imagine writing "if the event warranted it." Nothing in the way of a public demonstration in the annals of American political history has so moved the Congress to legislative action in the name of justice!) Following my sermon-report the next Sunday, something like 50 families left the parish. After the service, one prominent deserter said to me, "I admire your courage, but I deplore your judgment." Translated, this meant to me then and still means, "You are a damn fool!" I hurt for myself and for all the departed parishioners, but within two years as many as had left now made the Church of the Redeemer their new spiritual home. The experience made it clear to me that a silent church on the great social issues of justice and peace is self-defeating. More than that, church silence on the great political and moral issues is seditious!

Many friends in the parish joined me in the pain of seeing people leave. Some of them even wrote letters of criticism, saying that I was splitting the parish. To each one, I answered that I did not see it that way. I was not splitting the parish. I was simply revealing the splits already present and thus exposing them to the healing possibility of reconciliation. We Christians are charged with a reconciliation ministry, and the very exposure of alienation is the prompting cause for exercising a reconciling ministry. This is the Gospel according to St. Paul: "All this is from God, who reconciled us to himself through Christ, and has given us the ministry of reconciliation" (2 Corinthians 5:18). In strict terms, this verse does not exhort to reconciliation between Christians and Christians or between parishioners and their pastors. The exhortation applies to persons and God. But Christians are commanded to love one another, not for God's sake but for their own peace. Thus in terms of

Jesus' command that his followers love one another, the exhortation to a ministry of reconciliation clearly applies to the healing of any alienation in the body of Christ.

In the recent seasons of multiple social challenges that have caused pain in the church, too many of us clergy have stood aside from issues of social justice that affect minorities, including blacks and women and gays and lesbians. The reason for the failure of clergy to boldly witness for public justice may be as much our training in pastoral sensitivity as it is our lack of prophetic courage. But we clergy need to heed the prophetic dimensions of our calling in times of societal convulsion on issues of war and peace, gender equality, and human sexuality. We need to hear and obey at deep levels of our souls the calls to social justice by the great Hebrew prophets Isaiah, Jeremiah, Amos, and Micah.

Institutional timidity in the mainline churches seems to me heavily responsible for the growth of a virulent fundamentalism that is focused away from the world with promises of heaven for the faithful. This kind of disguised discipleship tends to be a moralistic individual piety, unconcerned with the larger issues of unjust suffering across the world. Worse, our silence is a betrayal of allegiance to Jesus Christ. His compassion and courage in the face of religious bigotry wrought the cross, and the cross is the badge of discipleship that he made mandatory for all who aspired to follow him (Matthew 16:24, Mark 8:34, Luke 9:23). And further, it is crucial for clergy and lay leaders to face the truth that courage of the Christ among his followers will never please many in conventional congregations. But that kind of courage will unfailingly attract the many who long for a vital voice that challenges injustice in the world, especially now in the face of an unjust war and the imperial ambition of present political leadership in the United States.

The Reverend Daniel Berrigan, SJ, jailed protester of our vain war in Vietnam, wrote a ringing indictment of the prophetic and social timidity of the churches:

I would like to say as simply as I know how, to other Christians, that I'm convinced that in our lifetime we have no contribution to make to one another or to the world at large except a modest and consistent NO to death [by violence]. Our churches can go tomorrow, our schools could have been closed yesterday, our institutions ground under by the next wave of tanks or the next phalanx of violence. And what will remain of Christianity except that we will have said audibly and consistently and patiently over our lifetime: "We are not allowed to kill. We are not allowed to be complicit in killing. We are not allowed to commit the crime of silence before these things."

— Daniel Berrigan, SJ, in *Peacemaking: Day by Day*,
Pax Christi USA, Erie, PA, 1985, p. 104
(www.paxchristiusa.com)

Chapter 20

Harvard and Homelessness

Does everyone have occasional sharp moments of unbidden illumining? And do they come while engaged in something quite alien to the moment? One Sunday morning about nine months after the March on Washington, I was preaching in the always crowded Church of the Redeemer and was suddenly struck by a totally vagrant question. Why do all these people come here? The question was so alien to the Sunday morning reality in front of me that I must have stumbled over my words or halted in midsentence. I now realize that the question was an intrusion into consciousness by a lively unconscious, an unconscious furnished with many prior repressed thoughts about a sense of alienation from my parish. In retrospect, I should have disclosed this sensation to Bea and the children. They would have been far better prepared for my response to an invitation in the summer of 1964 to spend an academic semester as a Merrill Fellow at Harvard Divinity School.

At some deep level, I had known for many months that it was time to go. I was 44 years old and still in my first parish out of seminary. Several opportunities to leave Redeemer had turned up since returning from our world tour. In the post-Japan years, I had been visited by vestries from large parishes in Chicago, Charlotte, and San Francisco. Even the bishop of Missouri had visited our home with a beguiling invitation to think about the deanship of his cathedral in St. Louis. All these oppor-tunities, despite their beguiling qualities, seemed sideways moves to me, and I declined them. But when the Harvard invitation came along, I was ready for something stimulating even though it meant absence from my family for several months.

I knew that I could not ask my vestry for another leave, and I did not need to since it was time for me to resign and find another arena for ministry. What also interested me was a visit by the vestry committee of a congregation in the small industrial town of Corning, New York, head-quarters of the world-renowned Corning Glass Works. I was committed to Harvard by this time, but the vestry committee asked, "Would I think about coming to Christ Church in Corning after completing my fellow-ship?" To go to a place of no great standing in size or reputation and seek to reinfuse a far smaller church with fresh vision and energy seemed like a call from God, and I would be following a faithful rector who had been at his post for many years. Bea and I spent a couple of hot summer days in Corning. We met many folks, all of them cordial and especially the chairman of Corning Glass Works, Amory Houghton, Jr., who at 38 was only a few years younger than I. We saw the rectory, a big frame house a few doors down the street from the church. Promises were made to put the house in any new order that seemed desirable to us. Corning seemed right, and I greatly admired George Barrett, the bishop of the Episcopal Diocese of Rochester. It all looked reasonable, and, most of all, Bea was warmly agreeable. So we accepted.

A few weeks later I went off to Cambridge after an uncomfortably muted ceremonial send-off dinner by the Redeemer vestry. My ves-try very subtly demonstrated their sense of betrayal that evening even though the mortgage on the new church had been prepaid by a full year. But I dismissed my discomfort. Too much lay ahead. Bea was generous in agreeing to oversee the arduous move and get the two older children into new relationships with their schools. Laura moved from being a

With my father, 1921.

With my mother Sarah and my father Lewis,
Davenport, Iowa, 1921.

An early indication of my abiding
fascination with cars, 1921.

With my grandparents
Harvey and Lucy Jones, 1922.

My brother Edward (right) and I, Davenport, Iowa, 1928.

My mother, my brother Edward (right), and I in front of the family Terraplane, 1934.

My father Lewis and my mother Sarah,
Kansas City, 1938.

My graduation photo,
Baker University, 1943.

The USS *Badger, DD-126*, commissioned in 1919.

Coming aboard the USS *Badger*, 1944.

The USS *Caperton, DD-650*, commissioned in 1943.

Bea, my brother Edward (right), and I at Princeton Theological Seminary, 1947.

Class of 1949, Virginia Theological Seminary. I am second from the left in the middle row. We called the seminary "Zabriskie's Embalming School," a reference to the graduates' grim looks and to Dean Alexander Clinton Zabriskie.

Virginia Theological Seminary
(Zabriskie's Embalming School)   *Class of 1949*

In front of the 1858 Church of the Redeemer, Baltimore, 1958.
The new church (left) is under construction.

The new Church of the Redeemer, Baltimore, 1959.

The rector's secretary Mihoko Takahasi and her family, Tokyo, Japan, 1962.

With staff of the Church of the Redeemer, Baltimore, 1963. I am second from the left in the front row.

My children Laura (16), David (10), and Grayson (13), Baltimore, 1963.

Aspinwall Hall, Virginia Theological Seminary, where I served as founding director of continuing education from 1966 to 1972.

My official portrait when I
became bishop of the Episcopal
Diocese of Atlanta, 1972.

The bishop's house in Atlanta, built in 1927.

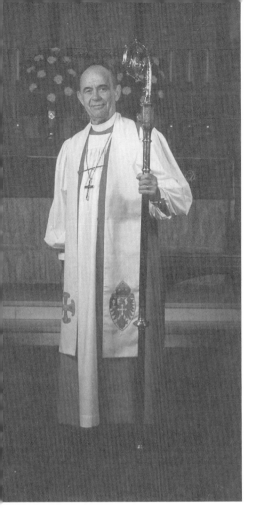

At the chapel altar, Cathedral of St. Philip, Atlanta, 1973.

As adjunct professor in the Candler School of Theology at Emory University, Atlanta, 1984.

In the bishop's office, Cathedral of St. Philip, Atlanta, 1982.

Mary Page and I on our wedding day, Mikell Chapel, Cathedral of St. Philip, Atlanta, August 27, 1988. (Photograph by Robin Boylan.)

The 50th reunion of the class of 1949, Virginia Theological Seminary, 1999. I am second from the left in the front row.

At Windsor Castle with Queen Elizabeth, Prince Philip, and the primates of the Anglican Communion, 1995. Archbishop George Leonard Carey is seated next to the Queen and Mrs. Carey next to Prince Philip. I am at the back center.

My grandson Nathan Sims and the 1929 Model A Ford Phaeton, Hendersonville, North Carolina, 1990.

Donald McDonald (left), my boyhood friend from 1927, and I in our late 70s.

My son Grayson with Mary Page, Brattleboro, Vermont, 1996.

Bill Jamieson, second president of the Institute for Servant Leadership, 1999–2004, and his wife Kennon, who was administrator for the institute during Bill's tenure.

Our expanded family circle at festivities honoring my retirement from the Institute for Servant Leadership, Kanuga, April 1999. (From left to right) Jane Bender, Jane Arrington, Debbie Anderson, Anne Greene, Tom Greene, Peter Anderson, David Anderson, Matt Boucher, Margaret Anderson, John Boucher, Mary Page Sims, Sarah Sommers, Bennett Sims, David Sims, Nathan Sims, Katie Sims, Mary Sims, Laura Boucher, Elizabeth Jane Sims, and Edward Sims. (Photograph by Robert Smith.)

In bishop's vestments, 2005.
(Photograph by Expressions Photography, Flat Rock, North Carolina.)

day student at Garrison Forest School to residential status, and Grayson made the same move at the Gilman School for boys. David went to Corning with us.

After 40 intervening years, it has grown steadily harder to think of these changes and now to write about them. The moves did not turn out well. Although Harvard was a splendid stimulation for me in some ways, the changes were traumatic for the boys. Grayson was deeply saddened, and David was uprooted from his friends at school and in Boy Scout Troop 35. By contrast, Laura blossomed, and she won an exchange scholarship to England on graduation from Garrison Forest. For Bea and me, it was a wrenching time and may have been the slow beginning of the end of our marriage that came 20 years later in separation and divorce. I was a long way from understanding the dynamics of our move at the time, but it stands now as the single most destructive decision I ever made. If everyone has a moment in life that they would painfully negotiate for the power to undo, mine would clearly be this wrenching shift from Baltimore to Corning. I would even give up the flattering invitation to Harvard if I could, because it only confirmed and rigidified in me the adolescent drive to be a greater achiever in life than my father.

In the wake of that move, I suffered the deepest despondency since my terrible soul-distress at Pearl Harbor in 1945. It was now 20 years later, and I had to find my way through another thickening gloom. Christ Church-Corning was a nineteenth-century stone Gothic building, soot-begrimed on its exterior walls and lifeless with a gray painted interior. It was so dimly lighted as to suggest a monastic setting, although the interior was a bit redeemed by a high, vaulted ceiling painted in faded blue tones. Of course, Christ Church was cherished by the congregation, but it stood in bleak contrast to Redeemer and the bright interior of St. Alban's Church in Tokyo. I felt lost in a sickening thicket of depression. One night in the cold of January 1965, I walked the streets of Corning wrestling the demons of darkness. I vividly remember my soliloquy:

"Bennett, you felt called to be here, but for what? Just to prove that you could do a pride-diminishing thing and win the approval of the angels of humility? This may have been your motivation, but what does God want to do with you?" It was a confrontation with the sly workings of the garbage-can side of pride, the keenly felt but self-deluding sense of "I'm not good enough for good fortune, so I'll choose a comedown." That was an insult to both Christ Church and myself. The saving question in the soliloquy was, "What does God want to do with you?" Almost immediately, I felt a slowly quickening rise in spirit, and with it came a new recognition. As I had been given the exquisite privilege of missionary duty in Japan, so too may I be the receiver of a missionary challenge here under the gray skies in the snow-sided valley of the Chemung River!

Three life-deepening lessons came from the trauma of the Corning move. Since life at its best is an adventure in learning, the Corning adventure may represent the very gift of God that I judged it to be when Amory Houghton and the Christ Church vestry sought me out as their new rector in 1964.

The first lesson is touched on above. I see now the extremity of my vulnerability to the ego boost in the Harvard invitation. I clearly see as never before that my whole life up to these years in my mid-80s has been an ego trip. For all the seasons of my long pilgrimage, I have been driven by a need to be better than I think myself to be. This terribly distorting need may be, in some measure, everyone's Achilles' heel, everyone's core of emptiness that only the supreme gift of God's forgiveness and the parallel acceptance of one's self can remove. Many are the symptoms of that crippling emptiness: the scarcely admissible ambition to be a bishop someday, the aspiration to be thought of as an intellectual, the certainty that a professorship is of higher vocational standing than a parish rectorship, the drive to write a book that runs to multiple printings, the rejection of personal appearance in the face of advancing baldness, the rejection of others on grounds of their appearance, and on and on.

My secretary in Atlanta once said to me, "Bishop, many of your clergy wish they could occasionally praise you, but they have given up because you seem never to allow it or to take it seriously." Bull's eye. Anyone too modest to receive genuine compliments is really not modest at all. The truth is that such a person is too diminished by the lacerations of an unforgiving pride to believe the genuineness of praise. And such push-offs of praise make for an increase in the self-rejection that one relentlessly practices, whereas a true modesty and self-acceptance would respond to praise with self-enhancing appreciation and other-enhancing gladness. This new understanding has made me such a ready receiver of praise that I can hardly wait to thank all bouquet throwers. Try me, friends and family!

The second lesson in the move from Baltimore to Corning via Harvard is that a person ought never to leave a relationship of long association in anger. Never use anger as the motivation to make an important interpersonal or vocational move. In retrospect, I clearly see that I was angry with the Church of the Redeemer for their refusal or inability to move with me from their cultural conservatism up to my superior and decidedly Christian brand of social and political liberalism. Never leave any relationship in a pout. Never leave any relationship in condemnation. Never leave any relationship for the quick satisfactions of retaliation. I remember thinking about my departure from Redeemer, "I'll show them that I don't need the approval of wealthy conservatives in their big, fancy parish. I'll just go to an ungainly parish in a small, ugly town." The problem here is plain. Such a motivated move is a destructive insult to both places as well as a deep, self-inflicted wound. Little wonder that things turned out badly for my family in the move to Corning. Little wonder that it is hard to write about this episode. And some big wonders might be added — that the Church of the Redeemer has been so forgiving as to invite me back many times, that Amo Houghton remains a close and generous friend, and that Christ Church invited me to return for a preaching engagement soon after I left for Virginia Theological Seminary.

The third lesson in that disruptive move is also the gift of much retrospective pondering. The lesson is this. Never move to a post for which you feel the least contempt or to which you feel superior. Never succeed a predecessor whom you cannot honor for his or her work and person. Never make significant changes in institutional habits and routines quickly nor without careful preparation and explanation. The message to the congregation in quick, imposed changes is that your predecessor was wrong or stupid or both and that you are contemptuous of traditions that many people love and are nourished by. Little wonder that I saw hatred in the glances from the pews in the case of several senior members of the congregation, especially at the early Sunday services. Little wonder that Christ Church was half-empty at the benediction on the Christmas Eve of my first service in which I announced some changes in the administration of the sacraments. Little wonder that, several years after leaving Corning, a nearby diocese was visited by members of Christ Church who lobbied against my election as the new bishop.

Still, the time in Corning had its ups as well as downs. Attendance at services grew, the giving levels went up substantially, and the interior of the church was brightened by new lighting, new carpet, and new paint. But too many good people suffered a sense of loss and alienation. When I announced my resignation to accept a call as a teacher and program developer at my old seminary in Virginia, the senior warden at Christ

Church, Art Weber, came to me with a look of relief. Were I not leaving, he told me, he would have had to handle a small mutiny of parishioners who were ready to instigate procedures with the vestry and the bishop of Rochester to have me ousted.

As for Harvard, there is more bleakness than brightness in recalling the experience despite the boost it gave me in exposure to a great university. The upside remains considerable, but the downside has to do with a case of despondency that drove me home as often as I could spend Friday and Sunday afternoons on airplanes between Boston and Baltimore. I probably sensed that something was deeply amiss in my decision about Corning and in my retaliatory leave-taking from Redeemer. Still, I relished the intellectual stimulation of both Harvard Divinity School and the graduate architectural program in Harvard Yard. My fellowship made it possible to audit courses anywhere in the university, and architecture had become a new passion under the influence of Belluschi, Rogers, Taliaferro, and Lamb.

I can still remember a youngish professor of architecture and his power to inspire. His students gave him a standing ovation after a lecture in which he told them that a Harvard education was so singular a privilege that a Harvard degree obliged its bearer to life-long service for building a more humane, just, and beautiful world. And I can remember the outline of a lecture by Richard R. Niebuhr, professor of theology, and the interfaith wisdom of Krister Stendahl in New Testament when he said in a tutorial, "We Christians are just honorary Jews." My favorite teacher at Harvard Divinity School was J. Lawrence Burkholder, a Mennonite theologian who flew his own airplane and often slept in his office at the school for having to work late preparing lectures. His course in church renewal was a groundbreaker in the era of reform that was just beginning to emerge in the 1960s and has since overtaken the institutional church in spades. Liberal-minded renewal and reform have led to controversies that continue to sunder congregations. These controversies have forced many former active church members into exile while stimulating the growth of fundamentalism as a fear-driven reaction to change.

Controversialist is my deserved name in the church. Controversy began at the Church of the Redeemer with the eruption over the striking departures from convention in the Belluschi design. It continued through my driving many good people away in the wake of the March on Washington, through the Harvard episode of liberal-intellectual stimulation, through the havoc of my shake-up at Christ Church in Corning, through the introduction of new theological currents at Virginia Theological Seminary.

All this personal history climaxed during my 12 years of leading the Episcopal Diocese of Atlanta through the tangle of controversies over civil rights, radical revision of *The Book of Common Prayer*, the ordination of women, and the leading edges of the most divisive issue, homosexuality. My position on this threatening issue, which now tears at the fabric of church unity, is clear after a period in which I rejected the normalcy of homosexual preference in a benighted minority. I now stand squarely on the conviction that homosexuality is a bestowed ontological identity as basic and unchangeable as skin and eye color in the overwhelming majority of cases and that the few Biblical prohibitions are all amenable to the liberating insights of historical critique and modern medical science. My 1997 book *Servanthood: Leadership for the Third Millennium* carries a chapter that elaborates an embrace of homosexuality as an entirely legitimate and unchosen identity.

Anyone familiar with most denominational churches, including my own Episcopal Church, will know instantly that my certainty about the normalcy of homosexuality in a special minority remains feverishly controversial. Although I have tried to be kindly disposed to those on opposing sides of the multiple controversies that have torn religious institutions, I have probably failed more often than succeeded. God forgive my arrogant use of power as a church and educational leader in contradiction to my expressed commitment to use power as a servant. In this retrospect on my life, I can see that I have done what I accuse others of doing. I have unknowingly wielded the Bible and theology as weapons to demolish opposition rather than as servants of the living God for up-building the beloved community. Maybe some of us write books to persuade ourselves of truths that we know we need to learn.

Chapter 21

Return to Virginia Theological Seminary to Invent a New Educational Enterprise

Not many weeks after my spirit-lifting soliloquy that winter night on the streets of Corning, a phone call came from my old school in Alexandria. It was March 1965. Dean Jesse Trotter wanted to know if he could send his professor of homiletics, Jack Beckwith, to Corning to talk with me about a professorship at Virginia Theological Seminary. Here I was, struggling to embrace an unfamiliar ministry and valuing a professorship as a highly esteemed calling, when suddenly I was asked to consider a plum job at a plum location in the church landscape. I thanked Jess for his call and waited eagerly for Jack's visit. He came to Corning with a beguiling invitation. Would I join him as a full professor of homiletics and pastoral theology?

I was thrilled, but two problems loomed. First, I had been at Christ Church only a few months and could not in good conscience leave any time soon. When did the seminary want me to come? Jack replied that they were ready now. "Come to the faculty in time for the fall semester." No go! I could not renege on Christ Church's expectation of a respectable season of leadership by a new rector even though I knew my departure the very next day would cheer the hearts of quite a cluster of communicants. There was no written longevity contract with Christ Church, nor had I made any verbal commitment for a specified number of seasons there. Still, decency dictated a reasonable stay. Would the seminary consider my personal need to remain at Christ Church for a couple of years? Jack didn't know. He would take the question to the dean.

The second inhibitor to an acceptance of the seminary's call was even more serious. My experience, both in the closing years at the Church of the Redeemer and in the immediate past at Harvard, convinced me that the pressing need of seminaries was to invent ways to address the critical needs of already-ordained clergy. Such a continuing education program would add to the traditional seminary work of training preordination candidates. Clergy in the field were being called to a vocation for which they had received little or no preparation, and many were suffering. A convulsively changing social order was challenging clergy to become agents of change in a church that was, in most places, reluctantly awakened to the social justice that is implicit and explicit in both the religious and political documents that define the American republic. Was Virginia Theological Seminary prepared to address this issue? I had to be honest with Jack. I told him that I genuinely honored his work in preordination education but that I believed I needed to concentrate on the already ordained as a prospective seminary teacher. I needed to find ways to help myself and my colleagues in the church's ministry to an understanding and practice of institutional leadership in a swiftly changing social order.

Jack Beckwith returned to Virginia, and I heard quickly from Jesse Trotter. He and I needed to talk. Would I come to the seminary for a heart-to-heart? Nothing would suit me better. A visit was arranged, and I flew to Washington. I shared my deep gratitude for the honor of the call and my honest inhibitions about accepting it as we crossed the Potomac to the 90-acre seminary campus. Jess assured me that he understood my position. He may have already anticipated my response because he said that he had launched the raising of funds for expanding the scope of the seminary, and the expansion would include the addition of a new department of continuing education. The department would be a research and teaching enterprise mounted exclusively as a ministry to the already ordained. His only problem was that he had tentatively approached another and much younger graduate of the seminary to head the new department. However, the seminary could well use the talents of the younger graduate to add to the school's muscle in teaching prophetic social ethics at the preordination level. A call to me could work well for another reason. Not only did the younger candidate lack the years of convulsive parish experience that I could bring, but he would not conclude his doctoral work in social ethics for another year or more so that both his and my availability for teaching posts at Virginia might coincide.

Meanwhile, Jess proposed that I chair a committee to study work already underway in continuing theological education at other seminaries, especially where any kind of emphasis was given to casting the role of parish clergy as change agents. With alacrity, I agreed. Jess offered a modest budget to cover travel and housing costs for me and for a committee that Jess and I would collaborate in choosing. My only reservation in accepting the invitation to form and chair a study committee was that I had to be circumspect with my vestry and the parish. I did not wish my work to be understood as preliminary to leaving Christ Church. Therefore I had to guard myself against any such understanding, refusing for a considerable time to decide one way or the other about the call to Virginia. To that end, I told Jess that I would not think of the committee leadership as a prelude to accepting a call to the seminary faculty. In fairness to all concerned, I would withhold any decision for another year, allowing the work of the committee to guide me about the future. Bea was cheerfully agreeable to all of this.

The committee assignment in 1965–1966 was both exhilarating and discomforting. On the upside, I had nearly a full year to work with a select group of clergy and laity in researching and blueprinting a whole new enterprise in ministry education. On the downside, I had to wrestle in relative silence with a confusing decision about where my moral and vocational obligations lay. Bea was my only confidant, and she left the matter entirely to me. Later, when Laura returned from England, I confided in her and her brothers, trying to get a feel from the family about another major move that could be looming on the horizon. As I look back, it seems a miracle that the secret was kept.

When I decided to accept the seminary's call in mid-1966, both the parish and the committee were surprised! In response, there was both glee and sadness. An uncounted but slim portion of the parish was moved to high spirits at the news of my departure, but others were abashed. One very prominent member of the parish faced me directly with the accusation that I was a rat fink. Ever the controversialist! However, both the vestry and the parish as a whole were generous and congratulatory. Over the years, my memory of this response from the great majority of the people has eventuated in a positive valuation of my 22 months as rector of Christ Church in Corning.

Two great values accrued. First, the time at Christ Church equipped me far more broadly for the ministry of teaching clergy. Had I gone directly from the Church of the Redeemer and Harvard Divinity School to Virginia Theological Seminary, I probably would have been narrowed as an elitist priest. I greatly needed the valuable lessons that only a ministry of multichrome coloration could teach me. Christ Church was and is a healthy cross section of humanity, unlike the relative monochrome character of privilege that marks the social makeup of Redeemer. Also, a graduate fellowship at Harvard tends to fashion an elitist posture, narrowing one's grasp of the dynamics of leadership.

Second, my relationships with many people at Christ Church have remained cordial and even affectionate during the 39 years since I left there, proof of the friendship and love that allegiance to the norms of Christ's teaching can cultivate. This enduring friendship is especially noteworthy in the case of Amory Houghton, Jr., who was chairman of the Corning Glass Works. No one at Christ Church had better reason to switch me off than Amo. He was the one who most encouraged me to accept the vestry's invitation to come as rector. He was also the one who supported me by accepting membership on the seminary committee to blueprint a groundbreaking enterprise in continuing education, not knowing that the committee work might wean me away from Corning. And he was the one who, after my decision to leave for Alexandria, remained a faithful attending member of the committee until its discharge after a full year of occasional meetings and a report to the faculty and trustees. He and I remain special friends, exchanging letters and political challenges. He and his wife Priscilla accepted my invitation to come to Hendersonville in 1994 to participate as leaders in a seminar of the Institute for Servant Leadership. Until his retirement from Congress in 2005, Amo was the only close contact I have had with the federal government. He was a Republican congressman in the House of Representatives from the 17th district of New York state for several terms. I write him often, and he responds unfailingly with a personal reply. Our relationship is proof that political partisans who share a superordinate allegiance to Christ can enjoy a mutual fondness and respect that endures through all seasons.

We moved into a brand-new house on the campus in Alexandria, and within some weeks afterward I had recruited six specially selected clergy from around the United States to test the six-week format that the committee and I had taken a year to blueprint. From the start, the continuing education program was to be ecumenical rather than limited to Episcopalians. The design committee itself represented a denominational spread. Over the ensuing seasons, the program enrolled many from the Anglican tradition, but it began with a marvelous mixture. Although he was not a member of the design committee, Gordon Cosby, founding minister of the ecumenical Church of the Saviour in Washington, DC, was a special mentor to me in launching what came to be called the Center for Lifetime Theological Education.

The six original fellows in the pilot seminar were the Reverend John Claypool, Southern Baptist of Louisville, Kentucky; the Reverend Conald Foust, Roman Catholic of Atlanta, Georgia; the Reverend Robert McMillan, Presbyterian of Atlanta, Georgia; the Reverend Timothy Pickering, Episcopalian of Toledo, Ohio; the Reverend Hiram Weld, United Methodist of Columbus, Ohio; and the Reverend William Youngdahl, Lutheran of Minneapolis, Minnesota. These men were six gifted pioneers who risked immersion in the currents and whirlpools of an untried six-week venture in continuing education almost 40 years ago. We melded into a close and affectionate community while we tested a program design that I called "The Dynamics of Change."

The seminar opened with a three-day silent retreat in the Maryland countryside northwest of Washington. The intention was to anchor the experience in quiet detachment from the rigors of parish ministry and in some depth of spiritual nourishment. As the retreat leader, I offered an occasional meditation.

The next component was a long weekend of exposure to what was then called sensitivity training. This was a carefully guided experience in interpersonal dynamics designed to open the fellows to one another and to an invited group of another 10 or 12 laity, both women and men, who joined us. This larger group was convened at a nearby conference center. Its purpose was to get in deep and honest touch with one's personal makeup and emotions and to learn directly about one's impact on others.

By intention, the contrast between the first and second components was quite radical. The ensuing weeks proceeded under the tutelage of a variety of resource scholars and practitioners in theological studies and management theory. In the first hour of each morning after chapel, I tried my wings as a teacher of clergy, assuming the mantle of theologian. I did not think I fitted that exalted designation, but I wanted to build the center's curriculum on a solid foundation of Biblical study and doctrinal reflection. So I named my lectures and discussions "A Theology of Change," and I found that teaching the courses was deeply fulfilling. So, too, did many of the fellows who rated the course well in their evaluations.

Halfway through the fellowship period, the wives were invited to join their husbands for a relaxing weekend. Private rooms had been assigned to each fellow in one of the seminary dorms for the duration of the course. In each of the series of seminars during the six years that followed, designs were kept fluid so as to reflect the evaluations of those who participated in the preceding event.

Of the six fine men in the pilot seminar, I have had ongoing contact with only one, John Claypool, until his death in 2005. John turned out to be a closet Anglican and left the Baptist tradition a few years later to become a distinguished Episcopal priest. During his fellowship at Virginia, he avidly read in the works of one of my first-magnitude heroes, William Temple, who became Archbishop of Canterbury in 1942 during World War II. I believe that John, as a natural scholar, comprehended Temple far more deeply than I. Hiram Weld, my favorite undergraduate teacher at Baker University, has since died after a long and notable ministry as a college professor and parish minister. Timothy Pickering also had a distinguished career but gradually moved away from an embrace of most of the changes in the Episcopal Church in subsequent years. Tim and I had to accept a steadily widening theological and liturgical rift between us. As for the other three, I have lost track, but I hold all of them in deep gratitude as pioneering with me in the development of what has since become a vigorous and renowned program of continuing theological education. The Center for Lifetime Theological Education at Virginia Theological Seminary now offers a doctoral degree, and its graduates are at work across the world.

The little Sims family of five lived at the seminary for what turned out to be six turbulent years, not unlike the lives of hordes of families in America who underwent the convulsive social changes of the late 1960s and early 1970s. There was a certain steadiness for me in the development of my department, but all of us endured the currents of rebellion against many traditional habit patterns in varying degrees. These currents were probably far more severe in the coastal sections of the country than in the insular cities and schools. I was invited to lecture at Oklahoma State University during that time and could scarcely believe that the young people looked so straight-arrow. The Oklahoma crowd contrasted sharply with the long hair and sloppy garb of the teenage generation in and around Washington that reached across the Potomac and turned my sons into real hippies — much to the confusion and consternation of their parents. At age 20, Laura seemed to escape most of the hippie momentum and costumery, but the boys plunged headlong into the convulsion.

In addition to the cultural currents that strained and rent relationships during our six seminary years and beyond, two other unanticipated influences worked profound changes in me. One of them, the vocational current, I write about easily here. The other, the theological-scientific-historical current, runs so much more deeply and enduringly that I will only touch on it here, saving two chapters toward the end of this chronicle to elaborate its broader meaning to me in terms of the world's need for peace.

As for the new vocational current that mounted during the years at Virginia Theological Seminary, clergy members of certain dioceses of the Episcopal Church began importuning me to enter their election contests for a new bishop. The first was the Episcopal Diocese of Bethlehem in northeast Pennsylvania. I was excited by the approach and fully expected to win. This was the contest to which a small group of Bennett resisters from Corning made a visit to lobby against my election. The result was that I came in second to my friend Lloyd Gressle. Since it all worked out in the years that followed, the Corning delegation did everybody a favor. Lloyd was very happy as Bishop of Bethlehem. Had I been chosen, I would have been disqualified for entrance into three more Episcopal elections. In two of the three, I also scored second. In Kentucky, I lost to an old seminary friend, David Reed. In Southern Ohio, I had to bow to a distant friend and eminent scholar, John Krumm. Prominent clergy from two other dioceses asked me to run, one in Michigan and one in New Mexico and Southwest Texas (later named the Episcopal Diocese of the Rio Grande). However, I felt that I would not be suitable for either jurisdiction and declined to be a nominee.

I had become a little weary of these close brushes with destiny and wanted no more of them. But one night, a call from a beer and pizza bistro in Macon, Georgia got me out of bed to talk with the Reverend Harwood Bartlett of the Episcopal Diocese of Atlanta (middle and northern half of the state). Woody said that several of my former students in continuing education who had returned to their parishes in the diocese wanted me to run for bishop in an election almost sure to go to the popular and handsome dean of the cathedral, David B. Collins. I remember saying, half in sleep, that I was an experienced loser of Episcopal elections and that Atlanta seemed to promise to add to that experience. Still, Atlanta intrigued me. If he and others wanted to raise the sails and see what the wind might blow, they were welcome to it. I think I added that I was happy in my ministry at Virginia and expected longevity as a teacher of clergy. And so back to bed.

About three weeks later, a phone call came from California. On the line was the esteemed historical and liturgical scholar Professor Massey Shepherd of the Church Divinity School of the Pacific in Berkeley. He invited me to visit his seminary for a serious talk with the faculty about becoming their dean. I went and felt honored to be there. Every member of the faculty, including Dr. Shepherd, encouraged me to think well of a possible call, but I felt a vagrant sense that I did not belong in that setting. Who knows whether I would have been called as dean, but the Atlanta prospect took lively precedence in my sense of vocation.

As the days went on, I got acquainted with the Georgia road map and began to feel an excitement about the South that was rising again, especially in Atlanta. In addition, I knew several of the Atlanta clergy as former students and admired them as competent and adventuresome. The election was held in early November 1971, and I won quickly on the third ballot to the total surprise of the whole diocese. No other vocational summons, save for my call to be rector of the Church of the Redeemer, lifted my spirits to such soaring. I called Dr. Shepherd and thanked him for the honor of thinking of me. True to his reputation as a pastoral scholar, he graciously wished me well in my new work.

Before proceeding to Atlanta, I want to tell more about a basic shift in my conceptual apparatus that confirmed a steady emotional and intellectual transformation from a conservative to an eagerly progressive view of life and history. As hinted in Chapter 6, the intellectual segment of my transformation is anchored in a discovery of the work of Pierre Teilhard de Chardin, the controversial Jesuit scientist and mystic whose great corpus of writings cover roughly the middle years of the last century. Any record of my life journey would be sharply incomplete without a distinct reference to Teilhard. So the next chapter is devoted to a brief synopsis of the influence of a great contemporary saint's life and thinking in my saga of transformation.

Chapter 22

Progressive Shift to a Timeline
of Divine Immensity

The leading edges of an immense change began to reshape my conceptual life as a teacher at Virginia Theological Seminary from 1966 to 1972. Those six years with faculty colleagues also got me one more dubious medal as a controversialist. The controversy was a subtle thing at first, but a slight dissonance grew as I got into a fresh construction of the Christian worldview through the scientific mysticism of Pierre Teilhard de Chardin. Looking back, this shift in my worldview was inevitable. Following 16 years as a parish priest, I returned to the seminary in 1966 convinced that theological education needed to move beyond some of the old paradigms that perpetuated a kind of medieval assessment of humanity and the world.

A restless society, with its values turned to social justice and world peace, was aborning. Clergy needed preparation for it. Most of us in parish leadership were prepared for a ministry of pastoral care with almost no accent on the rigors of the prophetic challenge in the record of Jesus and the Hebrew prophets. Often we were lambs led to the slaughter when we dared to use the pulpit to pronounce God's care for the poor and racially oppressed and to plead for social justice. When we dared to teach a dynamic worldview that takes evolution and constant change as basic to the Bible and the flow of human history, we became threats to the peace of the parish. In the middle of Chapter 6 are three paragraphs on the controversial dynamism of Teilhard, but he needs a fuller salute and elaboration here to do justice to his place as the original architect of my new and ever-advancing evolutionary worldview.

Teilhard entered my life in 1962 by way of a gift of his signature book, *The Phenomenon of Man*. During summer holidays in the early 1960s, I became the world's foremost expert on the first 15 pages of the book. I struggled vainly to comprehend the man's turn of mind, his self-invented terminology, and his substitution of lavishly mystical prose for plain reasoning. Words like *noosphere* and *sidereal vastness* simply did not compute. But his certainty that science and faith could be mutually enhancing disciplines of the spirit kept me wanting to find a way into his beckoning system of thought.

Two years later, after periodic struggling with a few essays on Teilhard by other authors, someone gave me an anthology of Teilhard's own collected essays called *The Future of Man* (translated from the French by Norman Denny, Harper & Row, New York, 1964). This small volume of his essays spanned the years of 1920 to 1950. Some of the essays had been unpublished until brought together in this book. The writings cover three decades of his burgeoning spiritual and intellectual life from age 39 to 69. For me, they became the clearest window through which to perceive and follow his soaring insights. A note in my handwriting on the fly page says, "Reading begun November 17, 1968; completed November 27, 1968." This closely compacted span of 11 days is emblematic of how I devoured and heavily underlined those luminous essays. A further note on the fly page, again in my handwriting, reads, "Until now the greatest book I had ever read was Dostoyevsky's *The Brothers Karamazov* in 1958. It must give way in 1968 to Teilhard de Chardin's *The Future of Man*."

Since those pivotal 11 days with Teilhard's luminous mind, I have not been able to think or to pray in any other than a processive framework about the history of the cosmos, life in the earth, and the future. Years before, in a college course on comparative anatomy, I had been enthralled with a glimpse of life in evolutionary terms (see Chapter 6). Thus I was prepared for Teilhard, but only he, as a scientist and theologian, gave me the confidence and the tools to move confidently beyond the static framework of traditional theology. One of Teilhard's categories of process is what he calls life's diminishment. He died of a heart attack at age 74, but he began to recognize his loss of energy and strength for a time prior to that.

Now, at age 85, with prostate cancer lurking in my loins for the past 11 years, I appreciate Teilhard as a spiritual director. Although my years outnumber Teilhard's, I sense my advancing diminishment acutely and am learning to accept it with the help of my towering hero. Our present home is on a golf course. There was a time when I used it frequently with friends and neighbors. Now it is simply a lovely green vista punctuated by stands of trees above streams and ponds. No longer do I have the energy (or humility) to go the ladies' tees and watch my drives run out of steam at 75 to 80 yards. On the golf course, I feel like the old man who remarked that he used to spit over his chin but now spits all over it!

In 1969 at Virginia Theological Seminary, there was ample time in my teaching schedule to enroll in a doctoral program across the Potomac at the Catholic University of America. Under the tutelage of two scholars at the university, Robert Fairicy and David Tracy, I wrote papers that gave my love of Teilhard some conceptual coherence. Although they are too technical for this chronicle, they deserve some summary. The best way to capsulize the insights gained at the Catholic University is to make three brief points and then elaborate on two theoretical absolutes in Teilhardian thought.

First is the series of three capsule convictions about the future. They rise from a Teilhardian perspective on the human experience of time. Humans, according to Teilhard, are the creatures of divinely overseen evolution that thrust up a type of being who "knows that he knows." Teilhard coined the word *noosphere* from the Greek term *nous*, meaning *mind*. The term *noetic* therefore means *of the mind* or *of consciousness* or, better still, *of advancing self-reflective consciousness*. This third meaning seems to me best because the unique self-consciousness of *Homo sapiens*, or self-transcendence, participates itself in the evolving character of the cosmos. Here, then, are the noetic propositions that, in my view, derive directly from the bold futurizing of Teilhard:

> Reality is far more than what is precisely measurable.
>
> Everything and everyone are interconnected.
>
> We are participants in our own evolution.

These three capsule convictions summarize, for me, the principal intellectual propositions essential to an evolutionary understanding of life.

As for the theoretical absolutes, the first in this tight review of Teilhard is his conviction that the forces of human evolution rebound unevenly on themselves to produce ever higher states of consciousness and interconnection. He sometimes called this the planetization of mankind and predicted in the 1930s the modern phenomenon of globalization. What he foresaw was the compression of humanity into an increasingly tight network of interaction by three kinds of temporal realities: (1) a limited planetary sphere in which to expand, (2) an ever-expanding human population to press the physical limits of the sphere, and (3) an increasing level of spiritual and intellectual sensitivity to the complexification of human interaction.

In addition, he predicted an increase in the wizardry of technology that would make global communication the great medium of exchange. This would involve the use and further development of the noosphere and inevitably bring about a quantum leap in the consciousness of the human species. Teilhard remains today a controversial theologian, and my adoption of his evolutionary and hopeful worldview won me a mildly controversial place on the seminary faculty. I often felt more tolerated than accepted as a colleague. Many people, and especially a classically trained theological intellect, find it difficult to move from a medievalist mind-set and embrace new conceptual adventuring, which, in Teilhard's case, seems to me to be precisely on target in forecasting the character of our world experience. Teilhard foresaw the planetization of mankind as including the present crisis of environmental threat and the possibility of nuclear self-destruction, but he was convinced that the future, however it might be threatened, would climax in a divinely designed fulfillment at an end point that he named Christ Omega.

So far, in my own evolving perceptions, I am unready to accept Teilhard's consummation in Christ Omega. Evil remains critically powerful. It breaks the created oneness of the cosmos by humanity's exercise of free will in self-aggrandizing competitiveness and protective fear. In my view, this perverse sundering of created oneness prohibits so optimistic a view as Teilhard's. But this reservation does not diminish my gratitude for Teilhard's hopefulness. I simply yield my theological limitations to the unlimited love of God for all life and to God's power to bend the history of evolving humanity to the frequent admonition of Jesus that we "Be not afraid" (Matthew 28:10, KJV). For me, fear is the prohibiting menace that cancels any forward-moving linear proposition that the human experience will inevitably get better and better.

The second of Teilhard's theoretical absolutes that I briefly summarize here bears on the issue of the ultimate goal of evolution. From his keen observation of the mechanisms and outcomes at every level of both organic and biological evolution, Teilhard deduced the principle that "union differentiates." Instead of a mush of undifferentiated components as evolution advanced, the basic ingredients of atoms, molecules, and cells combined to flower into a breathtaking variety of identifiably distinct combinations. From the primitive simplicity of snowflakes to the intricate complexity of the human species, no two entities are precisely identical. Teilhard's theoretical absolute that union differentiates evolved the cunning of highly differentiated *Homo sapiens*, but it makes two radically different forecasts of the human experience. One is the negative expectation of nuclear and environmental doom. The other is the achievement, by a global advance in human maturity and interdependence, of the finest quality of life the planet has ever spawned and humanity has ever experienced.

The outcome can go either way, given the reality of human freedom, competition, and fear. That is why an easy optimism about a preordained fulfillment of Christ Omega does not seem to fit human realism. Still, there is reason for hope. For me, hope lies in the faith that the unremitting thrust of evolving life by God's design will prevail. It may be that humanity on planet Earth does not need to survive as part of the vast living cosmos in order for God's purposes to prevail.

Still, I find hope on earth in two immense realities. On the one hand, differentiation lies at the base of all competitive striving, fear, and violence. On the other hand, union is the prior energy that produces differentiation. Therefore union is the precondition to differentiation. We know from the experience of love that this is true. Love as the power to unite makes it ever more safe and enriching to be individually different and distinct. An enduring marriage, bonded by cherishing and forgiveness, supports and enhances the individuality of those so married. Therefore what needs to happen for the world's survival is a spiritual triumph over the principalities and powers of accusatory fear and Jungian projection in self-protective blaming. No one knows whether this triumph can emerge in time to keep alive and safe the tightening web of human presence in our imperiled planet. We only know that the newest insights of quantum science and the oldest deposits of prophetic religion both insist on the divinely ordained oneness of all life as the precondition to life itself. Thus the great thinkers in both fields speak as one with the Dalai Lama of Tibetan Buddhism in proclaiming that only a spiritual revolution will suffice to preserve the world from the mounting threats of environmental plunder, factional scapegoating, and armed violence.

My personal bias in favor of a decidedly progressive view of history tilts me toward a conviction that the world-redeeming spiritual revolution is already incipient and growing in our time. This is a diametrically different theory of the world's end from an anticipation of the end-time in cosmic fire and death. Theorizing about the world's end is called eschatology in the theological disciplines. Eschatology in fundamentalist outlook awaits a so-called Rapture when believers in Christ will be lifted bodily from a perishing earth "to meet the Lord in the air" (1 Thessalonians 4:17). This is the lone reference in the whole of the New Testament to such a specific conclusion of history, although it has become heavily popular in fundamentalist circles to weave together from many biblical references a convincing narrative of a God-decreed violence as the end of earthly history. This popular doomsday theology is called biblical prophecy and dates its modern beginning among evangelical preachers and scholars to a little more than 100 years ago.

Forecasting this kind of divinely vindictive end-time is shaped by a now scientifically discredited historic time frame that sees the cosmos as having been created by divine fiat in the year 4004 BCE. Fundamentalist theology accords the Genesis accounts of creation as having contemporary scientific validity. Thus when the world's past is robbed of its verifiably immense longevity, especially in our own time of vast planetary crisis and change, despair of the world runs high, and the time remaining seems correspondingly robbed of its longevity. Thus eschatology must necessarily be apocalyptic, or violently calamitous, in a static, or time-constricted and nonevolutionary, worldview. The fundamentalist view of history is positioned backward, yearning for the now fallen but once-perfect creation to be restored. It understands the present as waiting for a future convulsion to bring with it a lost past.

By diametric contrast, eschatology in an evolutionary frame of reference is positioned forward. In its dynamic worldview, the future awaits an accumulating present to bring with it a completed past. Eschatology in an evolutionary framework is a conceptual basis for hope in this world — not optimism, but hope. These two postures of mind are profoundly different. On the one hand, optimism seems a one-dimensional, secular good cheer, which is not altogether without its own beguiling merit. Jesus himself enjoined his disciples to "be of good cheer" (John 16:33, KJV). On the other hand, and at a far deeper level, hope springs from a multidimensional faith in the undefeated Lordship of God. It sees beyond all temporal outcomes, trusting St. Paul's cherished promise. "For I am convinced that neither death, nor life, nor angels, nor rulers, nor things present, nor things to come,…nor anything else in all creation, will be able to separate us from the love of God in Christ Jesus our Lord" (Romans 8:38–39).

Chapter 23

Bishop of Atlanta: Challenging Billy Graham

As I walked one morning across the campus of Virginia Theological Seminary after the opening chapel service, I heard the familiar whine of jet engines as an airplane powered for altitude. It was on a vector for takeoff from nearby Washington National Airport. The jet was a DC9, the tail emblazoned with the triangular red, white, and blue logo of Delta Airlines. I knew from many flying trips that Delta was headquartered in Atlanta, and maybe that particular plane, appearing so soon after prayers, was sending a message. In chapel that morning, I had done what had become habitual during the two preceding and preoccupying weeks. I had offered a private prayer that, whatever the outcome of the election of a bishop in the Episcopal Diocese of Atlanta, it would be pleasing to God.

In earlier such elections, I did not develop much anticipation or hope of winning any of the three contests in which my name was put forward, but the Atlanta run was strikingly different. I ardently wished to win there, and I have never known why the prospect of being bishop of Atlanta aroused so much hope and excitement. Maybe it has to do with sensing a personal place in the mysterious unrolling of God's design in history. But I knew better than to pray for it. So my petition each morning at chapel was that God would take from me all undue ambition and guide the election to an outcome pleasing to divine wisdom. And when I saw the Delta jet climbing above the roof of the old chapel on that bright November morning in 1971, I thought, "Mmm, maybe this is a sign; maybe Bea and I will be flying to Atlanta soon." And so it was. I was elected on the third ballot.

Before our first visit to Atlanta ended and before accepting or declining the election, Bea and I met with all the clergy and their spouses in a series of convocational soirees around the diocese. Afternoons and occasional evenings were given to this exercise for several days. We were ferried to Columbus, Macon, Athens, Rome, and several locations in metro-Atlanta. The people attending these meetings were a blend of mostly eager enthusiasm and a scattering of courteous caution. One memorable conversation occurred during the convocation of Athens when a clergy wife confronted me with less than enthusiasm. She allowed as how the whole exercise seemed a waste of time. "Didn't you already know that you would accept the election when you consented to run? Why don't you just come out with it and let us get back to the work of the church?"

No doubt several people in those get-acquainted circles had the same thought, but I needed to know something of what the key people I would be working with wanted in a bishop before accepting the call. I had decided in advance that I would go to each of the seven or eight gatherings with a simple question, "What are your expectations of a new bishop?" The answers covered the whole spectrum of a pastoral executive job description, but the characteristic expectation in all the answers was a quality of personal caring. What I heard them saying was, "If you decide to be our bishop, we want you to know us personally and to care about us."

Remoteness is a bishop's severest handicap. That is true not only in the experience of the clergy's relationship with their bishop, but also — and painfully — in the personal experience of many bishops. It was so for me. Almost all bishops come from experiences involving close pastoral ties with their people in parish ministries or with students in classrooms and seminars. However long or brief the stay in a parish or school, the sense of being at home is characteristically keen. Love happens! Not always, of course, and not with everyone, but in most cases fondness flourishes. We clergy know that we are gypsies, in allegiance to the Christ who had no place to lay his head and in service to a system that presupposes much moving about. But the universal longing for love opens our hearts to our people and theirs to us. By contrast, one of the rude awakenings that confront a bishop sooner or later is that a diocese is not a parish church writ large. It is a regional system of more or less independent components, some of them fiercely independent. The reality of remoteness may be the leading reason for looking back on my 12 years as bishop of Atlanta as the most taxing work that I undertook in all the 56 years of my ministry since ordination.

Phillips Brooks (1835–1893) is widely regarded as the greatest preacher that the Episcopal Church in the United States ever produced. For all of his mature years, he served as rector of Trinity Church in Boston and was loved and listened to by overflowing Sunday congregations. At age 56, he was elected bishop of Massachusetts. After a year of that new work, he confided to a friend, "The fire of prophecy has gone out of me." Never married, he died only a year later at age 58, a lonely man at the pinnacle of his profession.

Brooks is hardly typical, seeing that most bishops live long lives, but his case is testimony to the sense of isolation that almost always accompanies the move from the intimacy of the parish to the top of a regional hierarchy. I have been a parish priest, a seminary teacher, a diocesan bishop, and, in retirement, an educational innovator. Nothing along the way compares in challenge and difficulty with the work of bishoping in the Diocese of Atlanta. And yet I would not exchange those days and nights of toil, anxiety, and high reward for anything. The blossoming story of those incomparable years follows in this chapter and the next.

The Cathedral of St. Philip, which seats 1400 when full, was the setting for my consecration in February 1972. The great Gothic-idiom church was filled to overflowing, and the processional from the narthex to the chancel required 25 minutes of solemn trudging. Included in the colorful parade were two choirs, all the clergy of the diocese, the entire faculty of Virginia Theological Seminary, several visiting and vested prelates of other major church bodies, 25 active and retired bishops of the Episcopal Church, the executive board and lay officers of the Diocese of Atlanta, the mayor of Atlanta, my attending clergy plus the preacher, and my four co-consecrating bishops, who included my honored predecessor Bishop Randolph R. Claiborne, Jr. Finally I myself came along. I was followed by the chief consecrator, John Elbridge Hines, who was then the presiding bishop of the Episcopal Church and who, along with his chaplain, brought up the blessed rear! A weary choir and congregation were at last relieved of singing what must have been five or six multiverse hymns.

After the two-hour service, a reception was convened in the cathedral's great Hall of Bishops, where everybody ate, drank harmless punch, and worked at sober merrymaking. At one point in the party, I was ushered to the stage to receive some tokens of office accompanied by speeches, after which it was my turn to make remarks. I still have a photograph of the presentation routine in which I am at the microphone. Not surprisingly, all the presenters who preceded me at the mike show painful signs of boredom and fatigue, and not one of them is looking in my direction while I speak! One comes away from such elaborate installations of a modern potentate suspecting that Simon Peter was ushered in as bishop of Rome with simple prayers and candlelight in a catacomb.

I made my first parish visitation a weekend later. I remember vividly an insight that suddenly erupted from the depths of history and from my own consciousness while I was laying hands on the waiting heads of young people and adults. The location was the altar rail of Grace Episcopal Church in Gainesville, Georgia, a county-seat town about an hour's drive northeast of Atlanta. What suddenly came to me as I moved down the rail, calling each person by name, was that I now occupied the second most ancient role of Christian identity of anyone in Grace Church that Sunday morning. My place was second because ahead of me for antiquity was Nat Parker, the rector of the parish. In his priesthood, Nat was a historic eyewink ahead of me in my episcopate. Local priests came before regional prelates.

As a bishop, my vocation stretched back to a dimly discerned point in the development of the apostolic church, back at least to Simon Peter, whom ecclesial memory names the first bishop of Rome. The 19th presiding bishop of the Episcopal Church, whom I knew personally, was the distinguished, bony, and tall Henry St. George Tucker. Bishop Tucker, decidedly a low churchman, knew very well the fog that beclouded early history of the New Testament church. From his certainty about our ancient uncertainty, he held his own theory about the appearance of the episcopate. He said that the early church went through a tunnel about the year 115 CE and came out a few years later with a bishop riding on the cowcatcher.

The recognition that Nat Parker represented a more venerable office than mine was a palpable thrill, and it quietly opened my heart to all the priests of the diocese. While I was their superior in status, they were my superiors in point of time as servants of the gospel, and my role was somehow to be their servant as a leader. St. Augustine knew this truth long before it came to me. In an address to his clergy in the North African Diocese of Hippo, he said this:

For you I am a bishop, but with you I am a Christian; one is an office, accepted; the other is a gift, received. One is danger; the other is safety. If I am happier to be redeemed with you than to be placed over you, then I shall, as the Lord commanded, be more fully your Servant.

— St. Augustine, 354–430 CE

It is recorded somewhere that Augustine had only 11 priests in his jurisdiction. Seeing that statistic, some wry bishop along the way remarked that he knew how the bishop of Hippo had time to write all those enduringly great books, some of them still in print after 1500 years. I myself wrote only two passing volumes while bishop of Atlanta. The first was a five-chapter rewrite of a series of lectures delivered in 1975 at the Episcopal Theological Seminary of the Southwest in Austin, Texas. That book, which never sold well, was titled *Invitation to Hope*. The other book was a compilation of essays on issues of the day that I had written for the monthly diocesan newspaper. Included were various sermons, addresses, and pastoral letters on the heavily controversial issues that overtook the Episcopal Church in the 1970s and 80s. It was titled *Purple Ink* after my practice in those days of writing everything in longhand for typing later by a secretary. While appreciated by some, *Purple Ink* aroused scornful amusement in one of my clergy, who re-titled it *Purple Prose*. Both volumes are now out of print.

I took office in Atlanta while the Vietnam War mounted. It was late 1972, and the war was a source of personal and ethical offense to me, although I did not make a public statement in protest. I simply fumed in private. But a lavish flier and personal letter from the Billy Graham organization smoked me out. The mailing, which came by first class just before Christmas, announced a Graham crusade to be held in Atlanta in June 1973. It asked for my participation in the crusade along with other church leaders in Atlanta and urged that I prompt my clergy and their congregations to attend.

A few days later, President Nixon ordered what came to be called the Christmas bombing of Haiphong Harbor in Vietnam. Instantly, I connected the Billy Graham appeal for support of his crusade with Graham's frequent visits to the Nixon White House. So I sent a night letter by Western Union to the renowned evangelist the day after Christmas. In the letter, I acknowledged receipt of his organization's appeal to support the forthcoming crusade but pointed out that I could not give it the sanction of the Diocese of Atlanta without some response by Billy Graham to a particular appeal by me. In the light of his close ties to President Nixon, I challenged him to intercede with the president and ask that such wholesale assaults on quasimilitary and civilian targets cease. Furthermore, I asked that he write me an explanation of his disinclination to intercede if he felt that he could not do so. I closed the letter with a statement that my support of his crusade in June was contingent upon receiving some kind of reply to my appeal. I did not ask to be agreed with, but only said that his reply, however he chose to position himself, would prompt my support of his crusade.

That was brash. Put it down to three things: (1) youth in the office of bishop, (2) a strong liberal bent in politics, and (3) a conviction that violence only compounds the violence to which it responds. I could only have sent that letter out of my deeply felt opposition to the whole Vietnam undertaking. A copy of the night letter went to all clergy of the diocese. I thought it important to let them know how I was dealing with a Billy Graham appeal since it included them and their congregations. I asked that they keep the letter to the evangelist confidential until he had time to answer. Live and learn! Within days, an outraged column appeared in the *Atlanta Journal*. Bishop Sims was blackmailing Billy Graham. How dare he so misuse his office! Angry letters soon began piling up from the congregation of the Cathedral of St. Philip and from the several churches in the city. Someone, or perhaps several, of the clergy had ignored my request for confidentiality, but I did not want to know who. Such knowledge could only escalate the whole sordid business of recrimination and misunderstanding.

In conservative circles, offended feelings and their accompanying recriminations tend to endure. My reputation for stirring the pot remains alive and well. I was 52 when the crusade controversy erupted. I write now at age 85. Just two years ago, I had a leading role in a series of experimental worship services held in Brevard, North Carolina, a lovely town near our home in Hendersonville. In reaction to the services, it was noised about that, years before, I had prevented Billy Graham from conducting a crusade in Atlanta!

The truth is that Billy Graham sent me a gracious, three-page reply to my challenge within a week of that night letter. I have rifled my files in vain looking for our exchange of correspondence, but many such records have taken wing in several housing moves since then. In substance, what Dr. Graham said was that his theology did not embrace a social or political component and that his conceptual relationship to the gospel was exclusively individual. Furthermore, he kept all his relationships with the several presidents he knew strictly sealed against any political or social implications. I replied that he had graciously met my conditions for support of his forthcoming Atlanta crusade and that I hoped to participate myself. However, my understanding of the ministry of Jesus and the gospel embraced the whole of life, particularly on issues of social justice, war, and peace. The day after the crusade opened in June of 1973, Billy Graham telephoned the bishop's house. We talked for several minutes, and he invited me to sit on the platform with him one evening of the weeklong event.

All of this is greatly to his personal credit! In my view as a pastoral ethicist and theologian, it is even more to his credit that he has since expanded his grasp of the evangel of Christ to include the communal and global as well as the individual force of the Christian message. In a recent lecture on fundamentalism, the renowned historian Karen Armstrong said that all fundamentalists are fearful, fearful of the erosions of modernism on what appears to them the unambiguous absolutes of the literal and inerrant Bible. She went on to declare categorically that Billy Graham, unlike so many other evangelists, was not a fundamentalist in her view.

I do not know Karen Armstrong's warrants for absolving the elder Graham of fundamentalism, but I would do precisely as she did on two grounds. First, he is neither compulsively angry nor afraid! Most fundamentalists whom I know and whose statements I have read communicate either harsh anger or smiling contempt or both. Billy Graham has never communicated contempt or wholesale dread in my experience of his ministry. Second, he has a clear grasp on the global perils of nuclear stockpiling and pleads for a nonnuclear sanity to preserve the earth.

By stark contrast, conventional fundamentalists see the future in fierce apocalyptic terms. They welcome the prophecies of certain portions of scripture that forecast a calamitous end of the world in fire and damnation, while their believers are raptured out of the perishing planet and into everlasting bliss. Billy Graham took a wise and enlightened position during the Cold War. In contrast, the evangelist Jerry Falwell, in a televised sermon that I heard him deliver, actually welcomed the arms race as a possible prelude to the convulsive apocalypse promised in the New Testament book of Revelation. Stepping beyond the tight boundaries of typical fundamentalist bombast, Graham wrote,

> Is nuclear holocaust inevitable if the arms race is not stopped? Frankly, the answer is almost certainly yes…I cannot see any way in which nuclear war could be branded as being God's will. Such warfare, if it ever happens, will come because of the greed and

pride and covetousness of the human heart...We cannot afford
to neglect our duties as global citizens.
    — Billy Graham, in *Peacemaking: Day by Day*, Pax Christi
    USA, Erie, PA, 1985, p. 76 (www.paxchristiusa.com)

This is my warrant for denying that Billy Graham is a typical fundamentalist, popular though this feverish brand of religiosity has come to be,
especially in the American South where I live.

Next in the Atlanta saga came the controversy over busing black
children to schools in the more privileged sections of the city. I publicly
supported this racial integration and received a heartwarming letter of
thanks from the federal judge in Atlanta who ordered it. But the consequence at home was an increase in the number of threatening and
obscene telephone calls. They came every day, sometimes several calls a
day, especially late at night. In the dark of one morning at 2:00, a wrecker
truck arrived in our driveway. When we answered the bell, we learned
from the driver that his office had received an urgent call to go to the
bishop's house in Ansley Park and take away a car for repairs. I hope we
thanked the man while explaining that this was just one more bizarre
effort at harassment and that any such request to go to our address in
the future should be ignored. Southern Bell was sympathetic to the daily
obscene phone calls but did not have the instant tracing technology that
was developed later. There was nothing the telephone company could do
except cancel our phone service and make it impossible to dial our number. While the volume of threatening calls gradually dropped off, they
continued almost daily for the first six years of our residence in Atlanta.

Meanwhile, another controversy erupted, this one an Episcopal
Church tangle over the long-cherished *Book of Common Prayer*.
Sequential general conventions of the Episcopal Church had passed
legislation that mandated the publication of revised liturgies for trial use
in Episcopal parishes and schools in every jurisdiction. In my view and

in the view of most parish and diocesan leadership, these revisionary steps were both crucial and timely. The old *Book of Common Prayer*, for all its beauty of language and honored use for generations, failed to address the real world of rapid change. Even some of its theological assumptions were dated and rigidified to outgrown convictions about God and the human condition. Still, even the most thoughtful Christians often find it difficult to be clear about the truth that God did not write *The Book of Common Prayer*. We did. We wrote and rewrote it through every era of church history from Hippolytus until now. Thus we can rewrite it in good faith — must rewrite it!

All words are human inventions, and the human pilgrimage continues to invent language to articulate our now swiftly advancing human experience. After nearly 20 years of trial use throughout the Episcopal Church, many rewrites by the liturgical commission, and three years of wide testing following a first authorization by the Episcopal General Convention, a new *Book of Common Prayer* was finally adopted in 1976 for general use throughout the church and was to be ratified for permanent use after three years. As diocesan liturgical officer, I directed that all regular Sunday services were to be conducted after the liturgies of the new book by the year 1979, giving the three intervening years for every congregation to grow accustomed to the new book. Of the 78 parishes then in the diocese, only 2 bucked my directive. I met with the priests who took exception in friendly pastoral consultations, and all went fairly smoothly among the clergy. But resistance among the laity grew feverish in many places. The heat was aggressively turned up by lobbying and printed pressure from the newly formed Prayer Book Society. They insisted on perpetuating the use of the 1928 prayer book, and I became the target of yet another round of attacking letters and telephone calls. So be it. After the prolonged siege over civil rights and the Billy Graham crusade, I had become almost inured to rotating forms of holy flame-throwing.

As if there were not enough to disturb the peace of the church, another eruption claimed the ardent attention of all Episcopalians. This one raged around the mounting pressure to ordain women to the priesthood and episcopate. Any reader of this chronicle can guess that Bennett was heartily in favor, not because I had grown enamored of controversy but because it had become my conviction that the rise of the feminist movement was one of the leading edges of a new paradigm of human social and political formation. Even more now than then, I believe that the world community is being reshaped at deep levels of human consciousness by the feminist and other movements. Such movements are challenging and correcting the prevailing male-dominant vengeance and violence that can portend a new planetary extinction.

I will write more about this in concluding chapters. For now it is sufficient to note that the confluence of the three roaring rivers of civil rights, revision of *The Book of Common Prayer*, and the ordination of women created three new congregations in the diocese. Providentially, none of the congregations of the Diocese of Atlanta were torn from their jurisdictional allegiance. The ties of all the churches to the diocese held firm, but disenchanted communicants in three locations in our territory formed new clusters of Episcopalians. Most of them affiliated with off-shoot leadership that sailed under the broad historic name of Anglican. One such newly organized congregation, which vigorously protested the ordination of women, ironically chose to call their new church none other than St. Hilda's. Poetic justice!

It was my experience as Bishop of Atlanta that there is great reward in being clear about one's position in ecclesiastical controversies. Perhaps the reward is late in coming. At best it may always seem delayed, but what is hidden in people's hearts does become manifest. My initial stand on busing and civil rights brought many accusatory letters and a six-year spate of threatening phone calls. But a special letter arrived from one of our black congregations, St. Paul's Episcopal Church in southwest Atlanta, and almost every member signed it. In it were moving words of thanks for my leadership. I was utterly undone by it. I took refuge in the privacy of the small lavatory in the bishop's office, closed the door, and sobbed out my own torrent of pent-up feelings. And there were other occasions when I felt undone by word and gestures of gratitude.

I believe that I seriously waffled only once in a controversy. I backed down a little in my first address as a new bishop to the diocesan convention. I felt undone by all the public flack that had erupted over the Billy Graham episode and said in my address that I meant every word of my letter to the renowned Christian leader and retracted nothing, particularly in the light of Graham's generosity of reply. In the future, however, I would call upon the Standing Committee as a council of advice before sending hip-shot letters of challenge to celebrities when confronted with a public issue of such magnitude on which I felt compelled to speak. That was waffling. It seems even more so in retrospect because at no time in the 11 years that followed did I make good my pledge to use the Standing Committee as a council of advice on controversial matters. But then, I never again hip-shot a night letter of challenge to a celebrity.

Of the many expressions of gratitude for strong stands on controversial issues, two public actions and one very private action are particularly memorable. First is the over-the-top response to my initiative in launching a $2.5 million expansion drive that we called the Diocesan Development Fund. The drive asked for funding for four major initiatives, only three of which I can recall: (1) expansion of critical facilities at our diocesan camp and conference center, (2) major funding for pre- and postordination education for clergy, and (3) a healthy boost in our invested land-acquisition funds for new congregations in our fast-growing diocese. I clearly remember the outcome of the effort. We did not raise the $2.5 million. Instead, we raised $3.2 million, and that was in spite of tacit resistance by the diocesan finance department! I took that stunning result to be clear ratification of a Midwest Yankee in King Cotton's Court.

The second major funding salute to liberal leadership came just before I retired in December 1983. As president, Ronald Reagan led the nation in cutting public welfare severely and closing many mental hospital facilities. At the same time, he danced the usual conservative caper of cutting taxes, giving everybody a quick tax saving while challenging the churches to take up the slack on seeing to the welfare of the poor. About that same time, the diocese received a whopping gift of $250,000 to be used for any purpose at the discretion of the bishop and executive board. As an ardent Democrat, it occurred to me that we ought to use that gift to fund something really big by way of stepping up to President Reagan's challenge. Why not go for a million dollars to create a substantial foundation for making wise grants to people and agencies impoverished by the Reagan initiative! More than that, why not challenge every Episcopalian in the diocese to give or pledge their Republican tax savings in 1983 to the effort to create an Episcopal Charities Foundation! I would be the first to give if the executive board would authorize the effort and add their tax savings. They did most heartily, and the effort went forward in every parish.

The initiative was a winner because of a vigorous bipartisan appeal. Conservatives liked it because it would help reduce government welfare handouts. Liberals liked it because it was a way to put the Episcopal Church on the line to help the poor while telling the government that we knew how to handle partisan political challenges. Within a few months, we had a million dollars for canny investment and a new agency of the diocese with the mandate and the means to strike a blow for concrete compassion. On its 20th anniversary in 2003, the Episcopal Charities Foundation of the Diocese of Atlanta was handling an invested corpus of $3.5 million and has distributed an almost equivalent amount of $3.6 million in grants and subsidies throughout the state of Georgia.

The third salute came in a totally unsolicited letter on the heels of the decision by the Episcopal General Convention to admit properly educated and qualified women into ordination for the priesthood and episcopate. It was a typewritten note from the most dyed-in-the-wool conservative and over-the-top Anglo-Catholic priest in the diocese, the rector of the Church of Our Savior on Highland Avenue in Atlanta. Although poles apart on almost every ecclesial issue, Father Roy Pettway and I had developed a friendly working relationship of mutual respect over the years. He had come some distance in seeing the importance of lay ministry that went beyond genuflecting at the daily mass and twirling great billows of holy smoke at the altar. He telephoned my office one morning to invite me to meet with his vestry for a get-acquainted gathering. He said an utterly astonishing thing as an opener to that phone call. "Bishop, I want you to know that, after 25 years as rector of Our Savior, I have begun to let my vestry meet. Now I would like you to come and talk a little about the responsibilities of service on a vestry." Astounding! That was a meeting I would not miss. It was as happy a dialogue with any vestry of the diocese in all my 12 years in Atlanta. But Roy's letter was even better. It endures in my file of important mementos. It was dated on a Tuesday in the spring of 1983. I retired later that year as bishop of Atlanta, and his letter remains high on my list of treasured testimonies.

Dear Bishop:
At the early mass this morning it suddenly came to me that you are the only bishop in the whole Episcopal Church that I am not mad at. However, I still do not approve of women priests.
Love,
Roy Pettway

Chapter 24

Bishop of Atlanta:
Confronting Homosexuality

When serving as bishop of the Episcopal Diocese of Atlanta, all five of my predecessors faced the tribulation of change in both church and society, especially my immediate predecessor, Bishop Randolph R. Claiborne, Jr. Gallantly, he bore the opening brunt of the most convulsive social controversy of the twentieth century — the era of Atlanta's esteemed son, the Reverend Dr. Martin Luther King, Jr. Bishop Claiborne bequeathed to me a heritage of honor for having bravely faced the firestorm of racial integration. He served for 19 difficult years and died at age 80 in 1986. I wish that he had left us a written record of his moral wrestling with such tensions as Dr. King's attempt to enroll his children in the all-white Lovett School in upscale suburban Atlanta. Lovett was founded with organic connections to the Episcopal Diocese of Atlanta, but Bishop Claiborne cut all the school's ties to the diocese when the Lovett board of trustees refused to honor the King children's application for admission. Instantly he was bitterly condemned for offending the sensibilities of cultural privilege. He wore thereafter the prickly badge of honor that was mine to wear as his successor for my own several offenses to southern comfort.

For me, the most important gain resulting from the subsequent tremendous changes was the subtle emergence of a fresh theology, a theology that takes seriously God's gift of all-inclusive human dignity and moral freedom. At the deepest and most enduring level of human understanding, that theological shift represents a seismic change in our understanding of power. For all the centuries of war-drenched recorded history, humankind has conceived of power as dominance from above. That continues to be the singular definition of the word *power* in our unabridged dictionaries. In spite of the stubborn, power-as-control mind-set articulated in our dictionaries and perpetuated in the aggressive militarism of prevailing American political policy, the human pilgrimage has begun to advance on the leading edge of a new conception of power as relationships of equality. Given the current dominating human technical skill not only to despoil the earth but also to incinerate our only resource base, the future will never again come without human intention to bring it about. A more mature humanity must now create the future, or there will be none for much of the planet's abundance of life.

Beneath the surface of the presently popular American flag-waving, there moves a rising tide of conflict resolution by the wisdom of nonviolence, a world-preserving use of power in relational equivalence. Quiet evidence abounds that humanity is on an incipient spiritual move upward, up from the lower conception of power as unilateral privilege to the more mature conception of power as relational equality. Even as I write, hope is encouraged by the apparent shift in the level of public support for the Bush administration's policy of endless war and rising deficit spending to underwrite our calculated violence. The press is now reporting that a second-term presidency has never before in American political history so quickly lost the momentum of approval it enjoyed on election day. Less than a year into his second term, George W. Bush's approval ratings have sunk below the 50% mark in the waning weeks of 2005. Maybe the unilateral privilege exercised by the incumbent president and his cheerleaders is losing momentum precisely because of the carelessness of privileged power. The domination ideology could be hastening its own repudiation at a juncture in human history that is busy installing the higher powers of relational equality.

All the convulsions of societal and ecclesiastical change described in Chapter 23 represent the new forces of relational power: (1) civil rights for a hitherto oppressed minority, (2) ordination rights for women after protracted centuries of enforced second-class status for the feminine half of the human species, (3) new prayer rites for growing numbers of the Episcopal Church's faithful who were disenchanted with many medieval forms of a rigid worship book, and (4) the homosexual equality movement, which is emerging now with increasing force to endow with dignity and freedom the age-long repressed minority whose birth-bestowed gender orientation compels a same-sex attraction.

Just when the collective ascent into a more mature humanity first appeared in the course of history is unclear, but the spirit is evident as far back in time as the influence of the Buddha and the Hebrew prophets. Two familiar and poetic Old Testament passages forecast a transformation of the weapons of conquest into instruments of cultivation and nurture: "they shall beat their swords into plowshares" (Isaiah 2:4, Micah 4:3; KJV). This change in human valuing has not yet come to pass except in isolated religious and political cases. I have in mind the nonviolent Society of Friends, which was subjected to religious persecution in England in the seventeenth century but has vigorously survived. The Quakers now give global witness and humanitarian service in behalf of world peace. In the political arena, the tiny Central American nation of Costa Rica dismantled its entire military establishment in 1947 and has installed mandatory citizen participation in all elections, declaring all national voting days public holidays and assigning stiff penalties to those who fail to exercise the right to vote. These are leading-edge eruptions of a growing grasp of power as relational equality.

But for leading-edge Christians everywhere, this life-giving perception of power came to brilliant flower in the teachings and self-giving servant life of Jesus of Nazareth. And it triumphed in an Easter cross planted since on the skyline of the world. True power henceforward, as pockets of human understanding slowly grasp it, means the calling forth of powers in the human spirit created in the image of God. The political formation of this fresh truth about power is democracy. But because democracy stands as a fairly recent historical corrective to power by dominance, it continues to be imperiled by resurgences of male-dominant passion, a reaction of fear and revulsion over the erosion of imperial male privileges. We know this reaction as fundamentalism, which, in all its male-dominant forms, has become a great backward-facing force in our time. Fundamentalist Islam uses terrorism as a worldwide instrument of intimidation and subjugation. In the United States, the fundamentalist surge seeks to reverse the course of history. It has seized the levers of unilateral power in a feverishly militarized government, which, by many signs, seeks the reduction of democratic and social protections and their replacement by a government of the rich, by the rich, and for the rich.

Fundamentalism seems to be kept in place by an essentially negative assessment of humanity and the world. Fundamentalist theology, as well as some forms of orthodox theology, understands humanity as irretrievably fallen and consigned to damnation except by the rescuing intervention of a sacrificial atoning death by God's own son whom God makes the crucified substitute for an unworthy and sin-stricken humanity. As for the created world, fundamentalist theology understands it to be utterly fallen and headed for an ultimate undoing by a calamitous end of the world in a violent Armageddon of fire and destruction. But despair of ourselves and the world has begun to yield to a sunnier view.

Under the influence of an evolutionary time frame that stretches fore and aft into the grandeur of immensity and with the emergence of a new holistic science of the interwoven wonder of all life, we live in a time of redeeming assessments of God, humanity, and the world.

One of the most distinctive ways to see this emerging challenge to tradition by a more cheerful view is to compare the historic versions of the general confession in the succession of Anglican prayer books with its most recent revision in 1979. From Archbishop Thomas Cranmer's translation from the Latin in 1549 through all later revisions until 1979 in the Episcopal Church in the United States, the general confession has described humanity in terms of an invincible depravity. In the liturgy for Holy Communion, the confession reads, "We acknowledge and bewail our manifold sins and wickedness...Provoking most justly thy wrath and indignation against us...The remembrance of them [our misdo-ings] is grievous unto us; the burden of them is intolerable" (*The Book of Common Prayer*, 1928, p. 75). The confession at morning and evening prayer seems equally preoccupied with the Reformation doctrine of total depravity (p. 6): "We have erred and strayed from thy ways like lost sheep...We have offended against thy holy laws...And there is no health in us." But in our time and in sharp contrast, the general confession of Rite II in the 1979 American *Book of Common Prayer* (p. 360) never uses words that accent depravity. Instead, our new prayer rites understand human sin as the pervasive misuse of human freedom in the tragic fail-ure to love: "Most merciful God...We have not loved you with our whole heart; we have not loved our neighbors as ourselves. We are truly sorry and we humbly repent...have mercy on us and forgive us; that we may delight in your will, and walk in your ways." Here the controlling accent in our confession has turned from dread of God's wrath to delight in God's will.

While it was often a severe discomfort to preside over the Episco-pal Diocese of Atlanta during an era of disruptive change, it was a high privilege to have had a small hand in the transformation of a regional section of church and society. In the course of 12 volatile years as bishop, I met many able and courageous apostles of change. They were the clergy and laity in my diocese as well as apostles in other settings and allegiances. The most aggressive apostle of change with whom I was literally forced to deal was Louie Crew, Ph.D., at that time a professor of English in an all-black college in the deeply conservative southern town of Fort Valley, Georgia. In 1974, Dr. Crew founded Integrity, a national, nonprofit organization of lesbian, gay, bisexual, and transgender Episcopalians.

Louie Crew is a white man of incisive brilliance. I knew nothing of his presence in the diocese until he appeared on my calendar for an afternoon office appointment in 1974. Speaking plainly and without cordiality, he introduced himself as a gay man whose gay partner was a black hairdresser. He had just founded Integrity as a mission to homosexuals. It was to be a community of encouragement, membership, and national advocacy. He intended it to include all gay and lesbian Episcopalians and hoped to establish Integrity groups in churches and dioceses across the whole Episcopal Church in the United States. Not bothering with opening courtesies, he confronted me by saying, "Bishop, I am a member of St. Luke's Episcopal Church in Fort Valley, and I am here to claim the legitimacy of my gay identity and to press for your support of the Integrity movement. Now what are you going to do about it?" I was stunned. I had not given the issue of homosexuality a second thought since a dimly remembered, surreptitious approach by a man in the shadows of a parking lot during my high school days in Kansas City, an approach from which I instinctively withdrew as unwanted and bewildering. Now, in the formality of my office and years later, I was confronted with the same reality but this time with great intelligence and forthrightness. What was I going to do about it indeed!

That first meeting multiplied into a dozen or more encounters between us, most of them in my office. These encounters grew steadily more confrontational. In one meeting that included his attorney, Louie pressed for my personal and official acceptance of his sexual orientation and my support of Integrity. Louie's pressure and my mounting discomfort with his undisguised hostility forced me into research and writing. I gave the mornings of our family summer vacation of 1977 to fashioning as clear and compassionate a response as I could write. In my 1982 book *Purple Ink*, my response came to 19 pages as a pastoral letter to the churches and communicants of the diocese. In my letter, I drew on all the thoughtful literature I could find on the pros and cons of homosexuality using biblical, theological, psychological, ethical, and medical resources. In substance, what I wrote was an acceptance of homosexual persons as fully entitled to honorable membership in the Episcopal Church and the resources of its pastoral ministry. However, my research led me to conclude that the condition was, for most homosexuals, amenable to correction by spiritual and therapeutic intervention. The pastoral letter ended with a terse statement that it was entirely acceptable to be a homosexual but equally unacceptable to practice homosexuality. In other words, my reading and obvious bias led to an acceptance of gay identity but a rejection of gay behavior as disallowed by Christian moral standards.

I intended that pastoral letter for the Episcopal Diocese of Atlanta only. However, the issue had so much currency in and out of the church that my letter was widely distributed, and I became an instant spokesperson for conservative bias, near and far. The nondenominational periodical *Christianity Today* reprinted my pastoral letter in full. The Lutheran Church in Sweden made it their official position on the issue, printing it in Swedish in their official church organ. Not only did churches in the United States and overseas applaud the pastoral letter, but our very conservative presiding bishop of the Episcopal Church,

John Maury Allin, appointed me chair and principal writer of the pastoral letter committee of our House of Bishops. Over the ensuing five years, I wrote the annual bishops' pastorals to all the congregations of the Episcopal Church, and Bishop Allin and I became friends. Before that time, he and I had kept each other at a cool distance.

With all this acceptance from my own church and from most of the ecumenical community, I wondered when the other shoe would drop. When was I going to be sandbagged by gay-lesbian forces and by Dr. Louie Crew in particular? Only one contrary and contemptuous letter came to me. It was not from Louie. By contrast, the Integrity group in the diocese quietly invited me to visit their meetings at All Saints Episcopal Church in downtown Atlanta and to join them in worship. I did so with some trepidation at first but later with gratitude and frequency. There I discovered that a few of my ablest clergy, both men and women, were among them as well as a surprising number of highly placed laity of the city. At every such meeting, I was met with warmth and affection. This experience was completely unexpected and mind-opening. The years went by, and my contacts with the gay-lesbian community extended and increased. In time, I started my research over and came to a firm conclusion that was nearly the reverse of my earlier view. I newly understood homosexuality to be an ontological characteristic, as birth-bestowed as skin color and gender identity in the overwhelming majority of gay men and women. Homosexual intimacy was almost never a matter of behavioral choice but rather a response to the engine of sexual desire implanted in all human beings by design. It carried the name *natural*, as natural as my maleness and creeping baldness.

It was now 1984, and I had retired as bishop to become an adjunct professor of theology at Emory University. Meanwhile, the sexuality issue had heightened to the point of threat to the unity of the Episcopal Church. It was the most bitterly contested concern on the agenda of the forthcoming General Convention, to which eight deputies from the

Diocese of Atlanta would be dispatched and voting. Word came to me that some of our deputies held a firm conservative view and that those on the conservative side of the debate hoped to use their former bishop's 1977 pastoral letter as supporting their position against the moral legitimacy of gays and lesbians. So I wrote another careful pastoral statement that reflected my changed position, intending it for exclusive distribution among the Atlanta deputation to the General Convention. But as before, the statement went far and wide.

My pastoral statement came to Louie's attention, and he phoned me with an outpouring of thanks. By then he had become a professor of English at Rutgers, The State University of New Jersey in New Brunswick. Some years later, Louie invited me to concelebrate and to speak briefly at Integrity's 20th anniversary Eucharist held at the Episcopal General Convention of 1994 in Indianapolis. That service remains the most spirited and memorable experience of worship in all 56 years of my ministry. The cathedral was crowded to capacity and more. Worshippers stood for nearly two hours beneath the overflowing balcony, and many more stood for the long service against the cathedral sidewalls. Still more gathered outside on the street. Louie, in his doctoral gown, preached the sermon. He began with a salute to all of us who had defied the General Convention's rejection of homosexuality by coming for worship that night in a neutral setting. He opened with a great smile, saying, "Welcome to Samaria!"

I need to emphasize that my change of heart and mind was not the work of reading and distant research. It must have had its beginning years before in a totally unanticipated moment of seeing Louie in a different and deeper light. We were in my office for the umpteenth time one afternoon, and he was talking. Suddenly, as a kind of interior flash of recognition, I felt a current of affection for him. He and I were kindred, not in sexual orientation, but in our shared and struggling humanity. That must have been the opening moment of seeing the courage and authenticity of a man of sharply different sexual drive. It was a drive that neither of us had created but only claimed as an expression of God's design of sexuality across all the divides in the family of life. That experience of seeing authentic humanity and goodness in a person of very different sexual impulses was repeated and multiplied in later years as I met with the Integrity group at All Saints Church. In other words, I was not persuaded to alter my position by distant research and rational processes. I was changed by interactive human experience. By the mounting warmth of interpersonal trust, I was moved by the power of affection to abandon domination from above in favor of the far higher motivational ground of relationships in equality.

I published my third book in 1997, and in it is a chapter that elaborates my experience of inner change with all the supporting conceptual evidence that I could bring to bear. The chapter is titled "Servanthood and Sexual Ethics" in *Servanthood: Leadership for the Third Millennium*. However, that chapter, which was written in the late 1990s, does not include my most recent conceptual discovery that goes to the meaning of a key word in Paul's letter to the Romans. The word in Paul's use of Greek is *physikos*. It translates in English as the simple word *natural*, and it occurs in two connecting verses that those who reject the legitimacy of homosexuality rely on heavily (Romans 1:26–27). Importantly, St. Paul never uses the term *homosexuality* in those verses; however, that term might have been translated in his uniform use of Greek. In explicitly condemning homosexual behavior, he argues that it is not *physikos*, which translates elaborately as *according to nature*. For Paul, *physikos* meant *heterosexual* and nothing else. For him, it was against nature that women should engage sexually with women or men with men.

But today, in the latest medical research and understanding of homosexuality, this orientation is widely regarded as established very early in the human fetus in utero by a process known as the sexing of the brain. This process is connected to the level of the male hormone testosterone in the pregnant female. Once established, sexual identity is, in the opinion of credible medical research, not changeable. Sexual orientation seems to be located somewhere on a continuum. Most humans locate definitively on the strongly heterosexual end of that line. Many fewer humans locate strongly on the homosexual end, and even fewer appear to locate somewhere in the middle.

In his autobiography, Bishop John Shelby Spong quotes Robert Lahita, MD, a close friend and research doctor at Cornell Medical Center in New York (*Here I Stand: My Struggle for a Christianity of Integrity, Love, and Equality*, HarperCollins, San Francisco, 2000, p. 336). Dr. Lahita's research leads him to contend that, as Bishop Spong puts it, "All human beings have one sex organ, the brain. All else is equipment." Insofar as this is physiologically dependable, then the Greek term *physikos* can be re-comprehended, making St. Paul's polemical use of it far too limiting and understandably wrong in his first-century contention that homosexuality is not natural. As a bestowed sexual identity, homosexuality becomes ontological, a word that means *in the order of a natural endowment*. Once this interpretation of *physikos* is accepted, it becomes possible and even necessary in sound biblical scholarship to argue that homosexuality is a naturally occurring reality in an uncertain proportion of humanity (and perhaps in lower animals also) and that the critical matter is how that natural drive is expressed, whatever one's given sexuality.

The Christian sexual ethic holds that promiscuity, perversity, and all exploitative and dominating relationships are morally out of order for either heterosexual or homosexual identity. They are prohibited because such behavioral choices degrade our created humanity. Our souls are fashioned in the image of God, both in freedom and righteousness. The emblem of God's righteousness in human makeup is the mystery of conscience that whispers what is right and wrong in the exercise of healthy human freedom. The freedom of moral choice may be nowhere more severely challenged than in dealing with the clamoring engine of sexual appetite. Built in God's image for obedience to the best, the whispers of conscience will, soon or late, bring regret and remorse over all misuses of sex in recreational lust, in betrayal of vows, or in exploitative male dominance, of which rape is the towering malfeasance. By contrast, the whispers of conscience in obedience to the best bring the deep resonances of happiness and fulfillment in sexual relationships of intimate mutuality and fidelity. Relational equality is the wholeness for which humanity is made.

Chapter 25

Adjunct Professorship at Emory University

A 37-page booklet arrived with the office mail in 1974, two years after I took up work as a bishop. The little publication was *The Servant as Leader* by Robert K. Greenleaf. How it happened to come to me I have never known, and why I took the time to read it is an enduring mystery. Then and now, my habit with mailed pamphlets is to toss them quickly aside or into the trash. The arresting paradox of the title must have moved me. Intellectually, practically, and even spatially, the words *servant* and *leader* are nonsense when juxtaposed. Intellectually, the two words are mutually exclusive and sharply contradictory. In practice, leading means taking charge, not bending in servitude. In spatial imagery, a leader is positioned above and ahead, while a servant stands below and behind. Why then did that contradictory title draw me into reading what lay beyond it?

As I look back now on the timing and try to reconstruct my interior sense of readiness, I took the time to read *The Servant as Leader* for three reasons. First of all, I knew I needed help in handling a huge new responsibility. I was the elected leader of a voluntary regional institution spread over 27,000 square miles and comprised of roughly 25,000

Episcopalians in 78 loosely linked, nonprofit units overseen by more than 100 priests and their lay leaders. In quiet moments of reflection, the magnitude of the task gave me the willies. Second, I deeply believed that my first obligation as bishop was to my clergy. They were key to the vitality of their congregations, and all the clergy suffered the same occasional willies as they faced the magnitude of their tasks. Unless I could muster a sturdy, serving care for each of them, I would only lock them and myself into mutual isolation and varying degrees of fright. Third, there is that bewitching text in Matthew and Mark that confounds all human ambition. Overhearing a dispute about who stood the tallest in the hierarchy of his disciples, Jesus gently rebuked them with a bewildering formula for preeminence: "Among you, whoever wants to be great must be your servant, and whoever would be first must be the willing slave of all" (Matthew 20:26–27, Mark 10:43–44; NEB). Although still eclipsed by a centuries-old, male-dominant, militarist paradigm of command, servant leadership is clearly the first principle of being in charge of anything as a Christian. How could I not open the pamphlet?

The author of *The Servant as Leader* carried all the important credentials as a wise and experienced manager of people. In his business life, Robert Greenleaf (1904–1990) was highly placed as the executive in charge of all management development for what was then American Telephone and Telegraph, the largest corporation in the world before its dismantling into several regional and autonomous corporations. Robert Greenleaf had been reared a Quaker in Indiana, received his education in engineering at Carleton College in Minnesota, and had risen to a place of high eminence in the management ranks of AT&T. He never worked anywhere else. He was now retired and busy writing trenchant essays on the broad issues of management and leadership. That morning in 1974, I read his pamphlet with rising excitement and delight. He was saying what I knew viscerally to be true about effective leadership. He galvanized my resolve to shape my bishoping to the ancient Christian formula for the work of leading. More than that, the pamphlet aroused a sense of wistful longing to be a teacher again.

Prompted by this indelible sense of a vocation to teach, I started a series of learning retreats for regional clusters of the clergy, assuming again the role of seminar teacher in a pattern of mutual exchange. A group facilitator joined me as a staff person in each of these groups, and things went well. Hierarchical barriers between bishop and priests began to melt. By sharing our thoughts and our personal innerness, we warmed to each other. Even better, the usual competitive barriers diminished between clergy in big parishes and little parishes, in city and county, and of high-church and low-church persuasion. While remaining real, all these distinctions receded in favor of relationships of trust and even affection.

My only regret was that this program of interactive learning had to give way before the administrative demands of my office and particularly for fund-raising. The Episcopal Diocese of Atlanta was growing apace with the rapid expansion of metro-Atlanta. We needed a very large helping of new money in cash and greatly increased investment funds for land and buildings as well as for the educational and pastoral development of the clergy, both before and following ordination. Fund-raising is an institutional demand in all nonprofit institutions. The top leader cannot shirk this role except in peril of losing institutional momentum. Fund-raising can and must be delegated to some extent, but it will falter without vigorous cheerleading and push from the principal leader. Money raised is a concrete measure of achievement, superficial in some sense but an outward and visible sign of energy successfully applied. More than that, it goes to the heart of what I believe is the deepest satisfaction that attaches to money, namely the glow of giving it away.

There is a personal story here worth telling. About halfway through the years of my ministry, I faced the need to launch another fund-raiser for some good reason, and I quailed before it. I must have nursed that resistance for days, maybe weeks, until suddenly something clicked into consciousness. It was a brand-new recognition, never before heard or thought. Out of my struggle with resistance to fund-raising, it suddenly dawned on me that I'd like tons of the money back that I had spent on myself. There were shirts and shoes and ties that I scarcely used, and some of them I actually loathed. And there were a couple of cars that quickly disenchanted me. One of them turned me quite sour, and another, an antique Model A Ford, cost an ugly bundle of money to repair and maintain until I found another sucker to haul it away at far less than I had paid for it. In sum, there were whole checking accounts spent on Bennett that I would love to have back. But money that I had spent on my children, their mother, our church, and our family trips in those precious years — not a nickel of that did I want back, not a dime, not the bundles of cash that I had spent on others and given away over the years.

What a recognition! Suddenly, I clearly understood that the human soul is much more built to give than to get. This is the reason that there is never enough money when it is clutched. But let loose of money in acts of generosity and, presto, there almost always seems to be enough and more. From then on, I have believed that you are doing people a favor when you ask them for money, whether they think so or not or whether they give you a brass farthing or not. Asking people for money is knocking on their secret door of freedom and joy. God is the great giver who makes all this come true. Made as we are in God's image, what fulfills the cosmic soul is sure to fulfill us.

After 10 years as bishop, I hooked up with the Candler School of Theology at Emory University and taught a course in theology as a visiting lecturer. One of the most learned priests of the diocese, Charles "Ted" Hackett, served full-time as a professor at Candler with special expertise in pastoral psychology. In 1979, Ted and I teamed up to invent an enterprise that would test the suitability for advancement to seminary of the many young people who came to me in the course of every year with aspirations for the ordained ministry. We dubbed it Experiment in Ministry (EIM) and started with a dozen hopeful women and men. EIM was successful in helping people measure their desire for ordination against the realities of actual ministry. On average, about 50% of the aspirants qualified for seminary. Most of those who did not qualify said that they were actually well-served. Some of those who were disappointed felt misjudged, and there were doubtless some misjudgments. In one particular case, however, the 10-month experiment ended in a prolonged disaster.

A mid-30s woman of outstanding intellect who held a Ph.D. was already certified as a postulant for the first level of qualification for ordination. Next up the scale of readiness was admission to seminary as a candidate. In the course of 10 months, the tendency in this gifted woman to put others down had raised some questions about her readiness for candidacy. Ted, as director of EIM, and the evaluating committee asked her to postpone advancement for a season in order to be in deeper discernment of her call. Without the slightest warning, she exploded in accusatory rage, bewildering the committee and threatening a lawsuit for breach of contract and defamation of character. True to her threat, a lawsuit was filed seeking $5 million in damages. I was named the principal defendant along with the bishop suffragan, the chair of the evaluation committee, and the Episcopal Diocese of Atlanta as the nonprofit corporation of responsibility. She engaged an aggressive feminist attorney who began trying the case in the Atlanta papers. Our lawyers persuaded the court to quash the use of the media, but the succeeding year was a time of tedious depositions and occasional angry insinuations. The circuit court finally judged the case in our favor, but the plaintiff appealed her case to the next level. Another two years went by until the appellate court judged the case as having no merit. That was the end of it, but not quite.

Just a year ago, 20 years after retiring as bishop, a letter came to me in Hendersonville from the woman who had brought suit against me and the diocese. In it, she thanked me for my stand on the issue of homosexuality and for her learning experience with the Diocese of Atlanta. Wonder of wonders. Even though her experience cost our insurance underwriter many thousands of dollars and cost me three years of lurking preoccupation, her letter brought bright sunshine for me and, I trust, a significant sense of reconciliation for her. Whereas I used to dread the possibility of ever seeing her again, I now hope that we can trade personal greetings and gratitude before my lights and hers go out.

Out of my deepening relationship with academia as an adjunct professor at Emory University from 1979 to 1983, my desire to return to the role of seminary teacher grew apace, and I quietly began to design a new educational enterprise that I wanted to lead when I retired as bishop of Atlanta. It would take the shape of five-day, interactive learning seminars for managers in all kinds of profit and nonprofit institutions, including business, government, education, foundations, public administration, and the church. Jim Waits, who was dean of the Candler School of Theology, and I had many conversations, and I also talked occasionally with Emory University President James Laney. Together, we fashioned a lively dream to create and fund a new enterprise in higher education called the Institute for Servant Leadership. We planned to link the resources of Emory's business school and the Candler School of Theology. George "Chip" Parks, the dean of the business school and an Episcopal layman, responded warmly to the idea.

I took up this new work of founding a teaching institute at Emory with a relatively untested assumption about truly successful leadership. The assumption was rooted in the quality of leadership reflected in both the life and teachings of Jesus of Nazareth. I have written earlier in this odyssey about the capital distinction between unilateral and relational modes of interaction. In combining resources of the business and theology schools at Emory, I wanted to translate these differences into fresh leadership styles. The unilateral style is heavily predominant in America's competitive culture, and it probably comes as if by nature to those with management and leadership responsibilities. The relational style may be even more profoundly natural to the human spirit and its longing for relationships, but it is trained out of us by the inescapable demands of competition. Still, I believed that relationality is a need so deeply ingrained in the human soul that it should be possible to lift that impulse into a rational and teachable category of successful leadership. The unilateral mode of management assumes a triangular shape with a singular head at the peak and a descending arrangement of ancillary command and compliance, all this with a minimum of feedback loops that tend to be structurally omitted. The contrasting relational approach roughly takes the shape of a circle, with the leader as the focus of shared authority and responsive to the automatic feedback loops that are part of the structure of a circular model.

By the time of my retirement as bishop of the Episcopal Diocese of Atlanta, I was only 63 years old, in good health, and full of ginger for teaching and fund-raising as director of the new and experimental Institute for Servant Leadership. The dean of the Candler School of Theology, Jim Waits, had secured funding for launching the enterprise, and the school awarded me the salary of a full professor. It was a blue-sky start!

Bob Greenleaf was much involved in the development of the new institute. A year earlier, while still bishop, I had invited him to Atlanta for a day of blueprinting the institute, which was scheduled for start-up an academic year later. In addition to Bob and me, the design committee included the president of Emory, the deans of the theology and business schools, and three Atlanta people prominent in business. We met for a long day and agreed on several guiding principles. First, the institute would involve only those in leadership roles at every level and in a variety of institutional settings. Second, participants would include both women and men. Third, the learning setting would be circular, with lectures balanced by casework for interactive sharing. Fourth, the time frame would be a five-day, residential retreat venue in a conference center near Atlanta. Fifth, informal worship and scriptural meditations would be a voluntary offering at the beginning of each day. Sixth, at least three or four such five-day seminars would span the academic year with a return conference for follow-up at least every other year. From the start, we wanted Jimmy Carter to be the principal in the first return conference. And so it was. He was already on the adjunct faculty of Emory and carried a reputation for world leadership as a spiritually grounded public servant. When former President Carter led our first return conference, nearly 200 of our graduated seminarians attended from many parts of the nation.

A few weeks before my official retirement as bishop on December 31, 1983, we convened the opening seminar of the Institute for Servant Leadership at the Unicoi Conference Center in the north Georgia mountains. Unicoi is a state facility that was relatively new at the time, beautifully rustic, and amply furnished with every convenience for learning and community building. Unicoi was a special project of Jimmy Carter's when he served Georgia as governor in the 1970s. A total of 15 women and men from a wide variety of institutional leadership had signed on. They were educators, business leaders, physicians, public administrators, and clergy. The four instructors were James W. Rouse, founder of the Rouse Company of Columbia, Maryland, developer of the new city of Columbia, and later founder of the Enterprise Foundation for low-cost housing in cities across America; Dr. James H. Laue, an old teaching colleague from Virginia Theological Seminary days and subsequently a professor of sociology at George Washington University in St. Louis; Thomas Dolgoff, industrial psychologist from the Menniger Foundation in Topeka; and myself as theologian of servant leadership.

My new secretary at Emory, Georgia Carroll, and I were the support staff for the seminar.

In addition to teaching, recruiting, and fund-raising, I began a periodic newsletter that soon became quarterly and then bimonthly and was ultimately named *Turning Point*, an apt name for a publication of conscious Christian underpinnings. Jesus' first recorded public address begins with a summons to turn around (Mark 1:14–15, NEB). The Greek word is *metanoia*, a lovely term that means literally *a higher mind* or *beyond ordinary consciousness* and translates simply as *repent*. Understood in its original Greek, *repent* is not strictly a religious concept. It never means self-flagellation or self-despising. Repentance may indeed be accompanied by remorse, but its primary meaning is to begin again by facing a new direction. As Jesus used it, *metanoia* means moving to a higher level of self-perception and behavior. Or it could mean refocusing your life on a finer way of fulfillment in service and self-giving. All those meanings are sharply congruent with the whole thrust of Jesus' ministry, especially as he redefined personal greatness as a servanthood (Mark 10:43, NEB). *Turning Point* is also an apt name for the institute's newsletter because it clearly distinguishes our time of epic shift in the whole human pilgrimage in the planet. We live on a moving hinge of history, and it is the conviction of most thoughtful scholars and observers that our time is so crucial for the human enterprise that we must either grow up now or lose forever the race to preserve the life we prize. *Turning Point* is now mailed to all alumni of the Institute for Servant Leadership and to all whom we hope to recruit to our circles of learning and practicing a finer way of leading.

Early in the life of the institute, I wrote what I think still serves as a working definition of servant leadership:

> Servant leadership has both spiritual and behavioral meanings. Spiritually, it is a way of life committed to co-creating with

God a just, nonviolent, and sustainable world. Behaviorally, it is a way of managing systems and their people.

Servant leaders live as much for others as for themselves. In their leading, they work for the transformation of human systems and for a finer life for all.

Servant leaders use power for collaboration and not control, for cooperation and not conquest. Their use of power forges a robust dynamic that brings loyalty, productivity, and financial health to the interaction of leaders and the led.

Servant leadership reflects the paradox of compassion and command that defines the character of God in the world's leading religious traditions. Among Christians, servant leaders strive for the fine balance of velvet and steel that marks the ministry of Jesus of Nazareth.

Servant leadership seeks alignment with quantum theory, which sees the cosmos as endowed with advancing levels of consciousness, from the bottom to the top of the created order — leading to the recovery of a primordial human understanding that cherishes the whole creation as ensouled.

The most advanced scientific perception, quantum physics, suggests that love is the binding power in all relationships, from subatomic to macrocosmic levels in the chain of life. This translates into an urgent contemporary relationship with the planet that sees humanity as in the earth, not on it. Human beings are creation's lower-case consciousness become self-conscious and morally responsible. The soul of education for servant leaders is thus an education of the soul.

Servant leadership functions from trust in love as the energy to overcome the fear that distorts leadership into struggles for subjugation and control. Repressive power in any system eventuates in violence, from covert forms such as grudging compliance or running from home to overt forms of retaliation in violent strikes and armed revolution. In a world become too small for violence, power henceforth has no acceptable moral purpose except for empowerment to participate in power in freedom and dignity.

The resolute aim of servant-led systems in families, schools, businesses, and nations is the inclusion of all its members in proportional responsibility for decision-making and the success of the system. Organizations so aimed will be enlargers of life for their people. In political terms, this is the high definition of democracy.

Given the mounting challenge of an interdependent world of justice and peace for all peoples, there is nothing optional about servanthood as a way of leadership and life.

A profound and controversial implication about human nature is embedded in the foregoing definitions of servant leadership. The implication is that a human being is fundamentally good, not bad. As such, a person is worthy of the trust and freedom that are implicit in the collaborative assumptions underlying servanthood. Such a view of humanity flies in the face of a conviction cherished for centuries of Christian dogmatic certainty, and it continues to exercise a kind of conceptual tyranny in strict orthodox circles. It goes by the name of original sin and dates its origin as a doctrine to St. Augustine (354–430 CE) of the North African diocese of Hippo. The following chapter seeks to lay a fresh theological foundation for the kind of education of the soul that distinguishes an enterprise devoted to servant leadership.

Chapter 26

Old Heresies Never Die, and One of Them Shouldn't

Our home is on a golf course, and I used to play often. That was before prostate cancer reduced my energy to below par. My partner was almost always a special and longstanding friend, the Right Reverend William H. Folwell, retired bishop of the Episcopal Diocese of Central Florida. During one round some years ago, probably on the wicked 10th hole over water where despair comes quickly after dumping a drive into the pond, I lamented to Bill that I have been accused of heresy for years, especially by knowledgeable colleagues when I taught at Virginia Theological Seminary. He laughed and repeated a favorite comment by one of his seminary teachers. His professor of theology had said, "Anybody can be orthodox, but it takes brains to be a heretic." Of course, that is miles wide of the mark, but it lifted my gloom. On the par-4 10th hole that day, I recorded a nasty 8 without grief.

The fact is that it takes outstanding brains to achieve fame for being either orthodox or heretical. St. Paul, who wrote or had attributed to him about one-fourth of the New Testament, was so brainy that the personal letters he dashed off to congregations have been revered as defining orthodoxy for the whole Christian movement since. However, it is crucial to note that Paul was hounded all his Christian life as a heretic by former colleagues in Judaism. Three centuries later, St. Augustine, the renowned bishop of Hippo, brought to the work of theology an IQ that must have been off the charts. But Augustine wrote documents that have rigidified orthodoxy for a large part of the Christian population for 1500 years. He has saddled lots of us with congenital guilt by insisting that every human being is born bad.

Orthodox doctrine has held for centuries that wayward humanity can be saved only by the grace of God in baptism and lifelong penitence thereafter. These beliefs were administered by the medieval Catholic Church, subsequently by the sin-preoccupied formulations of John Calvin and Martin Luther, and currently by various offshoots of those reformers as well as by Huldreich Zwingli, father of the Anabaptist movement. If it be wondered why such a negative and imprisoning theology could win its way over the human soul and human systems, consider how the universal human sense of missing the moral mark opens a deep vulnerability to an accusatory theology that enthrones an angry and scolding deity. This popular picture of the deity vis-à-vis humanity is made clear in the response of a Sunday school child who was asked for his understanding of God: "God is the big inspector in the sky who looks for anybody who is having fun and puts a stop to it."

If hordes of us grow up with a nagging sense of shame about our sexuality, we have experienced the subtle power of St. Augustine. He traced the corrupting power of sex to the Garden of Eden myth. In keeping with prevailing custom at the time (and to Biblical fundamentalism now), Augustine gave the myth of Eden historic validity: Adam and Eve were real persons in human history, and he saw in the sexual encounter of Adam and Eve the original act of rebellion against God in eating the forbidden fruit. This deduction means that sexual intercourse is the perpetual engine for transmitting original sin to the human species since humans cannot come to life apart from a sexual liaison between a parenting male and female. Thus the guilt of Adam and Eve, understood as real historic persons, has been as inescapable in all humans as are legs and lungs. Of interest is the fact that nowhere in Jewish theological tradition is there any doctrine of original sin, even though the Hebrew Bible is sacred scripture to both Christians and Jews. Only in the literalist and inerrant Christian reading of scripture does the Garden of Eden episode translate into doctrinal certainty about the origin of sin as rooted in the gifts of ambition, lust, and sexuality.

Given a continuing liturgical concentration on sin, any worshipping Christian can come to feel that many church services are designed to organize human guilt and then, by the standing privilege of an ordained person, to offer a solemn pardon that only authorized priestly officials of organized religion can bestow. Carefully examined, this practice could mean that the church makes continuing use of the doctrine of original sin as a subtle control mechanism over the sensibilities and lives of its people. Such moments of seeing through the slightly hidden mechanisms of soul-control have moved some believers to propose another view of things. While sin is hideously real in human history and human behavior, it very well could have originated somewhere else than in the universal gift of sexuality. Furthermore, there is concrete biblical testimony to the original goodness of created humanity in the Bible's opening book:

> So God created humankind in his image,
> in the image of God he created them;
> male and female he created them....
> God saw everything that he had made,
> and indeed, it was very good.
> — Genesis 1:27, 31

All orthodox formulations invite challenge. Every kind of orthodoxy does. The challenge to orthodoxy is easily seen in the history of government. Democracy is a classic instance of rebellion against the orthodox rule by divine right of kings and queens, a challenge that appears to have erupted first in Europe when barons stood up to the medieval English monarch King John in 1215 CE. Our own American revolution is a more recent expression of this political challenge to orthodoxy. Theological challenge to Christian orthodoxy goes way back in time. Pelagius, a Celtic monk and contemporary of Augustine, stood up to the classic negative assessment of humanity. Pelagius denied its legitimacy as orthodox. There were even earlier theologians with sunnier views of humanity. Valentinus, Gnostic advocate of spiritual freedom in the second century, and Origen, apostle of hope in the third century, were both condemned as heretics. In the thirteenth century, the German monk Meister Eckhart brought the scorn of the Catholic Church down on his head. The hierarchy appears to have despised Eckhart as an apostate for insisting on the goodness of creation — that God is in all things and that all things are deeply interconnected. Eckhart's belief is a startling premonition of the most contemporary insights of quantum physics.

To bring the matter up to date with a personal reference, a former close colleague has roundly criticized me as an apostate Christian. Of course she is quite correct, given her reasoned devotion to Augustine and his sources and views. But I find myself unable to accept the great Augustine's orthodox deduction of original sin. Neither could the contemporary learned theologian Matthew Fox, a former Roman Catholic priest and now an Episcopalian after being drummed out of the corps by the Catholic hierarchy as a menacing disturber of orthodoxy.

So there are many friends of Pelagius in history, before him and since, who honor his memory and his irrepressibly cheerful mind and heart. Pelagius was a thorn in the side of Augustine and another contemporary, St. Jerome, because he insisted on such things as follows (written in the century contemporary with Augustine and Jerome):

> You will realize that doctrines are inventions of the human mind, as it tries to penetrate the mystery of God. You will realize that Scripture itself is the work of human minds, recording the example and teaching of Jesus. Thus it is not what you believe that matters; it is how you respond with your heart and your actions. It is not believing in Christ that matters; it is becoming like him.
> — Quoted in J. Philip Newell, *Listening for the Heartbeat of God: A Celtic Spirituality*, Paulist Press, Mahwah, NJ, 1997, pp. 11–12

The development of doctrine in any field of enduring mystery such as science and religion is the entirely natural consequence of the human need to know how the world works. Examples of scientific and spiritual assumptions that take on doctrinal force are the big bang theory in science and St. Paul's religious definition of the meaning of life in faith, hope, and love. These are attempts in the face of mystery to explain, clarify, and codify what seems self-evident to the clarifiers and codifiers. Just as natural and inevitable are the challenges to doctrinal formulations by explainers and codifiers who see the same mystery from a different angle. Any great field of inquiry at the frontiers of human knowing will spawn both orthodoxy and heresy. As written earlier in this chronicle, *orthodoxy* means straight thinking, while *heresy* means crooked or deviate thinking. My early training in Christian theology focused on the great Swiss theologian Karl Barth. Happily, Barth never took himself as seriously as did some of my seminary teachers back in the 1940s. For a few of them, Barth was the last word in what was then called neoorthodoxy to distinguish it from theological liberalism. Any deviation from the Barthian position and especially from the Augustinian doctrine of original sin was regarded as practically punishable.

In the 1960s, when I was about a third of the way through my own theological pilgrimage, I began to read and relish the work of the French scientist and theologian Teilhard de Chardin. In Chapter 22 of this chronicle, I examine Teilhard's influence as a visionary scientist and theologian on my own transformation from a conservative to a progressive vision of life and the world. Even before running across Teilhard, I began to find Karl Barth's neoorthodoxy much too grim and implicitly world-denying. When the Frenchman's soaring hopefulness and his love of the world began to sink in, I found myself connecting with excitement and gratitude. It did not bother me that Teilhard's writings had been repressed by the Roman hierarchy. Instead, his rejection by the Catholic magisterium was an encouragement to take him seriously.

In retrospect, I can see the reason for this positive personal response. Teilhard brought two of my own budding intellectual passions into partnership. Since college days when I was captivated by comparative anatomy, I have been a biological evolutionist with a growing interest in archeology and paleontology. Also, my college major in philosophy, combined with my certainty of a call to the ministry after I was "born from above" (John 3:3) at Pearl Harbor, made me a natural candidate for discipleship to any passionate scholar who could make friends of science and religion. Deep inside me, there lurked for years an inchoate feeling that science and theology ought to be natural partners in advancing the frontiers of human life and learning.

So Teilhard walked into a waiting place in my heart. What he did was to show me that my love of God and my excitement with the world belonged together to make a holistic friendship that joined transcendence and immanence, heaven and earth, life now and life forever. What gripped Teilhard was an ardent "holy worldliness," a phrase that is linked to Dietrich Bonhoeffer, the 1940s German theologian and martyr to fascism. From my own reading and deep kinship with Teilhard, I believe that the cosmos is an ever-evolving natural phenomenon and that humanity is moving unevenly to ever-higher levels of consciousness. In other words, creation is God's book of life, and humanity is a turning page.

These deductions about the world and humanity are implicitly ratified by historic knowledge of the Hebrew-Christian scriptures. The Holy Bible itself is an evolution, having taken approximately 1000 pre- and post-Christian years to acquire its present form. These conceptual departures from many honored forms and formularies of tradition have made me somewhat a stranger in my own house. My attachment to the Episcopal Church and to my ministry as deacon, priest, and bishop remains keenly important. These attachments continue to define me in many ways, but I find that I can no longer recite the Nicene Creed with integrity. That historic formulary, which I used to repeat with ease and relative thoughtlessness, seems to me now less a confession of faith than a sophisticated theological argument. It seems more fashioned of ice than of fire in support of a partisan conniption in the fourth century over what was orthodox and what was heretical. Moreover, it says nothing about human behavior, which is the only truly ratifying reality about any earnestly held faith.

As the product of an era in history, the Nicene Creed is clearly locked into an outmoded and superceded time frame in comprehending the world and the work of God. Karl Barth's neoorthodox cosmology is totally at variance with an evolving worldview. He held that Jesus was an invasion into history from outside history, conforming nicely with the creedal statement that Jesus "came down from heaven." Jesus did no such thing. In an evolutionary cosmology, God is continually creating the world, always acting within history and never outside it. An evolutionary cosmology comprehends Jesus theologically and loves him spiritually as emergent from within the world, fully human and fully divine in the profound paradox of all surpassing truth. Jesus is not a spatial invader like some first-century E.T.

By many testimonies of scripture (John 1:1–3; Colossians 1:15–17; Revelation 13:8), Jesus the Christ is the eruption into vivid historic visibility of that creative, commanding, and forgiving love of God that has been life-giving in the evolving world from the beginning of the world. This makes the world eminently good, not a rotten place that is the object of holy scorn or pious indifference. Nature itself is one of God's own books intended for our love and learning. And humanity, again by clearest testimony of scripture, is made in God's image and is originally blessed for bearing the image of God. Looking into the face of a newborn child is not to see the visage of a soul already corrupted but rather a visage alight with the beauty of God's goodness. To be sure, each child is corruptible, and some are corruptible more easily than others for want of an embracing and saving parental love. Evil is real, sinister, and powerful, and humanity bears the heavy burden of free moral choice to go one's own way into darkness or light. As Teilhard insisted, all evil is disunion in a cosmos shaped to vast interdependence and connectivity. It is precisely here that modern science and old religion join hands.

Baptism does not make a person suddenly beloved of God. Nor does it bestow an otherwise unavailable salvation. Baptism is akin to the coronation of Queen Elizabeth II. She was already queen for having been born the first child of a king. Her coronation simply declared in a public ceremony — that invoked the presence of God — what had been true all along. She was a queen from her beginning. This understanding does not demean baptism. It heightens its meaning and extends its reach into all the world as a God-infused sacrament of proclamation about human worth. Baptism into Christ declares to the one baptized and to the beholding family of God that this person has been a child of God from the moment of conception, dearly beloved and honored with the tracery of God's own image.

Still, my argument is to suggest a risky question. The straightest thinking in both science and religion knows that Adam and Eve are not the original flesh-and-blood specimens of *Homo sapiens* and that sexual intercourse is not the invention of humanity but the design of the Creator for the perpetuation of sexually reproduced species. In humanity, sex is a gift for the most endearing exchange of interpersonal love. Therefore may it now be appropriate to propose that Augustine and Pelagius trade places as heretic and orthodox on the capital issue of sin and evil? Which of the two is the straighter thinker and which the more crooked?

This is probably a cheeky question since it suggests the reversal of a long historic assessment of two contending theologians. But it does go to the heart of servant leadership. If the Augustinian view of sin has blown itself into a vast, self-perpetuating and self-aggrandizing system of soul control (no doubt without any such intention by St. Augustine) and if the true vocation of the church and all sacred and secular authority structures is not to subjugate but to serve, would it not help to recall the church to its God-given role as servant by installing the sunnier and straighter thinking about the mystery of goodness and badness in the Pelagian system? Such a choice does not diminish Augustine. His place in the annals of Christian thought remains secure. He is a towering and saintly intellectual who was perhaps misled on the issues of sin and evil by his own obsessive remorse about his early years of sexual adventuring. Do we have to saddle the entire, world-wide Christian family, especially our Roman Catholic sisters and brothers, with a guilt trip and hang-up about sex? Not in my view. But it will take some intellectual courage and pastoral kindness to rescue old Pelagius from what I believe has become his unholy doghouse.

Pelagius was a Celt. Like Teilhard, he loved the world and encouraged others to cherish the earth. Pelagius deserves sainthood bestowed

by the Sierra Club, if not by the church. Long before human prodigality
and greed began to imperil the environment, Pelagius wrote this:

> Look at the animals roaming the forest: God's spirit dwells
> within them…Look at the fish in the river and sea: God's spirit
> dwells within them…When God pronounced that his creation
> was good, it was not only that his hand had fashioned every crea-
> ture; it was that his breath had brought every creature to life.
> Look too at the great trees of the forest; look at the wild flowers
> and the grass in the fields; look even at your crops…The presence
> of God's spirit in all living things is what makes them beautiful.
> — Quoted in J. Philip Newell, *Listening for the Heartbeat of
> God: A Celtic Spirituality*, Paulist Press, Mahwah, NJ, 1997,
> pp. 10–11

Celtic spirituality has emerged in our time as a discipline of partnership in the preservation of the planet. Another Celt of honored
fourth-century Christian history has become important along with
great Pelagius. He is St. Patrick, who arrived in England from his native
Ireland as a Celtic Christian missionary to the natives. He is credited
with hymn 370 in the 1982 Episcopal hymnal. The verses are blood-
stirring, and they ring with both Trinitarian orthodoxy and the wild
pagan earthiness of the old Celts. In our hymnal, the song is called "St.
Patrick's Breastplate," suggesting a suit of holy armor. It begins with an
invocation of the Trinity and then, in the fourth verse, soars into a song
of creation:

> I bind unto myself today the virtues of the starlit
>   heaven,
> The glorious sun's life-giving ray, the whiteness of the
>   moon at even,

The flashing of the lightning free, the whirling wind's
    tempestuous shocks,
The stable earth, the deep salt sea, around the old
    eternal rocks.
— *The Hymnal 1982 According to the Use of the Episcopal
    Church*, no. 370

Karl Barth used to say that the British are incurably Pelagian. As an Anglican of the Episcopal Church in the United States for whom England and Ireland are both holy lands to me, I need to say, "Thanks for the compliment, Professor Barth!"

Chapter 27

Leadership as the Exercise of Power

When I founded the Institute for Servant Leadership in the Candler School of Theology at Emory University in Atlanta, a partnership was arranged between the institute and Emory's business school. In plain truth, the reason for this was the overwhelming power and presence of business and industry in the institutional life of the United States and all of Western-shaped world culture. If the Institute for Servant Leadership was going to speak truth to power, we had to find ways into the hearts and minds of business leadership. The narrow but highly significant common ground for the separate schools of business and theology was that both were educating leaders in two fine but unlinked academic institutions.

My question in those early days was how to conceptualize a partnership between a discipline devoted primarily to getting and another presumably committed to giving. Of course, the reality is that both business and religion are eagerly into both activities. Business must give in order to get. Products come with warranties, and services must be offered with a smile. As for the church with its salaried hierarchies and tall steeples, ecclesiastical establishments must get in order to give. As an ordained clergyperson in a wide variety of assignments, I have had to be a fund-raiser for more than half a century. Facing the need to raise $750,000 in the late 1950s to build a new church and related buildings in Baltimore, my canny senior warden Dr. Huntington Williams cautioned me about being too optimistic. "Remember," he said, "money isn't everything for Episcopalians, but whatever is in second place is a long way behind!" Because we ultimately met the goal, Dr. Williams' remark was a cryptic joke, and he knew it. While the lure of money can be a corrupting lust, the human spirit knows deep down the higher power of a commanding love.

My critical problem in launching the Institute for Servant Leadership was to find a way to define leadership in such a way as to bridge the conceptual and practical gaps between for-profit and not-for-profit leadership. How could we harmonize an understanding of leadership that could bring a sense of inner unity and wholeness to the minds and souls of leaders in all kinds of institutions so that they could be the same persons in all settings? We conducted seminars and conferences for a few years without a clear answer to the question of wholeness of heart for leaders in disparate institutions. Then, in one intuitive moment when something crossed my path (as Robert Frost might say of an unbeckoned gift of the spirit), it struck me that all leadership is the exercise of power.

From parenting to presiding, from the family house to the White House, all leaders use power. But almost never does it carry a servant ring. Webster defines the word *power* as control, subjugation, and the capacity to compel compliance. That is exactly the meaning of the word *superpower*, and that is the way in which the United States is exercising power in expanding our military dominance as we stride across the world. We are busy spending our substance on the capacity to compel compliance with subjugational force at the expense of manifest needs in education, health care, and environmental controls.

But if we go from the dictionary and politics to the New Testament and look closely at one of history's undisputed great leaders, a more profound and more enduring form of power emerges. At every turn in the record, Jesus of Nazareth used power for a different purpose than dominance. Since then, history has underlined a paradox. While Jesus did not aim to dominate, his life and death and continuing life have become dominant in defining the spiritual and ethical odyssey of Western culture. The same paradox applies to the Buddha. His life and teaching in the Hindu tradition have shaped the character of human values in the Asian world ever since he forsook the dominant privileges of princely birth for the simplicity of nonviolent care for all forms of sentient life.

In essence, what we are looking at in the lives of Jesus and Buddha is the power, not to dominate, but to make a difference. To make a difference: that is the true meaning of power, and the best thing about true power is that everybody has it! Power in its deepest and most enduring terms is every person's gift from womb to tomb and well beyond. Power in the womb is exercised by every expected life. In expectant parents, the power of a fetus to prompt response runs the whole gamut of sensations, including joy, foreboding, wonder, anxiety, and outright rejection. And this fetal power is both private and public. In the womb, its privacy lies in a pregnant mother's intensely personal response. In the public domain, fetal power lies in the intensity of political contention between the forces of prolife and prochoice. In the public domain, real tomb power lies in the levels of esteem and disesteem of all who hold anyone in memory. Public tomb power is exemplified by history's heroines and heroes and equally by history's hooligans.

Soon after Nathan Pusey was installed as Harvard University's 24th president in 1953, his wife Anne was invited as guest of honor to a fashionable tea at the Beacon Hill home of a Boston socialite. Impressed with the variety of lovely hats in the circle of guests, Mrs. Pusey was moved to ask her hostess, "Tell me, where do your friends get their stunning hats?" Quickly came the answer, "Oh, my dear, in Boston we don't get hats; we have them!" Just so in the case of every human being: at the base of life we don't get power, we have it! All forms of life, including the lower forms, have power by virtue of the gift of life itself. The question for every human is therefore not whether we have power but how our power should be used.

I have come to understand the temptations of Jesus in these very terms. How shall I use my power? That is the question that goes to the heart of personal freedom and to all constructs of human governance. The classic saga of temptation is in the very private experience of Jesus of Nazareth. As reported in Matthew and Luke, the experience is so private that it can only have gotten into the record by virtue of Jesus' personal disclosure. That he chose to tell about his deeply personal confrontation with the choice of how to use his power must mean that it was of capital significance to him. It stands at the headwaters of the ever-flowing river of his teaching.

There are three highly symbolic thrusts of the tempter to use personal power for either dominance or for what I want to name servanthood. These three temptations are in both Matthew and Luke but in different sequences.

In the Matthew version, the first lure is to exercise dominance over nature. Jesus staggered with hunger after a lengthy fast, making him extremely vulnerable to the challenge "Turn these stones to bread." Whether he really could have done that is not the question. All three temptations are symbolic of human capability. In Jesus' time, this was a temptation to use power for personal gain. The need for bread among the poor was a clamoring requirement, often unmet and leading to malnutrition and starvation. To be able to turn stones into bread implies the power to command the rulership of the masses, that is, the power to dominate rather than to serve. In our time, we know the immensely critical character of human power over the natural order. If contemporary human power to dominate and exploit the natural order goes unchecked, the planet must perish as the resource base for all of life. Jesus' answer takes the challenge up to a higher level than bodily craving. His answer defines the enduring hungers of the human heart, the hungers that no feasting on food can ever slake. "Man shall not live by bread alone, but by every word that proceedeth out of the mouth of God" (Matthew 4:4, KJV). Jesus does not deny bodily hunger; he simply elevates human need to the level of soul. That is where real power resides — in choices of the soul where decisions about the use of true power are made, whether to dominate, subjugate, and exploit or to serve.

The second address to the lure of dominant power raises the ante from the personally manipulative level to the level of public pageantry, again for purposes of dazzling domination. The tempter took him to the parapet of the temple. "If thou be the Son of God, cast thyself down: for it is written, He shall give his angels charge concerning thee" (Matthew 4:6, KJV). This temptation is a summons to hypnotize and subjugate people with demonstrations of the miraculous. But in terms of scripture and real life, this is not miraculous. It is magic, and magic requires secrecy, sleight of hand, and a practiced skill in fooling the public. The miracles of Jesus are never in the dark, never for the purpose of dominance or exploitation. Some reported miracles, such as walking on water and stilling a storm, look like editorial additions by the writers in the early believing community when the record of Jesus' ministry was transmitted orally and not written as gospels for another generation or more after his death. Such reported occasions are most likely exaggerations characteristic of literature that seeks to commend and exalt history's high heroes. In these possibly fictional cases, it is important to be clear that they were in service to others and never done for self-aggrandizing dominance. Also, the great bulk of reported miracles are in service to health and normalcy. They never take the normal and convert it to the abnormal. Jesus never makes gold of goldfish or compels cows to jump

over the moon. Even in reports that he raised the dead, his action was to
convert the abnormal to the normal. It is not normal for a 12-year-old
girl to die or a widow's son to go early to the grave. No doubt the early
believing community remembered and orally embellished the memory
of Jesus, but not one of the reported miracles is performed in terms of
the tempter's seduction to use power for bedazzlement or manipulation.
Every miracle, whether real, embellished, or invented, precisely fits the
high norms of servanthood.

The historically convincing miracles seize the disordered and restore
order. The lame walk, the deaf hear, the blind see, the hungry are fed, the
diseased are made whole, the possessed are repossessed of their composure. This is servant power. It exalts others, not the self. Servant power
is recognizable by its fruits, and its chief fruit is that it makes others
powerful. Servant power calls forth the powers implicit in the gift of life.
Servant power forces nothing. It implants nothing. It works by evocation
of what is already there, seeing intended wholeness in what appears only
partial or unsummoned. This is the power that must have turned Simon
Bar Jonah, the courtyard coward on a Thursday night, to Peter the Rock
50 days later on Pentecost when he boldly confronted the Jerusalem fes-
tival crowd who had acquiesced in the bloody murder of the crucified.
This is evocation, not manipulation. This must be the meaning of Jesus'
reply to the tempter when he returned the challenge by refusing to tempt
God, by refusing to do tricks and manipulate reality. The manipulation
of reality is not power. It is weakness, as all lying and distortions of the
truth are capitulations to weakness. Lying sets the seal on its own demise
because it violates the character of the cosmos ruled by its creator in
truth and self-giving love. God, in the revelation of Jesus, is not a divine
dominator, never a manipulator, and never a high-and-mighty, self-
serving subjugator. In the crystal image of Jesus as the face of God in
history, the ruler of the universe is supreme in the exercise of servant
power:

Here is God: no monarch he, throned in easy state to reign;
Here is God, whose arms of love aching, spent, the world
    sustain.
— Words by W. H. Vanstone, *The Hymnal 1982 According to the Use of the Episcopal Church*, no. 585

The third lure is to empire-building, perhaps the most pernicious and fatal of all temptations open to human choice. Surely empire-building is the most public and the most open to the inevitability of violence, injustice, and tyranny. The tempter took Jesus to a panoramic view of all the kingdoms of the world. "All these things will I give thee, if thou wilt fall down and worship me" (Matthew 4:9, KJV). Capitulation to this lure must be what Lord Acton had in mind in laying down the axiom that power corrupts and absolute power corrupts absolutely. What he refers to is clearly the dominating and controlling force of power in popular and dictionary terms. We know that this is the subjugating power he had in mind because of the long history of human corruption in the use of power, but it does not square with our attribution to God as absolute power. The prayerful address to Almighty God is a statement of trust in the absolute incorruptibility of divinity. If we keep in mind the orthodox insistence that Jesus Christ is the incarnate face and action of God, the life and death of Jesus become our warrants for a theological certainty that God's power is not a subjugating force but clearly a servanthood. This unequivocal biblical fact unconditionally declares the evolutionary character of the Bible. Earlier portions of scripture reveal God as wearing a warrior face in battles that sanction the slaughter of Israel's enemies. Almost the whole of the 10th chapter of Joshua is a record of ruthless carnage against Israel's neighbors, all of it sanctioned by Israel's God. The evolution of scripture's image of God is indisputable when Joshua of the eighth century BCE is compared with the revelation of God in John's gospel of the first century CE (John 14:9). When Philip asks to be shown the Father, Jesus replies, "Have I been with you all this time, Philip, and you still do not know me? Whoever has seen me has seen the Father." Soon thereafter, Jesus endures execution, responding in total personal nonviolence.

History is uniformly unkind to violence. The organized violence of empires appears to have erupted into human formations of power 6000 to 5000 years ago and later with the appearance of Egypt, Sumer, Persia, Babylon, and others in their train. All are now gone save for Communist China in its takeover of Tibet and the United States in our contemporary lust for using dominant power to force regime changes in a variety of nations. American imperialism may have begun rather modestly when Theodore Roosevelt authorized the occupation of Nicaragua, the Dominican Republic, and Haiti soon after the Spanish American War. Our interference reached noteworthy proportions on August 19, 1953, when Kermit Roosevelt, Jr., grandson of Teddy and a CIA operative, orchestrated the ouster of Iranian prime minister Mohammed Mossadegh. Mossadegh was a populist leader who had aroused the wrath of the British by nationalizing the British-owned oil industry. He also frightened Washington by failing to oppose Communist influence inside Iran. Now, in 2006, American imperialism runs in high gear with the use of dominant military force to prompt a regime change in Iraq, all with lively hints of moving this imperial power into other nations on Bush's "axis of evil." The temptation to imperialism remains both powerful and fatal. History is not mocked. Empires fail.

This is not to suggest that dominant power is fundamentally bad or never applicable. All leaders set boundaries. These are the acceptable parameters of behavior, established for the good of both the leaders and the led. Everyone in a leadership role sets boundaries. This makes boundary-setting itself a form of servanthood. Mothers are good at this: "Get your elbows off the table." Bosses set boundaries: "Get to work on time." So do teachers: "Do the reading and get to class." Jesus did likewise: "For whosoever will save his life shall lose it; but whosoever shall lose his life for my sake and the gospel's, the same shall save it" (Mark 8:35, KJV).

Jesus capsulized God's own boundary-setting in answering a religious lawyer's query about how he might inherit eternal life. Jesus said nothing about sexual behavior, be it heterosexual or homosexual. Evil must have been rooted for Jesus somewhere else than in sex. In answer to the temple lawyer's query, Jesus simply asked the man to answer his own question from a lawyer's knowledge of the Hebrew tradition (Luke 10:27–28). The lawyer quickly repeated the biblical summary: "You shall love the Lord your God with all your heart, and with all your soul, and with all your strength, and with all your mind; and your neighbor as yourself." Jesus nodded approval: "You have given the right answer; do this, and you will live." Earlier than the four gospels in the history of Christian writing, a convert from the elaborate rigidity of Hebrew rule-making wrote, "Owe no one anything, except to love one another...Love does no wrong to a neighbor; therefore, love is the fulfilling of the law" (St. Paul in Romans 13:8–10). This, then, is the enduring paradox of real power: love and law go together to complete the meaning of servanthood. This is the balance of velvet and steel in all expressions of servant leadership. Or to put it differently, there is no real servanthood without the service of boundaries.

Monty Roberts is a horse trainer who works with this same mystic balance of velvet and steel. Famous as the "Horse Whisperer," he does not use the force of whip and bronco-busting dominance. He does not break a horse's will to the superior force of a rider from on top while the horse bucks and snorts and tears the turf. Monty Roberts uses the mystic balance of iron and eiderdown to tame a horse to an experience of controlled horsepower. The iron in his taming process is a rope, a long restraining leash. The eiderdown in his method is his use of eye-to-eye contact. In the taming process, he never rides the horse from a coercive position on top. He is on the level of the horse in a posture of relational equality. He gets inside the horse from his sense of kinship with the animal. For Roberts, taming is a soul-to-soul exercise. Using the rope, he walks the horse in a slow circle while trusting the mystic connection between the leader and the led. In 30 minutes, the horse will receive a bit and bridle and a blanket and saddle without resistance, and it is ready for riding or racing or pulling in the traces. As the horse's servant leader, the Horse Whisperer simply releases the already-present horsepower for the animal's own servanthood.

Monty Roberts uses a long loop of rope as a rein. But the rope is never a weapon. It is a tool for implementing the process of trusting a horse into a voluntary claim on horsepower. It is a leash for unleashing the coiled body and soul forces native to the horse. Its message is "Be not afraid. I care for you." As for religion, we need to be suspicious of any theology that uses the Bible as more than a leash, a leash for unleashing our created human powers. Beware of a biblicism that wields the Bible as a weapon, playing upon and compounding our fear. Much of that abounds these days. From a tragic (and perhaps unintended) misreading of biblical righteousness, it supports the violence of war and commits the violence of denigrating and denying the full humanity of gay and lesbian persons who are made so by endowments of sexual identity in the womb. In Chapter 24, two resources are identified to substantiate the claim of normalcy for homosexual identity: (1) scripture itself and (2) advances in medical science.

Violence is the capital difference between dominant and servant power. Dominance always carries with it an implied or explicit threat. Dominance either whispers or shouts "Do this or else." What dominance means is "Be afraid." This is characteristic superpower behavior. By contrast, servanthood is explicitly nonviolent and seeks to eliminate fear in the manner of the velvet and steel of Jesus of Nazareth. Servanthood means "Be not afraid."

Peace I leave with you; my peace I give to you. I do not give to you as the world gives. Do not let your hearts be troubled, and do not let them be afraid.
— John 14:27

Important as it is to rebuke and oppose the current American use of dominant power in preemptive war, it is infinitely more important for our hope to claim that another superpower has blossomed forth, unbidden by a single charismatic leadership and uncontrived by manipulation of some dominant power. In a speech at a program of the United Nations Association of San Francisco on February 5, 2003, former assistant secretary-general of the United Nations Dr. Robert Muller said, "The miraculous outpouring of millions across the world in protest of an American-led rush to war represents the emergence of a new force for peace never before seen in the history of the world. There are now two superpowers, the United States and the merging, surging voice of the people of the world."

The world's counterresponse to the Iraqi war looks like greatly added energy for turning the massive hinge of history on which the world now moves — pulling humanity up from a long adolescent addiction to dominant power and concomitant violence to the maturity of nonviolent, relational equality in a new global civilization. This reality clearly seems to me a fresh power up from the depths of our collective unconscious. Humanity, although forestalled by long habits of war and conquest, has clearly begun to evolve beyond coercive violence as a method of opposing one another.

Instantly this evolving capacity to negotiate instead of moving against an enemy means that servant power has moved from option to necessity. A mission in servant leadership thus fits hand in glove with the emergence across the world of an advancing momentum of the healing power in nonviolent resolutions of conflict. Extinction is a continuous exercise in the long, protracted emergence of life in the planet, and the human species may be calling down that same ineluctable engine of evolution in our nuclear capacity to burn the world. But there is a counterengine that throbs with increasing muscle in the rising tide of commitment to a servant posture in personal and institutional leadership. Human extinction, along with much of the planet's life, may yet be forestalled. A world imperiled by the lust and swagger of dominant political power now cries out for a rapid increase in the numbers and self-giving power of servant leaders. If we want a world for ourselves and our progeny unto the seventh generation, servanthood appears the only way open to a human future.

Chapter 28

Transitions:
Divorce and Remarriage

There is an admonition in most marriage rites that sounds like thunder on the edges of a sunny day: "Those whom God has joined together let no one put asunder" (Episcopal Church, *The Book of Common Prayer*, 1979, p. 428). Somehow this never seems to fit the bright internal weather of a wedding. The reason must be that, as some wise commentator put it, "No one gets married to get divorced." But divorce overtook my first marriage long before it was declared ended. My divorce was a sorrow that took years to face up to, then more time to accept its inevitability, and still more years to heal from the lacerations of guilt. One of the reasons for my guilt lay in a written defense of Christian marriage that had long been my ethical and theological posture. Now I was in violation of my own declared convictions.

Years before, in 1979, I had given voice to what I called the "indelibility of marriage" in a pastoral letter to the Episcopal Diocese of Atlanta (published in *Purple Ink*, 1982, pp. 87–89). Much later, in 1985, I accepted the radical brokenness of my 42-year marriage, for which I bore large responsibility, and initiated divorce proceedings. By then I was teaching at Emory University. However, I felt obliged to send notice to the clergy of the Diocese of Atlanta that Bea and I had come to a mutual decision to divorce. With the consent of my successor, a personal letter that I signed as bishop emeritus went to all the clergy. At the same time, I was fearful to read again what I had written in the 1979 pastoral letter, particularly since I did not recall exactly what I had said. So it was months before I could summon the courage to reread it. Honor dictated that I had to revisit at some point what I had put into print. Facing that old pastoral letter was like plunging into an icy lake, but the waters turned warm when I came to end of it. For all who must face failed marriages, I hope the conclusion of my letter will bring the sense of deliverance from guilt that it brought to me. The old pastoral letter follows in its entirety.

Everybody makes a good start, but broken endings wound too many lives. Therefore the thunder at every wedding — as a solemn warning that most marriages are assaulted occasionally by howling winds. The storm warning in the middle of the marriage rite is intended to gird our love for each other with the resolve of lifelong commitment against the inevitable day when romance is revealed as inadequate to the strain of ugly weather.

Marriage is by far the most challenging of all human relationships. The very nature of marriage is to place two naturally self-centered persons in close and daily contact. This arrangement is bound to evoke the best and the worst — our darkest rages and insecurities as well as our most luminous devotion. Due to the worst in us, all marriages experience endings, somewhat repeatedly. The conflict of wills and the stubborn residue of wounded childhoods assure this. It is the function of the Christian tradition of lifelong commitment to ring us round with hoops of spring steel, flexible but tough, holding two persons together so that the nobler self in each may have opportunity for reemergence, to make a new start — to reenact that bright beginning from a healed and truth-filled posture of forgiveness and new maturity.

The tender mystery of enduring marriage must lie in the odyssey of repeated deaths and rebirths — each rebirth making the dying worthwhile — thus forging sturdier commitment, deeper friendship, and easier devotion. The vows of Christian marriage anticipate the howling winds, the endings, and the new beginnings. We pledge our love to each other "for better for worse, for richer for poorer, in sickness and in health…until we are parted by death" (Episcopal Church, *The Book of Common Prayer*, 1979, p. 427). By death is meant, not the death of feeling, but death of the body — in advance of which partners in marriage can experience repeated dying of the worst that the better in each may emerge and grow.

The theological word for the power to live this way is grace. It is a mystery as deep as Christmas — and just as real. And it is of God. So strong is the church's commitment to lifelong marriage and so deep our belief in the empowering grace of God that our marriage canons (regulations) require all of us, laity and clergy alike, to seek the reconciling ministries of pastoral counseling or professional therapy when marriage is imperiled. No one may justly seek permission to remarry in the church who has not done the work of reliance on the ministries of counseling or therapy. Those ministries seek the opening of a light upon our dark dreads and angers and our unsearched memories, exposing them to the grace of God so as to effect the rebirth of what, in one degree or another, is bound to die — in order that a chastened self may be reborn!

That is the use of death in a universe ordered and governed by God — death is instrumental to life! This is the meaning of the cross as our central emblem — that in yielding to the

sovereignty of God all human dying is the gateway to resurrection and new life. Thus all endings become the mystic seeds
of new beginnings. In the Christian understanding of life, it is
expected that all human relationships will feel assaulted by the
tempests of selfishness, enduring occasional deaths — in order
to claim the cleansing and bracing joy of a livelier bonding than
ever before.

Thus the sacramental doctrine of the indelibility of marriage.
Divorce has reality only in secular terms, not at the spiritual level
— of which the sacrament of marriage is the outward and visible
sign. Marriage is inwardly indelible. Something happens in the
living out of marriage that makes total and absolute unmarriage
impossible. Even under secular auspices, marriage impinges on
two people at mystic levels. In any marriage, each person leaves
the mark of the other on his or her life and memories. Marriage
between serious and practicing Christians sharpens and deep-
ens this reality. Thus, in spiritual terms, marriage is an indelible
bond. That is why the church only marries and remarries. The
church does not sacramentally unmarry people.

But we live in a broken world which Christ comes to redeem,
not to condemn. Long ago, the Episcopal Church made a pastoral decision, reflected in our marriage canons, that acknowl-
edges the possibility of irreparable marital brokenness, allowing
us to begin again. Canonical provision is made for remarriage
after divorce, requiring of those who seek remarriage a personal
readiness to assume a real measure of responsibility for the dis-
solution of the earlier marriage.

So it is that our marriage canons imply two functions of
grace. The first is for the repair of what we sunder — the grace
that energizes our reapproach to each other in repentance and
forgiveness, claiming thereby love's fulfillment in peace. The

second work of grace in marriage is to enable our recovery from failure when nothing prevails to save a marriage. Marriage is not immune to failure. Like all holy gifts offered us, marriage participates in the defeats of a broken world. Thus we give thanks for the grace to effect repair — and the grace to endure and recover from failure.

So we perceive two functions, but it is the same grace. It is the grace that upholds us in our weakness, married or divorced, and uses failure as raw material for fashioning new life. The lesser doctrine of indelibility must yield to the overarching doctrine of justification by grace through faith, for the Gospel admits of no superiority of one human being over another — of the married over the divorced. "For there is no distinction, since all have sinned and fall short of the glory of God; they are now justified by his grace as a gift, through the redemption that is in Christ Jesus" (Romans 3:22–24).

I know, for being with many in anguish, that God is not absent from the pain of divorce. And I have seen new life bloom in a new bond of matrimony when the old has been laid to rest, its shroud of guilt replaced by the mantle of joy. So let there be not stirred among us either pride or guilt, but thanksgiving — for "There is therefore now no condemnation for those who are in Christ Jesus" (Romans 8:1).

Bea and I divorced. She took up residence at our mountain house in Eagles Mere, Pennsylvania. I moved to a condominium in the Emory neighborhood, and my new work as founder of the Institute for Servant Leadership became the focus of my attention and energy.

In the course of time, Mary Page Welborn, my administrative assistant in the Episcopal Diocese of Atlanta, reemerged in another professional role. I was told by mutual friends that she had become a licensed consultant in teaching and applying the Jungian personality test called the Myers-Briggs Type Indicator® (MBTI). It seemed to those friends that the MBTI might be a useful component in our seminars on leadership. I telephoned Mary Page at her home in Anderson, South Carolina and found her responsive to the idea that she consider teaching the MBTI as part of our developing seminar curriculum. Periodically thereafter, she joined our teaching staff in Atlanta, and her component became integral to the formation of a quality of self-understanding that all accomplished leaders must develop.

For the next two years, Mary Page and I saw each other frequently, and out of those contacts there grew a deepening love. But it was hindered by the nagging pain of divorce and the emotional clutch of 42 years in a first marriage. Added to my confusion was the desire to remarry, but standing in the way was a convention that looked askance at clergypersons who divorced and took a second spouse. Even though I was now retired from the office of bishop and teaching in a large university, I felt afraid and forestalled. Providentially, I had developed the daily habit of walking two or three miles in the evening since moving from Alexandria to Atlanta. As I walked day after day near the Emory campus, a long-remembered hymn from my Presbyterian childhood came regularly to mind: "Guide me, O Thou great Jehovah, pilgrim through this barren land." And nearly every day there came to me a quiet word — courage! Since I had been in a ministry of frequent controversy for years, I knew the importance of courage and just as frequently knew my inner sense of quailing before the challenge. Now I faced another challenge. Should I ask another love to take on a refugee from a failed marriage and risk the censure that could come to a divorced and twice-married old bishop?

Finally, after living for many seasons into the quiet assurance that courage was a gift of prayer, a fine resolve solidified for me. So, at age 68, the accumulating energy of deliverance from fear moved me to risk disfavor again. Mary Page said yes to my proposal, and the decision to commit to remarriage stands out as a towering experience of being freed. Only the deliverance that came at Pearl Harbor compares to that gift of liberation. We both felt a sense of standing tall for sharing a high vision of our life together. We had talked often about marriage as a paradoxical vocation of being bonded in spiritual freedom — the bonding freedom of seeing ourselves as called to foster each other's growth in becoming the distinct and whole person God intended us to achieve. This vocation in marriage became our commanding vision as we looked forward to our wedding day.

Our vision of marriage brought us both the further gift of gratitude for our former spouses and for the children born of those unions: David, Peter, Laura, Grayson, and David. They, in turn, have given us altogether six grandchildren, one newborn great-granddaughter, and a second great-grandchild now on the way.

After my single life of three years and hers of ten years, Mary Page and I stood together with 100 invited guests in the chapel of the Cathedral of St. Philip on August 27, 1988. Awaiting us at the altar were the three highest principals of the Episcopal Diocese of Atlanta: the dean of the Cathedral, my successor as bishop of Atlanta, and his bishop coadjutor. We recessed from the chapel as if on wings.

Chapter 29

Transitions at the Institute for Servant Leadership: Fired and Freed to Meet the Queen

The fortunes of the Institute for Servant Leadership grew shaky after five years as part of Emory University. By late May of 1988, three developments were making the institute's future at the Candler School of Theology problematic. First, although our seminars had been well attended for most of our time at Candler, we had begun to experience increasing difficulty in recruiting seminar participants, and the number had grown smaller. Second, we were running short of grant money. Although I had secured additional funding from the Woodruff Foundation, it had declined any further approaches. Emory University itself proved unable to give us any funding encouragement. The institute was only a small subdepartment of the Candler School of Theology, and priorities had been properly assigned to much larger units of the school. While Emory President James Laney was sympathetic to my appeals, he keenly felt the pressing needs of the huge enterprise for which he was responsible. Third, and crucially, George "Chip" Parks had left the Emory business school for another academic deanship at Tufts University in New

England. In his place, Emory University appointed a man who later revealed that he regarded the whole theological enterprise as having nothing to say to the leadership of American business.

In the midst of these disappointing factors, I experienced another liberating grasp from beyond. The experience was totally outside the normal exercise of consciousness. It was briefer than the first such episode of mystic soaring and rescue at Pearl Harbor in 1945, but this second one was an unmistakable pointer into the immediate future — actually into all my futures. One early morning as I walked from my bedroom to the kitchen in the lonely condominium that I had bought in anticipation of a long stay at Emory, I was feeling lost in the gloom of Emory's unreadiness to provide much-needed support for my fledgling experiment in leadership education. Halfway down the hall on my way to a wake-up cup of coffee, a voice spoke from the silence. It was quiet, kindly, clear, and pointedly personal. The voice said, "I want you to do this for me." I knew instantly that I had heard from the Christ of my faith. It did not take long to decipher the meaning of that piercing experience of further liberation.

My mystic moment carried three great meanings. First, it meant that the work of the new institute was lifted from the realm of personal ambition. I was relieved of captivity to the burden of pride that, in my case, sought to glorify Bennett as an innovative educator. Very quickly, I felt deeply free. Second, it meant that I no longer needed to dilute the spiritual force implicit in the very words *servant leadership* in order not to discomfort the self-interested mind-set of a money-driven, secular culture. Henceforward the institute would articulate, as best we could, a quality of leadership in the pattern and power of Jesus. It was Christ who set the enduring standard of human success: "…whoever wishes to be great among you must be your servant" (Matthew 20:26). Third, it meant that my Lord was certified as ever-present, closer than breathing, nearer than hands and feet. There is no explanation for mystic initiatives like this. They seem unprompted and undeserved assurances that the limitations of our love never place limits on the love of God.

Later that day, I asked for an appointment with Jim Waits, dean of the Candler School of Theology. His keenness for my proposal to inaugurate the institute and his initiative in securing generous launching grants had made my work possible. In an earlier conference with him, the years of diminishing returns for the institute had prompted Jim to suggest that I consider the possibility of cutting loose from the Candler School at Emory and taking the enterprise to a private, nonprofit status in stand-alone independence. After that voice had sharpened the mission of the institute, I took him seriously and had called a meeting of our advisory board. We wrestled with the question for a long afternoon and concluded that we needed to spin off. By a serious error of my judgment, Jim Waits was not included in that meeting, even though I knew he felt badly. When I went to his office the next day to inform him that we had taken his earlier suggestion seriously and had decided to leave Candler, he exploded in anger. I was totally stunned. I anticipated just the reverse. I offered to call the advisory board back to meet with him and reconsider, but he would hear none of it. He abruptly offered to transfer the remainder of the institute's funds to whatever continuing enterprise we would establish. I left his office with a crushing sensation. For the first time since college days when Western Auto sacked me for being unfit as a tire and battery installer, I had been fired!

Putting the Institute for Servant Leadership in place as a private, nonprofit, educational corporation took some time, but my relationships with Jim Waits, Emory President James Laney, and the Emory community quickly recovered. Not only did both Jims and their wives attend our wedding some weeks later, but Jim Waits invited Mary Page and me to be the principal presenters at an annual meeting of the dozen or so seminary deans of the United Methodist Church and their wives

from across the country. We did so, at a grand event on Jekyll Island in
Georgia about a year after leaving Emory.

After the closeout at Candler, Mary Page and I both thought of
Kanuga Conferences in Hendersonville, North Carolina as the most
likely location for an attempt to make the Institute for Servant Leadership a viable private, nonprofit corporation. Kanuga is situated on 1400
acres of beautiful mountain terrain with a large lake, a modern inn, and
platoons of modernized cottages first built in the 1920s. In addition,
there are assembly facilities for all sizes of conferences, and it is open
year-round. Mary Page knew the lovely place from successive summer
childhood visits there with her family. When it became clear that we
would have to find a new setting for the institute, she and I knew immediately that we needed to make Hendersonville our home after we married. And so it was.

In 1988, we found a house in our new mountain town and named
it "Horizon" because it stood on a hillside with a view of the mountains
through 150 uninterrupted degrees. The view from the house was spectacular. Pinnacle Mountain loomed in the distance from all the front
windows, and the long, undulating line of lower ridges on the right and
left flanks of Pinnacle made the view breathtaking. Horizon had three
floors with four bedrooms and four baths. A two-story great room dominated the center of the house with a rock fireplace and exposed rock
chimney that climbed through the peak of the cathedral ceiling. There
was also a kitchen and adjoining den with another fireplace. In addition to all this, a solarium on the lower floor could seat 25 in a circle of
chairs with a mountain-facing glass wall. The house occupied the top of
a sloping, 3.5-acre lot and boasted a big, detached garage and shop area
with an apartment above. We knew that it would be easy to furnish the
big place. By combining our households, we had ample accumulations.
But our two former households differed, maybe even clashed. Whereas

Mary Page brought many beautiful family antiques, my additions amounted to used furniture!

Administered from our big house, the institute prospered handsomely. Each of us had an office. Mary Page handled all the financial and administrative details, while I did the recruiting, writing, and lead teaching in partnership with imported scholars and instructors. We awarded ourselves a minimal $5000 each in annual salaries, and the institute broke even on money as a mom-and-pop operation. Our seminar and annual conference participants came from the United States and Canada and from overseas as well. Our bimonthly essay and newsletter *Turning Point* was sent across the country and overseas to participants in Europe, South America, and Africa. Between events at Kanuga, I was invited to teach in many parts of the country and did so while Mary Page kept the store.

On my 74th birthday in 1994, a letter came from England in an envelope marked Lambeth Palace, the home and headquarters of the Archbishop of Canterbury, The Right Reverend and Most Honorable George Leonard Carey. Many pieces of mail came so marked, and I thought it was just another appeal for mission funds somewhere in the worldwide Anglican Communion. I was about to toss it away when something moved me to open the envelope. It was a personal letter from Archbishop Carey himself! He was inviting me to lecture on leadership before a biannual meeting of all the primates of the Anglican Communion from around the world, 35 of them at the time, along with their chaplains and interpreters. Among them, of course, would be Archbishop Desmond Mpilo Tutu, primate of South Africa and recipient of the Nobel Peace Prize in 1984. Wow! I could hardly take it in. Handing the letter to Mary Page in our kitchen, she read it and then smiled. "Bennett, you've received a birthday card from God."

The two weeks in England with the primates and Archbishop Carey were highlights of my life. I lectured twice and was well-received.

Encouragement to publish came from my own primate, Presiding Bishop Edmund Lee Browning, as well as from other primates such as Richard Holloway of Scotland and French Chang-Him of the Seychelles in the Indian Ocean. These affirmations led to my third book, *Servant-hood: Leadership for the Third Millennium*, which was published in 1997 by Cowley Publications. The book, a slim volume of 185 pages that went through a fourth printing, is used in theological seminaries and to some extent in business circles. When Cowley discontinued publication, Wipf and Stock Publishers in Eugene, Oregon picked it up in 2005, and the book continues in use across the country.

The spectacular standout of that fortnight in Britain was meeting the Queen and Prince Philip at Windsor Castle. In England, church and state have organic linkages dating from about 1534 when King Henry VIII repudiated the pope, designated the church in England as the Church of England, and declared himself the ecclesial head. The British Crown still functions as titular head of the church, which is what entitled Archbishop Carey and the rest of us to a formal tea with the Queen one afternoon. The memorable moment for me came about midway in the soiree when the Queen led us on a tour of Windsor Castle. I was not one of the primates, only a lecturer at the conference, so I stood back from the crowd and was looking at the Long Walk out one of the great bay windows. The Long Walk is a mile or so of paved avenue through the parkland between Windsor Castle and Cumberland Lodge, the great house where the primates and staff were housed and meeting. Suddenly I heard a highly cultivated Englishwoman's voice saying at my elbow, "Tell me, Archbishop, which is your province?" It was the Queen herself. In low heels and her ever-present black purse, she stood at eye level with me at about 5 feet, 7 inches, and we had a few minutes of one-on-one exchange. I explained that I was not a primate, only a retired bishop of Atlanta in America. Searching frantically for something further to say, I heard myself remarking that her eldest son, the Prince of Wales, had visited our Atlanta cathedral as lay reader on a Sunday morning during my incumbency and that everyone had found him an elegant and engaging person.

Out that bay window, I had been eyeing the equestrian statue of King George III, which is situated at the halfway point in the Long Walk. George III was the sovereign in England during the American Revolutionary War. He did not take our rebellion with adequate seriousness, making it easier for our George and his colonials to achieve the victory. Sometimes we are saved from speaking the first thing that comes to mind in tense situations, and I was so saved that afternoon. In the breathless moment of grasping for what to say to the Queen of England, I had thought first to thank her for her forbearer on the throne whose moderation had made American freedom easier to come by. What a stupid thing to have offered Her Majesty! "Thank you, ghostly protector of flustered clerics in critical moments!"

After returning from England at age 75, I realized that my physical zip was diminished. If the Institute for Servant Leadership was going to have an extended life, I needed to raise a million dollars as endowment to pay salaries for two successors, one for me and the other for Mary Page. No one substantially younger than I with executive and teaching ability was going to come as president of the institute for a measly salary, nor could we get an office administrator for $5000. We would need greatly enhanced income for the institute before we could hand the reins to successors. So I went forth. Mary Page and I agreed beforehand that a disappointing hunting trip would be a signal that the institute did not have divine sanction to endure. Although I was keen about prospects, Mary Page allowed that she did not relish the idea of tracking pledges and endowment funds and making reports to our small reconstituted board. I identified the four wealthiest friends I knew and made four trips to four cities, Washington, Charlottesville, Pittsburgh, and Atlanta. I asked each of the four to consider the rising momentum and reputation of our enterprise and my advancing age and then asked for a pledge of $500,000 in four- to five-year increments. I came away with a resounding result: not one brass farthing!

But Providence was preparing something very different. Heavenly headquarters didn't need four rich men to perpetuate the institute. About a year after my fruitless foray, a former participant in an institute seminar during the Emory days telephoned from Arizona. He was Bill Jamieson, experienced business owner, educator, political associate of Jimmy Carter in Georgia and Bruce Babbitt in Arizona, and an ordained deacon in the Episcopal Church. Bill said that his commitments to the bishop of Arizona and other Arizona enterprises were fulfilled and that he would like to come to work with me and Mary Page for as long as two years at his own expense. Another wow! I checked with our board and got a green light. None of them knew Bill, but I could boost him to the rafters. I had known him since his Jimmy Carter days in Atlanta when he served as senior warden in one of my churches and more recently as a gifted participant in an institute seminar at Emory.

Bill came in 1995, and so did his wife Kennon. She found a house 35 miles north of Hendersonville in Asheville, and Bill won his way with the board after one proprietary and resistant board member decided to resign. What this did was to give me an eager and brilliant understudy and get me going again on a money-raising gig. With some consultant help, I raised nearly a million dollars in capital and endowment funds. Bill worked without compensation for more than a year until the endowment kicked in and annual giving made it possible to award him an executive salary. Kennon relieved Mary Page in time as our unfailingly gracious and competent administrator. This shining outcome represents another mountain peak on the map of my liberated life. At age 79, I retired as president of the Institute for Servant Leadership, and Bill succeeded me.

Mostly on his invitation, Bill and I meet weekly for a long lunch at a sandwich shop halfway between our towns. We always have a gabby good time talking education, baseball, theology, and politics — especially politics. It can be imagined that two old liberals relish roasting the incumbent administration while accepting its popularity among many of our friends and associates.

But progressive hope endures. By God's grace, the Institute for Servant Leadership grows in usefulness as a servant enterprise. We are buoyed by the truth that a divine servant power spins the stars and has so constructed the interwoven world that service and generosity to others is the promised road to participation with Christ in a triumphant quality of life. Such a life prevails against every daunting challenge and every tug of personal despair in every era of hope-shaped human history.

Chapter 30

Global Warming of the Second Kind

This chapter is written close on the heels of the 2004 elections that reinstalled the administration of President George W. Bush. His incumbency treats the evidence of global warming as inconclusive. This posture of tacit denial is supported by an ideological despair of the future of the world, an ideology rooted in a determined conviction about the literal inerrancy of the Hebrew-Christian scriptures that foretell the imminent end of the world. "We'll soon be out of here" is the ardent belief of many literalist interpreters of the Bible. This despair of the world is paralleled by a happy certainty that true believers will be levitated to heaven by the Rapture — a pastoral appeal by St. Paul for the comfort of the believers to whom he is writing (1 Thessalonians 4:16). This appeal is found only in Paul's earliest written letter and never referred to again as the Apostle developed his own steadily maturing theology.

It is critical to note that the operating belief system of those who count on the imminent end of the world runs parallel to a rejection of the theory of evolution. Substituted in place of evolution is the timetable deduced in the seventeenth century by James Ussher, archbishop of Armaugh, Ireland, who scrupulously calculated from internal biblical evidence that the world was created by God in the year 6006 BCE. These calculations fly in the face of modern science and foreshorten the life of the planet by multiple billions of years. A shortened beginning of the earth is matched inevitably by a shortening of the end of the earth. This has a fatal effect on the Christian doctrine of hope by transferring vital hope from life in God's world to an afterlife in God's heaven and relieving such believers of all responsibility for the stewardship of creation.

Modern science is offended by this deduction, and so is any modern belief system that understands the Bible to have its own long-evolved history of oral and written records. The Hebrew Christian Bible did not descend full-blown from God's hand. Our sacred scriptures were fashioned over more than 1000 years of human striving after the truths of revelation and historical actualities. These actualities include the phenomenon of extinction. Modern science estimates that over 90% of all the once-living earth species have risen and fallen into oblivion. Extinction is thus an integral part of the process of evolution. Because premodern forms of humanity have appeared and disappeared before the emergence of *Homo sapiens*, we, too, may go the way of extinction, this time by our own hand in global nuclear war. This possible reality forecloses any long human future. Even more, it makes hope and the moral responsibility that hope engenders more keenly significant now than at any previous moment in human history.

Plainly much is up in the air, but one thing is certain: the massive hinge of history is slowly swinging. It moves under pressure from the two major sources implied in much of what I have shared so far. First is the rising momentum of nonviolence as a positive problem solver. Second is the increasing pressure to halt and eventually reverse the tide of environmental degradation. No one knows whether hope is healthy enough to swing the hinge of history soon enough to sustain the imperiled human and planetary odysseys. But we can know both the peril and the promise. At the moment, the peril looms far larger than the promise, given the immensity of nuclear capability in our own and other arsenals. This means that those who recognize the peril and who push hopefully on the doors of tomorrow need one another as pilgrims of the promise.

Meanwhile, both the practice of active nonviolence and the energy for environmental protection grow apace. This is global warming of the second kind.

Consider first the warming trend of nonviolence. To the charge that nonviolence is idealistic, the answer is "Of course!" Ideals are what energize the human spirit. If nonviolence were not an ideal, we could not use it. Ideals are embodied in all the structures of freedom that Americans cherish. The erosion of ideals is precisely what sickens the American spirit and polarizes the electorate. The first victim of all violence, private and public, is the commanding ideal of truth. All regimes that exalt violence use deliberate lies as perverse instruments of power. Nazi Germany was awash in lies about Aryan racial purity and an adulterating Jewish conspiracy. The Bush administration's deceit as preparation for citizen support of the Iraqi war is an alarming sign of social and political decadence. Ideals are the driving energy of all social constructs of freedom in both personal and public life. Jesus said, "…you will know the truth, and the truth will make you free" (John 8:32). To his teaching on truth, Jesus added the personal cost of it by enduring vicious resistance to truth and dying for its sake in nonviolent endurance and forgiveness of his executioners. The cross is a vile emblem of the most ruthless cruelty that, by an embrace of active nonviolence, has since become the luminous symbol of the enduring power of God's mercy.

It is no accident that modern history's most forceful user of nonviolence as an instrument of political change called his method *satyagraha.* Mohandas K. Gandhi (1869–1948) translated the word as truth force. Sometimes he interpreted the Hindi term as soul force or love force. The word is actually Gandhi's own invention, combining two Hindi nouns *satya* and *agraha.* As a religious leader, Gandhi used truth force in the political arena, saying that those who oppose the entrance of religion into politics do not know the meaning of religion. Following the teachings of Gandhi, Martin Luther King, Jr. used religious conviction as a force for working nonviolently in the American political arena. In King's doctoral studies at Boston University, the conceptual basis of his Ph.D. research rose from the life and work of Gandhi. In the successful nonviolent social change wrought by Dr. King and his followers, Gandhi's life and witness were the forces that lay behind the American civil rights achievement. In one of King's most memorable addresses, he gives vivid voice to the power of nonviolence:

> We will match your capacity to inflict suffering with our capacity to endure suffering. We will meet your physical force with soul force. We will not hate you, but we cannot in all good conscience obey your unjust laws…But we will soon wear you down by our capacity to suffer. And, in winning our freedom, we will so appeal to your heart and conscience that we will win you in the process.
> — Martin Luther King, Jr., in *Peacemaking: Day by Day*, Pax Christi USA, Erie, PA, 1985, p. 93
> (www.paxchristiusa.com)

Gandhi's influence now spreads across the world, making truth force the energy for political reform in such recent nonviolent victories as formerly communist Russia, formerly apartheid South Africa, and formerly violence-torn Ireland. Gandhi attributed his learning about nonviolence to the Christian scriptures, which he read while a law student in England as a young man. Returning to India after an important interlude in South Africa, he knew intimately the dominant white political and military forces that ruled the so-called Christian nations of his experience. Some of his biographies (of which there are nearly 400) contend that he considered converting from his native Hinduism to Christianity. In the four that I have read, it is clear that he decided to remain a Hindu because of the dissonance between the teachings of Jesus and the value systems of the Christian nations that he knew well. He is reported to have said that everyone knows Christianity to be a religion of nonviolence — except the Christians.

Despite the broad failure of Christian populations to live by the truth force of *satyagraha*, nonviolence blossoms and grows as a political engine of reform and renewal. The sanctity of the ballot is precisely an instrument of *satyagraha*, of truth force. The ballot belongs to the people, not to the government or to a powerful, money-influenced political party. Its protection as an instrument possessed by the citizens themselves is critically important to American freedom and the defeat of imperialist aggrandizement.

Environmental reform also blossoms across the world, especially in the northern hemisphere, where the crisis of global warming is exacerbated by petroleum usage. Environmental reform will continue to grow, I believe, no matter what the outcome of any next election. Only a nuclear catastrophe could halt its gathering momentum. Since April 2001, we have had a new set of wheels in our garage. It is a small emblem of global warming of the second kind — like the first green shoots of daffodils that brighten the face of February. It is a small car called a Prius, a daffodil name that means *first* in Greek. Born in Japan under the auspices of Toyota Motor Corporation, it combines the motive power of electricity and fossil fuel. It is an engineering breakthrough of such ingenuity that the travel-case-size engine in front intermittently recharges the oversize battery in the ample trunk behind the rear seat. The trunk easily holds two large pieces of luggage and incidentals. Not only does the battery get an occasional boost from the engine, but the friction-induced heat from the brakes also generates a recharge. The result is no need for external recharging. Our Prius gets up to 55 miles per gallon with exhaust emissions only 10% of those of its larger garage mate. The Prius is also a jackrabbit, rocketing on command and cruising easily at 65 on the interstate. There is something pleasingly spiritual about that car. It stands as an outward and visible sign of an inward and spiritual grace, an irreversible shift in the soul of contemporary humanity. It is the shift from careless consumption and pollution of the planet to a caring appreciation of our living and vulnerable resource base. The Prius is only the first mass-produced hybrid vehicle to honor the cries of the earth. Much more is to come. Honda also markets a practical hybrid car, and General Motors and Toyota have stepped beyond blind competition to collaborate on the design and production of fuel-cell vehicles that reduce carbon emissions to zero in the form of water.

All this represents a spiritual reformation, a transaction in our advancing human consciousness, and it comes at what looks like the last few minutes of opportunity to preserve life unto the seventh generation. *Consciousness* is the emerging word that makes it possible to speak of the inner life without confusing the conversation with partisan religious talk. Multiplying numbers of us who rejoice in global warming of the second kind appreciate the word *spiritual* because we believe in a deep distinction between religion and spirituality. Spirituality is primary. It is rooted in human prehistory as a genetically coded impulse, whereas religion is the later-developed organization and codification of our advancing spiritual development. Spirituality is etched into human prehistory as far back as Neanderthal burial practices of 100,000 to 60,000 years ago. Our early forbears added both implements and ornaments to the graves of their dead, clear signs of primordial belief in an afterlife. Archeology has uncovered grave sites that include hunting and cooking tools and even fossilized flowers as emblems of caring remembrance.

Paleoanthropology, the archeological science of the ancient, testifies to deep spirituality, as does the very new science of quantum physics. Both sciences add the weight of their empirical evidence to the reality of inborn and advancing spirituality. Quantum theory insists that everything is connected to everything else in a web of interlocking life. The newest scientific insights reverse the older, discrete parts-and-pieces reduction of the universe in Newtonian mechanics, and the new perception of cosmic interdependence means that any action that diminishes others in the great web of life diminishes the diminisher. A person is lessened as a person for any contempt of or heedless violence inflicted upon any other entity in the order of life.

In an interlocking system, what is done to others is done to one's self. This is the foundation of the golden rule that unites the ethics of all the religious systems in the human family. In Islam, the golden rule reads, "None of you is a believer until he desires for his brother that which he desires for himself." In the Buddhist tradition, it reads, "Hurt not others in ways that you yourself would find hurtful." This universal ethic instantly mandates the emergence of political arrangements that honor all lives in the intricate scale of life. That we are far from perfection in achieving the ideal is no reason for despair. The goal does not count nearly as much as the advance we make in approaching it. The question for our time is therefore not "Have we created a relationship-serious global civilization that cherishes all forms of life?" Not yet. But the real question is "Are we serious about moving toward such an outcome in our common life on the earth?" While the outcome is problematic and in the distance, the process is clearly underway, and the process is what counts in a creation still being created!

There is an ancient axiom in the Hindu tradition to encourage hope. Called *kami yoga*, it means that the key to success in any endeavor is to avoid preoccupation with the outcome in favor of attention to the process. This translates into the wisdom of good golf, which urges, "Keep your eye on the ball!" The key word in the title of this chapter is a process participle: *warming*. It is not *warmed*, as if the process were completed. *Warming* carries the same process force as our familiar word for a house or a public structure. We call these things *buildings*, never *builts*, even though they may be completed in the sense that the builders have left the property. But the fact is that they are never finished. Our current house is only six years old, and already we have had the builder back on several occasions. He has more than honored his warranty by virtue of his friendship with us to repair roof leaks and a foundation problem. Also, we have added one bedroom and have glassed in the screen porch. Every building is described in process terms, never in the language of finished products. So, too, is the earth, the planet of God's entrustment to human hearts and ingenuity. All life is one huge process, and it is never over.

Current political leadership in America is bent on policies that shield consumerist market capitalism against challenge by the rising tide of environmental passion. The same leadership presses for gargantuan sums for military investment to the impoverishment of American children and their education in deteriorating schools manned by underpaid teachers. But this is a predictable part of the process. Pressure to change any destructive addiction, personally or publicly, will always arouse denial and resistance. Talk to any member of Alcoholics Anonymous or to any of us in the privileged sector of American society who struggle against the addictive blandishments of our rich, materialistic life style.

Meanwhile the beat for liberation from cultural captivity goes on, and it mounts. In all sectors of American enterprise, there are leaders who pull the bell ropes that ring out for radical change from the practice of power as dominance to a conviction that real power lies in partnership, negotiation, reconciliation, and love — love of the natural order and love of one another across all boundaries. Two contemporary business thinkers and writers talk of power as love. Rosabeth Moss Kanter of the Harvard Business School says that power is like love — it is one of those precious commodities that grow by giving it away. Here is what

Dr. Margaret Wheatley, good friend and author of best-selling business books, writes:

> What gives power its charge, positive or negative, is the quality of relationships. Those who relate through coercion, or from disregard of the other person, create negative energy. Those who are open to others and who see others in their fullness create positive energy. Love in organizations, then, is the most potent source of power we have available.
>
> — Margaret Wheatley, *Leadership and the New Science: Learning about Organization from an Orderly Universe,* Barrett-Koehler, San Francisco, 1992, p. 39

All of the above leads directly to the current shift from power structures of hierarchy to circular network models of interaction in organizations. Leadership in such vital networks is exercised as a power center of participation in responsibility and decision making.

Knowing that spirituality is stamped indelibly into our genetic coding and that to be human is to be spiritual, I wonder how the differentiated religions of the world can add their ancient and honorable power to the fusionist energy of global warming of a second kind. The great religions are the most enduring of all the world's institutions. The oldest among them emerged in the mists many centuries before Jesus. Hinduism, Buddhism, and Judaism are all pre-Christian. Most of the remaining religions are centuries older than constitutional democracy, and nearly everyone knows that Abraham and Moses were famous long before Jesus of Nazareth. The renowned biblical scholar Marcus Borg sometimes refers to Christianity as "a way of being Jewish." His statement is precisely accurate historically: the Christian movement grew directly from Jewish roots, and half or more of the distinctly Christian scriptures are of Jewish authorship. This is a progressive way of getting at the problem of religious tolerance and cooperation. But religious tolerance in a globalizing culture is already fiercely resisted by the male-dominant, fundamentalist sectors of several world religions. This is simply another natural and inevitable expression of addiction and resistance to the irreversible unifying process.

Christians of biblical seriousness can be troubled by a verse that many interpret as forbidding any relativizing of Christian exclusivity: "No one comes to the Father except through me" (John 14:6). Dr. Borg writes that the key to freeing the text from rigid exclusivism lies in the introductory language of the passage. "I am the way" says Jesus in anticipation of what follows. A way clearly implies a path, a journey, a process and not a verbal formula or a dogmatic prescription. In other passages, Jesus vividly sets forth his way as the way of death and rebirth (resurrection). In an earlier text in John's gospel, Jesus is remembered as instructing a highly placed Jewish seeker, one Nicodemus, a preeminent member of the prevailing Jewish hierarchy who initiated a question about gaining eternal life. Jesus answered unequivocally, "Marvel not that I said unto thee, Ye must be born again" (John 3:7, KJV). Rebirth implies dying to an old and familiar way and being given a new and finer way of life, a life in allegiance to the indiscriminate love of God as mirrored in the life of Jesus whose mercy takes him to the cross.

Marcus Borg recalls a story he heard about a sermon preached by a Hindu scholar in a Christian seminary several decades ago (*Reading the Bible Again for the First Time: Taking the Bible Seriously But Not Literally*, HarperCollins, San Francisco, 2001, p. 216). The text on that occasion included the passage on the one way in John 14:6. "This verse is absolutely true," said the scholar. "Jesus is the only way. And that way, of dying to an old way of being and being born into a new way of being, is known to all the religions of the world." The way of Jesus is a universal reality of life, known to millions who may have never heard the name Jesus. Thus the way of Jesus as "the truth, and the life" (John 14:6) is not a set of beliefs about Jesus. Rather, it is a path of transition and transformation from an old rule-and-regulation religion to a way of being and behaving in freedom from fear and self-preoccupation. In a word, the way is to discover and to live by the grace of God, reborn to a life of justice, healing, and servanthood. Behold the beauty of this understanding: it offers common ground to fundamentalist and fusionist Christians alike.

When Billy Graham urges "giving your life to Christ," he is not prescribing anything uniquely Christian but rather using Christian language to declare a universal truth. It is the truth that a longed-for rescue from a life of self-destruction in any one of a hundred addictions to fear and me-first comes of dying to an old, self-preoccupied, and fearful way of life and being born again to a new way of fulfillment.

When the universality of this truth is seen, not just personally but prophetically in terms of social reform and rebirth, it will warm the fires of a new world now in process of aborning. What this truth means in global terms is clear: the way to a new world of economic justice and environmental sustainability is the way of the cross. This truth means the process of dying to an old way of untruth — the unsustainable way of inequitable consumption of the planet's diminishing resources. It means rising to a new way of being — of being a reunited human family in the intricately interwoven web of life. It means dying to greed-driven competition while accepting honorable competition as useful in adding zest to life. Even more, it means living into the dream of God and the dream of all healthy human aspiration for a finer world of compassion and peace. It means dying to dread of change and rising to embrace the overriding challenge of this swinging hinge of history. It means that we live into the advancing process of (1) simplifying our lifestyles, (2) reinventing our industrial systems and our fuel and power sources, (3) eliminating the monetary grip of special interests on our political processes, (4) disavowing war as a costly, counterproductive, historically outmoded, and violence-compounding conflict-resolution mechanism, and (5) resolving that human presence in this exquisite planet shall cause no callous and ill-considered harm to persons or to our living partners lower on the scale of consciousness.

The fact that substantial and increasing numbers of the human family are committed to the above is why it is possible to talk about global warming of the second kind. Of course, such a new vision of life raises fierce friction, but friction raises the levels of energy. We need not worry that current reality is loaded with manifest improbability. Visions are never justified by their plausibility. The human spirit goes for great dreams, not because they are plausible but because they are irresistible!

Chapter 31

A Way to Peace

I have a dream. I dream of a global human community able to restrain the frightened forces of violence that seek vengeance, endless warfare, and control by male-dominant ascendancy. I dream of a new humanity, not perfected but spiritually and politically mature beyond any previous development of the human spirit. I believe that my dream has the same force of moral possibility that fired the imagination of the immortal civil rights leader, our brother Martin. But all dreams of justice and a finer future carry only the power of possibility, not inevitability.

Still, I am hopeful. Not optimistic. Optimism seems to me a one-dimensional perspective on the world. The optimist is furnished only with what is humanly possible in contemplating the future. That is by no means a small thing: optimism has always fired the engines of human accomplishment. But for me, hope is a two-dimensional hold on the future. Hope includes the inexhaustible forces of God as sovereign of history. Hope is the intersecting vertical that sustains the horizontal trudge of humanity in holding fast our dreams in all unpredictabilities. Some canny theologian whose name I do not know wrote, "Hope is the future tense of faith and love."

As a Christian, I know that the human enterprise is situated in a moral arena as wide as the world and presided over by God — the God revealed in Jesus Christ as well as in all the justice-seeking spiritual traditions of the world religious family. I trust that this universality of faith is true from the fact that all the major historic religions enshrine a version of the golden rule as a distillation of their governing ethic. Moreover, my dream is shared by people in ever-expanding circles of energy and commitment, both at home and abroad. On February 15, 2003, more than 10 million people marched in major cities all across Europe, Asia, South America, South Africa, and the United States in protest of the contemplated American invasion of Iraq (David Cortright, *A Peaceful Superpower: The Movement Against War in Iraq*, Fourth Freedom Forum, Goshen, IN, 2004, pp. 30–31).

Present history turns on a great axis of change in the meaning of human achievement. We live at a momentous time in the evolution of human experience. We are shifting away from force-based competitive domination as the goal of human striving and toward collaborative and gender-inclusive ideals. This is a rising tide of global mind change, an epic shift away from male dominance to a balancing feminist ideal of cooperation and caring as the higher aim of human enterprise.

This epic shift is occurring as we breathe. It flourishes dramatically in the emergence of a cultural partnership between the new quantum science and the old religion of Jesus and the Hebrew prophets. This remarkable coalition of science and religion represents forces that have been opposing contenders for earlier generations. In my youth, brave science pushed at all the frontiers of fresh discovery and development, while religion floated in the rear on gossamer wings of moral invisibilities. But this new coalition brings with it what may be an irreversible power because it carries a capacity to fire the higher hopes of all humanity. Along with what must be millions of us, I long for a new world of compassion and collaboration to replace the prevailing feverish paradigm of materialistic competition that encourages fraud, alienation, addiction, and exhaustion of the human spirit. Whether the new coalition of science and religion can gain enough force in time to head off the ominous drift toward an Armageddon of planetary incineration by competing nuclear powers may remain humanity's most urgent question.

This urgency is exacerbated by the opposing coalition, the coalition of an old science and a new religion. As I behold my shrinking world and respond to the bombardment of the daily news, the marriage of old science and new religion is what drives the incumbent leadership of the world's most heavily armed nuclear power. By the old science, I mean the separatist atomism of seventeenth-century Cartesian mathematics and Newtonian physics. By the new religion, I mean the late nineteenth- and early twentieth-century emergence of fierce individualist fundamentalism. Alfred North Whitehead, distinguished mathematician and process philosopher of the twentieth century, wrote:

> The two most powerful forces in human history are science and religion. The future of humanity depends now more than anything else on how these two forces settle down in relation to one another.
> — Alfred North Whitehead, quoted in Bennett J. Sims, *Servanthood: Leadership for the Third Millennium*, Cowley Publications, Cambridge, MA, 1997, p. 131

My early schooling assumed the conventional truth about the universe as atomic matter in motion. The cosmos was governed by the laws of mechanics as developed by seventeenth-century thinkers and observers. From a dream that came to him in 1619, René Descartes of France imaged the cosmos as a clockworks machine. He deduced from his dream that human competence could manipulate and rearrange all raw matter for human convenience and material profit by the application of mathematics to the inert atomic structures of the earth. In 1687, the

Englishman Isaac Newton summed up the laws of universal mechanics in a series of algebraic formulations. The long-term effect of these works of genius was to reduce the mystery of the universe to confidence in the mastery of human ingenuity. For Descartes and Newton, the world is not only our inheritance to use and populate. For them and their con-quering mentality, the world is our possession to explore, deconstruct, and rebuild. Both men, along with Francis Bacon, taught that atoms were the irreducible and lifeless building blocks of the cosmos and that they floated in a void without any animated relationship. Atoms carried no living connectivity with each other. Relationship was only accidental or ornamental, as in the flow of colors in works of art.

This mechanistic isolation of parts has been the hard operational paradigm that created the most powerful knowledge base in the history of human accomplishment. Every modern technical achievement flows from that seventeenth-century assumption. Admittedly, the mechanistic worldview has brought the gains of four-wheel drive, improved human longevity, and the Internet. And it carries a liberating invitation: "Don't be a dishwasher, buy one!" That worldview remains in place today with diminishing but still pervasive force in the scientific, political, and corporate communities. The stridently individualistic character of the Cartesian-Newtonian paradigm enthrones competition as the principal enabler of human achievement. In spiritual terms, this is the old science buttressing and blessing the institutional religious mentality that sees the human population as individual consumers of religion and ignores all the prophetic accents of communitarian social justice and their shap-ing influences on the lives of individuals and societies.

This is the old fragmented and still powerful paradigm that dis-poses of the social seriousness inherent in such political gains as the United Nations on the world scale and as social security, Medicare, and the minimum wage in the United States. The old paradigm exercises a powerful influence on political decision makers. The incumbent president and U.S. Congress are busy proposing to diminish these communitarian provisions that honor the progressive mandate in traditional religion to care, to love one's neighbors. Currently, our predominantly conservative Congressional membership has voted itself seven increases in annual compensation since 1997 while raising the federal minimum wage by not a single penny in that same period (*The New York Times*, March 14, 2005).

Just as the Cartesian-Newtonian paradigm of atomized life shapes political decision making, it also shapes fundamentalist religion. Nothing demonstrates this more vividly than fundamentalist promises of the Rapture at the soon-to-occur end of the world. Based on a single New Testament citation in St. Paul's earliest written letter, the faithful in Christ will be levitated on high "to meet the Lord in the air" (1 Thessalonians 4:17) at the last trumpet sound that will end the world in a flaming convulsion. In Hendersonville, North Carolina where we live, there is a popular parking lot where religious bumper stickers appear with regularity. About a year ago, one such bumper sticker read, "At the Rapture, this car will be driverless." Notice the total absence in that slogan of any social conscience or concern. A driverless car at 35 miles an hour would be a roaring public menace. A few months later in that same parking lot, I saw a sassy bumper sticker that read, "At the Rapture, may I have your car?" In the same vein, a recent cartoon in *The New Yorker* magazine pictured a man in a business suit suspended a few feet in midair. Another man on the sidewalk near him was looking up and saying, "If you are being 'Raptured,' would you mind throwing me your wallet?"

The scientific corrective to the old Cartesian-Newtonian fragmentation is in the emerging truth of quantum mechanics. This new science came to birth in the early 1900s with the work of the German physicist Max Planck. He discovered that packets of vital energy exist below the empirical level of the inert atom, packets that he named quanta. Planck's research contradicted the prevailing scientific wisdom in which atoms were understood to be the irreducible and inert building blocks of material reality. For Max Planck and for geniuses like his countrymen Max Born and Werner Heisenberg and the Danish physicist Niels Bohr, a whole new world of reality opened up below the level of the atom. At the base of the material world are quantum elements named quarks and subquarks that whirl with life and energy. These lively components of the material order, which exhibit highly animated patterns of behavior, defy the fixed category of particles. They behave as waves as often as they appear to be discrete substances. Moreover, their behavior is both predictable and unpredictable, both regular and random. As photons, or elements of light, their actions are like cars on an interstate. Most speed predictably along as if on a superhighway, but some veer off as if onto an exit ramp. And as in the case of cars under observation, there appears to be no way of predicting which photons will do what. Quanta are thus like people — interrelated and unpredictable.

Albert Einstein resisted these discoveries since they opened a once-tidy world to vast unpredictability. Einstein never quite accepted what quantum science now calls chaos theory, by which is meant the untidy behavior of matter — like small children inside the boundaries of a cosmic playpen. Einstein remained relatively unconvinced, apparently because the further quantum theory took the thinking and observations of the physicists, the more untidiness was revealed. This essential randomness offended the great man's certainty that predictability at some deep level must be a fundamental characteristic of a universe created by the God who, as Ethel Waters reportedly said, "don't make no junk." But the burgeoning discipline of quantum physics forged ahead of Einstein, insisting that the elements of the observable universe in their relatedness resemble the behavior of living people in both random and predictable patterns. To quantum science, the cosmos appears as a vast, pulsing, sidereal aggregate in which no body behaves entirely independent of any other body.

In the new science, the macrocosm of humanity in our planet is an image of the microcosm of the entire lower elements writ large — the microbes, atoms, cells, and molecules. Humanity is therefore not a collection of separated parts and pieces. We are fundamentally a community of interwoven wonder. Instantly this means that what we do to others we do to ourselves, soon or late. This is the reason that hatred is soul-destructive of the hater and that love is life-giving to the lover. This is the reason that indifference to the plight of others diminishes the human capacity for compassion and that self-giving rewards one with ever-larger capacities for giving. This is the reason that the golden rule is shorthand for the personal and social ethics of all the world's major religions. This is why we are bidden to love God and one another, not for God's sake, but for our own.

Quantum science is sure that we live in a relational universe and that all the elements of creation to some mystical extent live for love. That is why neglect or abuse of anything, including the environment, will eventuate in withdrawal and a snarl. This includes spouses and children, all our relatives, the folks in the neighborhood, dogs, pigeons, your Buick, and even your lawnmower. Everything lives for love because all matter has life and because love is the primordial first need of all living matter. Antique car owners are therefore the great practitioners of quantum mechanics. Those who rebuild, repaint, tend, polish, and moon over old cars understand the longing of a machine for life and care. "God don't make no junk." But we do. We make junk as we live by the old science and behave toward the least of these brothers and sisters as disposable nobodies. And in the thrall of the old paradigm, we make planetary junk of the earth as if the living natural world were a feelingless object for human exploitation.

But the truth is that we are not on the planet. We are in it. We have known for a long time that each of us is composed of a high percentage of water, and we have known for even longer the tradition that "the Lord

God formed man of the dust of the ground, and breathed into his nostrils the breath of life" (Genesis 2:7, KJV).

The new religion of fundamentalist separatism scorns the earth as unworthy of environmental protection, while the old religion insists that "The earth is the Lord's, and the fulness thereof; the world, and they that dwell therein" (Psalms 24:1, KJV). Both the new and the old religions know about the wrath of God, but the old takes marvelous precedence over the new by insisting, over and over, that wrath is reserved for those who live in scorn of God's possession of the earth and in contempt of justice and compassion for all people. It is the old religion that thunders, "I hate, I despise your festivals, and I take no delight in your solemn assemblies…But let justice roll down like waters, and righteousness like an ever-flowing stream" (Amos 5:21, 24). It is the old religion that warns, "Put your sword back into its place; for all who take the sword will perish by the sword" (Matthew 26:52). It is the old religion that prophesies, "they shall beat their swords into plowshares, and their spears into pruning hooks; nation shall not lift up sword against nation, neither shall they learn war any more" (Isaiah 2:4).

The old religion is represented in the affirmations of two venerable Anglican Christians whose convictions confirm the light now supplied us by quantum theory. The first is from the dean of St. Paul's in London, the poet John Donne (1572–1631), whose pen is famous for a beloved line about the unbreakable bonds of human community. He wrote, "Any man's death diminishes me, because I am involved in mankind; and therefore never send to know for whom the bell tolls; it tolls for thee" (from Meditation 17, "No Man Is an Island"). This is the truth of the newest science.

The second affirmation for our time comes from Richard Hooker (1554–1600), an Anglican divine who intuited the truth of quantum theory and knew about the deep, bonded unity of the whole creation.

Hooker wrote this prophetic paragraph for a sermon in about the year 1590:

> God hath created nothing simply for itself: but each thing in all things, and everything in each part in other hath such interest, that in the whole world nothing is found whereunto anything created can say, "I need thee not."
> — Richard Hooker, quoted in Bennett J. Sims, *Servanthood: Leadership for the Third Millennium*, Cowley Publications, Cambridge, MA, 1997, p. 137

Another and cruder way of putting this axiom is to say that everybody is somebody's lunch in the evolutionary economy of God. Big fish swallow little fish. Microbes munch on human remains.

Human history in the planet may be so much dominated by the lust of empire and warfare that there is no chance of turning the human pilgrimage from its own demise by the deliberate folly of nuclear extinction. If so, I grieve for God in whose love humanity has the gift of free will along with God's forgiveness for the ugly use of freedom, such vile use as in the willful execution of God's life in Jesus. I grieve for God if, congruent with the desecrating evil of crucifixion, human willfulness brings about its own extinction as part of the long arrow of evolved planetary life. If this be the scenario of the world's tomorrows, God's mercy will endure, but I am glad to be old and soon to die.

But I can never accept that scenario. Nor do I accept the narrow and heartless expectation of the fundamentalist community in its anxious welcome of a predicted Rapture for only a smidgen of all who have ever lived. I dream of a new humanity learning the art of peace and redeemed by Christ whose love, I believe, enfolds the whole human experience in time and space, from our earliest appearance in the mists of prehistory until now — in all the nobility of human beauty and sorrow. The

providential confluence of the old religion and the new science promises the miracle of the very peace for which the world hungers. But it
cannot be perfect. A perfect peace in which conflict were totally absent
would put the human spirit to sleep. It would obviate all the life-giving
gallantry of forgiveness and reconciliation. However, a peace that leaves
room for all the dynamics of broken and restored relationships would be
a quality of peace that is promised in the church's familiar benediction as
a mystic gift beyond rational grasp.

The mystic gift is directly sourced in hope, the God-fashioned vertical dimension of our reach into every tomorrow. "And the peace of God,
which surpasses all understanding, will guard your hearts and your
minds in Christ Jesus" (Philippians 4:7).

> History says, Don't hope
> on this side of the grave.
> But then, once in a lifetime
> the longed for tidal wave
> of justice can rise up,
> and hope and history rhyme.
>
> So hope for a great sea-change
> on the far side of revenge.
> Believe that a further shore
> is reachable from here.
> Believe in miracles
> and cures and healing wells.
> — Seamus Heaney, from *The Cure at Troy:*
> *A Version of Sophocles' Philoctetes*, Faber and
> Faber Limited, London, 1990

Afterword

A Litany
for Envisioning a New World

A moment of silence follows each supplication.

Refashion our minds, O God, to a new way of thinking, that
seeing the peril in our power to cripple the earth and halt
the human odyssey, we commit our lives to the promise of
life for all in creation with whom we share the gift of life.
Hear our prayer and enlarge our compassion.

Reconcile our hearts to one another across all boundaries,
that human diversity may be experienced as enrichment
and differences honored as leading to wiser action.
Hear our prayer and strengthen our resolve.

Raise up a chorus of thanksgiving for the tide of nonviolence
that has risen in our time and, seeing the vast disparities of
wealth in the world, prompt us to see national security in global
terms — that priorities in all places of your dominion may be
turned from self-aggrandizement to sharing and servanthood.
Hear our prayer and open our hearts.

Kindle in each of us a resolve to dismantle our private arsenals of violence — our grievances, our blaming, and our hatreds — that justice may be dealt to offenders without vengeance and punishment applied for the purpose of teaching responsibility for relationships of care in an interdependent world.
Hear our prayer and cleanse us of all self-righteousness.

Enliven your church with a rebirth of welcome for all sorts and conditions of humanity, moving us to reorder our lives and our loves to such simplicity and good will as preserves the earth and makes for peace.
In the name of God: Creator, Redeemer, Unifying Spirit. Amen.

Bennett and Mary Page Sims at Kanuga near
Hendersonville, North Carolina, 1999.
(Photograph by Robert Smith.)

The Author

The Right Reverend Bennett J. Sims, DD, LHD, is Bishop Emeritus of the Episcopal Diocese of Atlanta. He served for 15 years as a parish priest in Baltimore, Maryland; Tokyo, Japan; and Corning, New York. He then joined the faculty at Virginia Theological Seminary for 6 years as the founding director of continuing education. He was elected bishop of the Diocese of Atlanta in 1972. Following retirement as bishop in 1983, he returned to education as an adjunct professor of theology in the Candler School of Theology at Emory University and founded the Institute for Servant Leadership at Emory in 1983. He moved the institute to Hendersonville, North Carolina as an educational corporation in 1988 and continued to serve as president until his retirement in 1999. Bishop Sims is the author of four previous books: *Invitation to Hope: A Testimony of Encouragement* (1974); *Purple Ink: A Selection of the Writings of Bennett J. Sims as Bishop of Atlanta* (1982); *Servanthood: Leadership for the Third Millennium* (1997); and *Why Bush Must Go: A Bishop's Faith-Based Challenge* (2004). He served in the United States Navy from 1943 to 1946 as a line officer on destroyers. He lives with his wife Mary Page Sims in Hendersonville, North Carolina.